Inquiry-Based English Instruction:
Engaging Students in Life and Literature
RICHARD BEACH and JAMIE MYERS

The Best for Our Children: Critical Perspectives on Literacy for Latino Students
MARÍA DE LA LUZ REYES and
JOHN J. HALCÓN, Editors

Language Crossings: Negotiating the Self
in a Multicultural World
KAREN L. OGULNICK, Editor

What Counts as Literacy? Challenging the
School Standard
MARGARET GALLEGO and
SANDRA HOLLINGSWORTH, Editors

Critical Encounters in High School
English: Teaching Literary theory to
Adolescents
DEBORAH APPLEMAN

Beginning Reading and Writing
DOROTHY S. STRICKLAND and
LESLEY M. MORROW, Editors

Reading for Meaning: Fostering
Comprehension in the Middle Grades
BARBARA M. TAYLOR, MICHAEL F.
GRAVES, PAUL van den BROEK, Editors

Writing in the Real World: Making the
Transition from School to Work
ANNE BEAUFORT

Young Adult Literature and the New
Literary Theories: Developing Critical
Readers in Middle School
ANNA O. SOTER

Literacy Matters: Writing and Reading the
Social Self
ROBERT P. YAGELSKI

Building Family Literacy in an Urban
Community
RUTH D. HANDEL

Children's Inquiry: Using Language to
Make Sense of the World
JUDITH WELLS LINDFORS

Engaged Reading: Processes, Practices,
and Policy Implications
JOHN T. GUTHRIE and
DONNA E. ALVERMANN, Editors

Learning to Read: Beyond Phonics and
Whole Language
G. BRIAN THOMPSON and
TOM NICHOLSON, Editors

So Much to Say: Adolescents,
Bilingualism, and ESL in the Secondary
School
CHRISTIAN J. FALTIS and PAULA WOLFE,
Editors

Close to Home: Oral and Literate Practices
in a Transnational Mexicano Community
JUAN C. GUERRA

Authorizing Readers: Resistance and
Respect in the Teaching of Literature
PETER J. RABINOWITZ and
MICHAEL W. SMITH

On the Brink: Negotiating Literature and
Life with Adolescents
SUSAN HYNDS

Life at the Margins: Literacy, Language,
and Technology in Everyday Life
JULIET MERRIFIELD, MARY BETH
BINGMAN, DAVID HEMPHILL, and
KATHLEEN P. BENNETT DeMARRAIS

One Child, Many Worlds: Early Learning
in Multicultural Communities
EVE GREGORY, Editor

Literacy for Life: Adult Learners, New
Practices
HANNA ARLENE FINGERET and
CASSANDRA DRENNON

Children's Literature and the Politics of
Equality
PAT PINSENT

The Book Club Connection: Literacy
Learning and Classroom Talk
SUSAN I. MCMAHON and TAFFY E.
RAPHAEL, Editors, with VIRGINIA J.
GOATLEY and LAURA S. PARDO

Until We Are Strong Together: Women
Writers in the Tenderloin
CAROLINE E. HELLER

Restructuring Schools for Linguistic
Diversity: Linking Decision Making to
Effective Programs
OFELIA B. MIRAMONTES, ADEL NADEAU,
and NANCY L. COMMINS

Writing Superheroes: Contemporary
Childhood, Popular Culture, and
Classroom Literacy
ANNE HAAS DYSON

(Continued)

Inquiry-Based English Instruction

ENGAGING STUDENTS IN LIFE AND LITERATURE

Richard Beach & Jamie Myers

FOREWORD BY JEROME C. HARSTE

Teachers College, Columbia University
New York and London

Published by Teachers College Press, 1234 Amsterdam Avenue, New York, NY 10027

Library of Congress Cataloging-in-Publication Data

Beach, Richard.
    Inquiry-based English instruction: engaging students in life and literature / Richard Beach and Jamie Myers.
        p.   cm.— (Language and literacy series)
    Includes bibliographical references and index.
    ISBN 0-8077-4102-7 (pbk. : alk. paper) — ISBN 0-8077-4103-5 (cloth : alk. paper)
    1. Language arts (Secondary)—United States.   2. Language experience approach in education—United States.   3. Interdisciplinary approach in education—United States.
I. Myers, Jamie.   II. Title.   III. Language and literacy series (New York, N.Y.)

    LB1631 .B355   2001
    428'.0071'2—dc21   00-067817

ISBN 0-8077-4102-7 (paper)
ISBN 0-8077-4103-5 (cloth)

Printed on acid-free paper
Manufactured in the United States of America

08   07   06   05   04   03   02   01   8   7   6   5   4   3   2   1

Contents

Foreword

In 1990 I was invited to keynote a conference on school reform sponsored by the State of Hawaii. At that conference I laid out what I called an education-as-inquiry model of education (Harste, 1990). There were three moderately radical things about this model. First, it was centered on personal and social knowing, the argument being that rather than organize schools around the disciplines (English, social studies, science, etc.), another way to organize schools is around the individual and collective inquiry questions of learners. The second radical thing about this model was that, while disciplines were not eliminated, they were seen as perspectives that inquirers could use to research inquiry questions of personal worth. The third radical suggestion was a call for a much-expanded view of literacy to include art, music, drama, dance, and other ways of knowing in addition to language. My argument was that a good English/language arts curriculum ought to expand communication potential rather than make students increasingly "verbocentric," or dependent on language.

I argued that the focus of curriculum should be on the underlying processes of inquiry rather than on specific pieces of content. Even the most basic "truths" we learned in school no longer hold. Atoms, for example, are not the smallest thing in the universe. Not everyone has an equal chance at becoming president. Complex problems call for complex solutions. Persons working alone are not likely to solve the problems our society faces at the beginning of the twenty-first century—pollution, depletion of natural resources, overpopulation, urban decay, sexism, racism, homophobia, drugs.

Now, 10 years after that speech, I wish I had gone further. Arthur Applebee (1997) studied secondary schools and argued that the best teachers organize curriculum in terms of the conversations in which they want students to engage, rather than in terms of the content they wish to deliver. Allen Luke and Peter Freebody (1997) saw "literacy" as a particular form of social practice. They argued that our society and its schools construct particular kinds of literate beings. If curriculum "is a metaphor for the lives we want to live and the people we want to be" (Harste, 1993, p. 1237), then as educators we have important choices to make. James Gee (1996) and Brian Street (1995) helped us see that "literacy" is never a single state, but rather societies are made up of "multiple literacies" that relate to multiple realities and multiple ways of knowing, a theme I picked up on when giving my presidential address at the 1999 annual meeting of the National Council of Teachers of English (Harste & Carey, 1999). Donaldo Macedo and Lilia Bartolome (1999) argue that we can never have culturally responsive schooling until we have a culturally responsive society. They argue that popular culture as represented through the media does more to educate our young than does anything we do in school. Barbara Comber (2000), Carole Edelsky (1999), Vivian Vasquez (2000), and Dennis Sumara and Brent Davis (1999) call for school curricula that support students of all ages in interrogating the dominant, and often taken-for-granted, systems of meaning that operate in society.

Together with Richard Beach and Jamie Myers, in this volume, these educators are calling for an inquiry-based curriculum with a critical edge, one that helps students understand how they have been positioned in the world and what they might do to transform the ways in which school and society have constructed them. The underlying issue in education is not what knowledge is worth knowing, but whose knowledge is worth knowing and for what purpose.

If the function of a foreword, like curriculum, "is to give perspective" (Burke in Harste, Short, & Burke, 1988, p. 51), then my hope is that this brief history of inquiry-based education serves this purpose for readers. What Richard Beach, Jamie Myers, and the teachers with whom they worked manage to do—and what makes this book so significant—is take all of these ideas and use them to re-imagine a new secondary English curriculum, one that doesn't walk away from traditional values, but that goes beyond and recasts everything in a new light. Their curricular focus is on "social worlds," the ones in which students live, the ones portrayed in texts, the ones students dare to imagine. The underlying processes they focus on are immersing, identifying, contextualizing, representing, critiquing, and transforming, a much-improved list over ours (Short, Harste, w/Burke, 1996) or that of Gordon Wells and colleagues (2000). Better yet, they demonstrate in chapter after chapter how these processes get played out in real classrooms with real teachers and real secondary students.

Like Richard Beach and Jamie Myers, I was fortunate in that a group of teachers took my ideas and ran with them, creating a new public school called the Center for Inquiry in Indianapolis. Unlike Richard Beach and Jamie Myers, I and the teachers with whom I worked had to learn the hard way that inquiry-based education wasn't good enough. To really work, it had to be critical, anchored in the life space of learners, and focused on interrogation and re-construction of real and possible "social worlds."

I see this as a landmark volume. It takes the best of what we know and pushes us at least two steps further. It simultaneously represents best practice, our current knowledge base, and possible new futures.

Jerome C. Harste
Indiana University

REFERENCES

Applebee, A. N. (1997). Rethinking curriculum in the English language arts. *English Journal, 86*(5), 25-31.

Comber, B. (2000).What really counts in early literacy lessons. *Language Arts, 78*(1), 39-49.

Edelsky, C. (1999). On critical whole language practice: Why, what, and a bit of how. In C. Edelsky (Ed.), *Making justice our project: Teachers working toward critical whole language practice* (pp. 7-36). Urbana, IL: National Council of Teachers of English.

Gee, J. P. (1996). *Social linguistics and literacies: Ideology in discourses* (2nd ed.). London: Taylor & Francis.

Harste, J. C. (1990). Inquiry-based instruction. *Primary Voices K-6, 1*(1), 7-8.

Harste, J. C. (1993). Literacy as curricular conversations about knowledge, inquiry, and morality. In M. Ruddell & R. Ruddell, *Theoretical models and processes of reading* (4th ed.; pp. 1220-1242). Newark, DE: International Reading Association.

Harste, J. C., & Carey, R. (1999). *Curriculum. multiple literacies, and democracy: What if English/language arts teachers really cared?* (Monograph). Urbana, IL: National Council of Teachers of English.

Harste, J. C., Short, K. G., & Burke, C. L. (1988). *Creating classrooms for authors.* Portsmouth, NH: Heinemann.

Luke, A., & Freebody, P. (1997). The social practices of reading. In S. Muspratt, A. Luke, & P. Freebody (Eds.), *Constructing critical literacies* (pp. 185-225). Cresskill, NJ: Hampton Press.

Macedo, D. P., & Bartolome, L. I. (1999). *Dancing with bigotry: Beyond the politics of tolerance.* New York: St. Martin's Press.

Short, K. G., Harste, J. C., w/Burke, C. L. (1996). *Creating classrooms for authors and inquirers.* Portsmouth, NH: Heinemann.

Street, B. (1995). *Multiple literacies.* Portsmouth, NH: Heinemann.

Sumara, D., & Davis, B. (1999). Interrupting heteronormativity: Toward a queer curriculum theory. *Curriculum Inquiry, 29*(2), 191-208.

Vasquez, V. (2000). Building community through social action. *School Talk, 5*(4), 2-4.

Wells, G., w/Davis, G., Donoahue, Z., Hume, K., Kowal, M., McGlynn-Stewart, M., & Tassell, M. (2000). *Text, talk, and inquiry.* New York: Teachers College Press.

Acknowledgments

WE WOULD LIKE to acknowledge the following people for their assistance with this book: for using inquiry instruction in their classrooms, Anne Andersen, Kelly Bertoty, Leo Bickelhaupt, Sarah Gohman, Kristen Konop, Barbara Lambert, Carol Paul, Jon Paulson, Brenda Robertson, Rob Robson, Amy Taylor, and Kim vanVoorhees; for their helpful comments and feedback on drafts, Brian Edmiston and Kathy Short; for his supportive foreword, Jerry Harste; for their assistance with permissions and the manuscript, Meg Courtright and Judy Nastase; for her thoughtful, thorough editing, Catherine Bernard; and for her ongoing support as acquisitions editor, Carol Collins.

Beyond these specific "adults," hundreds of adolescents have participated in activities initiated by the ideas in this book. We thank them for the enjoyable time spent together and their willingness to share their work and thoughts, and we wish them all the best in their future social worlds.

1

Constructing Social Worlds: An Introduction

MEET SUSAN, an 18-year-old, twelfth-grade student who is triracial: Native American, African-American, and Caucasian. In addition to taking high school and community college courses, she has a part-time job working with preschool and elementary students at a museum. Susan is quite outspoken and is involved in student government at her high school. She is highly artistic, composes music, lyrics, and poetry, and sings in a band with several other young women.

Susan therefore inhabits a range of different social worlds: high school, community college, art museum, student government, band, family, and peer group. Each of these worlds has its own unique set of social practices characterized by particular values, expectations, roles, relationships, and identities. These multiple and often overlapping social worlds are not fixed and objective. Instead, through social interaction, participants repeat the practices important within each particular world to seek a stable sense of cultural existence. At times the value and meaning of activities and language in these worlds are full of tension and ambiguity, given participants' allegiances to different, sometimes contesting social worlds.

In her work at the museum providing younger students with information about cultural differences, Susan experiences a multicultural world that reflects her own mixed-race heritage. As she notes, "Coming from three different races, I feel uncomfortable where there are homogeneous people . . . I just have to have a mix of people or I am super uncomfortable." She attributes her desire for different cultural perspectives to her experience working with Native Americans at a local museum:

> We have the greatest, on the second floor, mix of different things of different cultures. And I work closely with a lot of Native American people there. . . . It fascinates me how much their philosophies and theories have influenced me, even though I've never even been on a reservation.

Susan is also encouraged by her Norwegian mother to explore these alternative cultural perspectives shaping her identity: "I have these mixed cultures. My mom is really happy that I've found a balance in how I feel about that. And she pushes me to rethink stuff." In each of her "mixed cultures," Susan uses particular symbols—such as verbal expressions, dress, gestures, music, photographs, and written text—that enable her to negotiate and to share meanings for herself, others, and the world of experience.

As we participate in multiple social worlds, our possible identities become mixed, limited, expanded, or even contested in each world. If we use the slang, wear the clothing, read the texts, or dance to the music valued by one social world when we interact with others within a different social world, we may feel tension in the social relationships. We may assert our desired identity by using particular symbols, language, or activity to intentionally contest the valued symbols and activity of another social world. The tension may result in our exclusion from a particular social world, or a change in the practices of a social world. Ultimately, we must be able to openly discuss and negotiate the values and expectations of the diverse worlds we continually encounter so that we are better able to generate with others new shared social worlds.

As a triracial person, Susan refuses to identify exclusively with any one racial group in her school. She recalls incidents in which African-American students would ridicule her dress, which is generally overalls or jeans over a plaid shirt or cotton T-shirt. According to these students' code, this dress represents a denial of her Black heritage, because overalls are linked with a 1960s, White, hippie identity. Conversely, European-American students have judged her according to misconceptions or stereotypes of African-American students at their school, even to the point of harassment and physical threats. In the following poem, Susan explores competing meanings of dress as a marker of allegiances to different peer worlds:

MY SWEATER

blue, yellow, and brown,
my old golfer sweater is the subject of a
conservative, alternative,
OH HOW DO YOU PUT IT?
right wing
left wing struggle
who's sweater is it?
it's mine and it's on my body
and I suppose if you don't like it
DON'T LOOK AT IT

It's striped with a miss-matched face,
never lacking in social grace
and if you are displeased (let me say it again)
with my stylin' high-flyin' sweater,
DON'T LOOK AT IT

Susan explores her peers' conflicting interpretations of her sweater as a symbol of her conflicted identity within multiple social worlds. She writes more poetry to explore conflicts and tensions within her family world, such as the significance of her mother, the absence of her father, and her tricultural heritage. In one such poem, she describes her relationship with her mother:

watching my mother as sweat drips from her chin to her neck in
    the hot sun
and as the last of the wood falls from her weathered hands to
    the
wood pile, I realize
someday my hands will look as hers do and my children will be
    watching

The final line suggests that her mother serves as a role model for her own future activity as a mother. In contrast, in another poem, she describes her father as deceitful:

you were always his precious little girl . . . blinded you with
    the shine in his eyes
there was no way for you to see his lies
bruises from years gone past
reminded you how long it would last . . .

She uses this poetry to position herself within her family social world as her mother's daughter in opposition to her absent father. As she describes her experiences in different worlds, she constructs her desired identity and values in those worlds. She is typical of adolescents who continually negotiate the demands of competing social worlds (Phelan, Davidson, & Yu, 1998). Because social worlds are constructed, contested, and maintained through language and symbols in social activity, the English classroom, with its focus on students' language development, is an ideal place to study social worlds.

In this book, we propose a curriculum framework to help students reflect on their participation in their own social worlds, as well as the representations of social worlds in literature and the media. We provide examples of middle and high school students conducting inquiry projects into their concerns and perceived issues or dilemmas associated with their participation in or response to social worlds. In these projects, students are studying how social worlds in their own lives and literature are constructed and represented. And they are critiquing these constructions and representations with an eye toward proposing changes in these worlds.

WHY STUDY SOCIAL WORLDS IN THE ENGLISH CLASSROOM?

An English teacher might ask, Why would one want to study social worlds in the English classroom? Doesn't that topic belong in social studies? We have several answers to this question.

Students are more engaged with English when they connect it to their own lives. As former secondary English teachers and as English educators, we have experienced students' lack of engagement with traditional approaches to teaching English. This lack of engagement stems from a sense of disconnection between studying language, signs, and texts as intrinsic forms, and how texts and language are used within everyday life to construct meaning. At the same time, outside the English classroom, students are highly engaged with using language, signs, and texts to build relationships, develop a sense of belonging with others, and navigate the competing demands of institutions. Organizing English instruction about inquiry around social worlds places these engaging activities at the center of the curriculum. Adolescents are particularly motivated to study how they define their identities through participation in the activities of social worlds. As we began working with teachers who implemented this approach, we found that students' engagement with English improved because they perceived some connection between English and their everyday lives.

Students learn that worlds are constructed through language and texts. Students simply may assume that worlds are givens that are "out there" rather than continually undergoing reconstruction through their own uses of language and texts. They therefore may be reluctant to critically interrogate institutions because they presuppose that institutions are fixed entities immutable to change. We believe that inquiry into social worlds belongs in the English classroom because students need to examine how language, signs, and texts are used continually to construct our cultural practices and institutions. Students are particularly aware of the tenuous, constructed nature of worlds through drama activities (Wilhelm & Edmiston, 1998). In simulating the worlds of a courtroom hearing, teens at a school dance, a school board hearing, or a family dinner hour, they realize that they are "making it all up"—that through their talk and symbolic action, they are constructing and negotiating a world.

By engaging in social worlds, students learn that worlds are constructed through multiple literacies. We also have been dissatisfied with the focus of much English instruction only on understanding and producing written print texts. While written texts are central to constructing social worlds, social worlds also are constructed through a range of multiple literacies, including signs, images, icons, music, and oral discourse. The process of producing and sharing literate texts is only one activity in the entire collection of symbolic interactions that construct any one social world. Some social worlds, like the school English classroom, are constructed almost entirely through social practices that employ a narrow range of texts and grade written texts in a very particular way. How students engage in such school literacy practices has significant consequences for the social relationships and identities they can experience within their school and peer social worlds. Susan's band also uses literacy within its activities to create music and lyrics, but in very different ways from how literacy is used in the school context. In some social worlds, print texts are not part of any social interaction; however, visual texts such as television, film, or web pages form a basis for valued activity and symbolic representation of the self, others, and the world. When the English curriculum shifts to focus on the study of social worlds, the variety of texts and symbolic activity experienced in the classroom broadens as students and teachers inquire into how worlds are constructed through the whole range of different literacies.

In communicating across social worlds, students learn to employ "intercultural inquiry." Students such as Susan inhabit increasingly diverse worlds with competing cultural practices and values. These diverse worlds are not singular, isolated entities frozen in time, but continually are evolving and changing due to challenges and conflicts from other worlds. It is through exposure to and not isolation from the diversity of worlds that students and their worlds change.

In studying social worlds, we help students learn to negotiate these competing cultures through what Flower, Long, and Higgins (2000) describe as "intercultural inquiry." In their research on students' participation in inquiry about differences between each other's cultural perceptions related to gender, class, and race, Flower, Long, and Higgins found that students learn to understand others' cultural perceptions through recognizing and interrogating "rival hypotheses," that is, alternative claims about the world. By actively sharing competing cultural perspectives related to a problem, students engaged in

> a joint effort to use culturally different perspectives to collaboratively construct new readings of the problem and strong (rival) hypotheses about the best response to it . . . when urban teenagers enter the inquiry about youth, for instance,

their rival interpretations of the problem deny simple distinctions between "gang" and "good" kids, and locate the motivations for neighborhood gangs in urban teenagers' search for identity and respect and in the limited choices they see. (pp. 72–73)

Students acquire tools for coping with conflicts within and between social worlds. Another reason for studying social worlds in English is that the students we have worked with are particularly engaged in using literacy as a tool for coping with and understanding conflicts and tensions within and between diverse worlds. Susan uses her poetry to make sense of what were often bewildering experiences in multicultural family, peer, and community worlds. She values her writing because it helps her to make sense of her experiences in other social worlds and to reflect on the values of those worlds, on her position in those worlds, on her identity and relationships in those worlds, and on the actions and words that might help her realize her desired identity and relationships across her social worlds. Beyond representing personal experience and envisioning future social worlds, the resultant texts can become objects of further social activity, for when they are shared and read by others, social worlds are further negotiated and constructed. The development of these two literacy practices, the personal and the social, in the English classroom provides students with tools to negotiate meanings about self, others, and the world.

CHARACTERISTICS OF A SOCIAL WORLDS CURRICULUM

In proposing a reframing of the English curriculum around inquiry about social worlds, our overall goal is to help students employ and critique the multiple literacies used in social worlds. To best capture this critical role of literacy as both an activity and an artifact, we distinguish between "lived" and "represented" social worlds. "Lived" worlds are those actual peer, school, family, and community worlds in which we participate using language, symbols, and texts to interact, to engage in activities of shared value, and to produce artifacts. "Represented" worlds are texts that portray or comment on events and experiences in a lived social world. For example, when we talk with others about a past experience, we simultaneously represent a social world and engage in an activity that is constructing the immediate lived social world. Literature, the performing arts, and mass media are the typical texts of an English classroom that portray represented worlds. In responding to these textual representations of worlds, students draw on their own lived-world experiences. For example, in responding to *Romeo and Juliet*, students draw on their lived experiences with romance and family conflicts, and other textual representations of love and family from mass media and prior reading. As they merge the texts of their lived and represented worlds, they construct possible identities and relationships in past, present, and future social worlds. They may perceive their romantic relationship as "just like Romeo and Juliet," to quote a popular 1960s song.

In the English classroom, literature study of these representations becomes an opportunity to explore how the language, activity, and interactions of characters construct multiple social worlds full of tension and conflict. The social worlds that authors create for characters become relevant arenas for students to critically reflect on their own lived social worlds. When responding to literature or the media, students can be transported into a different verbal landscape that provides them with alternative ways of thinking about their lived world. Students enact the critical study of social worlds when the language and texts produced to represent their own lived social worlds, or to respond to the social worlds represented in classroom texts, are examined in reference to the perspectives and values of different possible worlds. This reflective activity heightens one's agency to actively participate in critiquing and transforming social worlds.

The shift to studying social worlds reorients the study of language in the English classroom itself. Language study traditionally is focused on the reproduction of convention. Writing, vocabulary, and grammar exercises emphasize a predetermined pathway toward valid meanings and linguistic forms. Reading consists of figuring out, with the expert guidance of the teacher, the authorized, official meaning held within canonical texts. Speaking and listening, reading and writing, commonly are defined as mediums through which we simply exchange static meanings. Language is treated as capable of precision whereby everyone struggles to make texts have exact and single meanings.

James Seitz (1999) describes this approach as a "literalist" model of English instruction in that it focuses primarily on conveying literal information or stated positions. Thus, "student writing is brought forward primarily for the 'points' it has to make, the 'views' it has to argue . . . for what they literally *say* (and for the purposes of assessment, how well they say it)" (p. 202). Seitz contrasts this literalist model with a "metaphoric" approach that emphasizes the uses or practices of language in constructing meaning. In this approach, students learn "what the writing does, for the action it takes—intertextually, historically, sociopolitically, culturally—and not just for the message it delivers" (p. 202).

Within a metaphoric approach, language meanings are invented in social interaction instead of simply shuttled between minds. Everyday interaction with common symbols and recurring language patterns constructs conventional meanings and literacy practices. But every utterance of language is open for negotiation, allowing participants to explore how the values, expectations, roles, relationships, or desires of their many overlapping social worlds can shape layers of meaning possible for any word, gesture, image, or sound. Language is constructive, symbolic, and metaphoric, even though we establish conventional meanings as a consequence of constructing shared social worlds. This suggests the need to move language study into the center of this dialectic between convention and invention.

Although we easily might understand that we live within social worlds, we seldom examine how a social world is constructed, especially the ones in which we participate. We know that the worlds represented in texts like books, newspapers, film, photographs, or television do not mirror our lived worlds, but always portray a lived world from some particular perspective and interest. But we often do not inquire into how the words and actions common in our everyday social worlds are defined by the larger practices and discourses of the social world in which we find ourselves, or to which we hope to belong or even create. Additionally, adolescents spend an increasing amount of time within the virtual worlds of interactive electronic spaces. Human interaction in the virtual activity is mediated completely through text representations, bringing a new sense to the idea of "social" in a social world. Often the lived experience of a video game overwhelms any conscious reflection, or study of the representations on which it builds the virtual experience.

By reframing the activity of the English classroom around the study of social worlds, students become more conscious of how language, symbols, and actions create and maintain social worlds. Through inquiry activity, they acquire various social practices that include uses of literacy and collaboration essential for coping with real-world concerns, issues, or dilemmas. They increase their own agency to construct more equitable and just social worlds because they have a fuller understanding of how the values of a social world are generated and contested through social interaction and literacy practices. As they engage in the study of lived and represented social worlds, their activity shifts the traditional purpose of language arts study away from the transmission of convention and culture, toward critical inquiry into the activities and texts we use to negotiate community belonging and difference, to construct desired relationships and identities, and to transform convention and culture.

CONSTRUCTING SOCIAL WORLDS IN THE ENGLISH CLASSROOM: AN AUTOBIOGRAPHICAL RECOLLECTION OF TEACHING

Given the value of building an English curriculum around the study of social worlds, the next question might be, How does this play out in the classroom? To illustrate an initial shift in teaching toward a social worlds curriculum, Jamie recalls his own experience teaching senior English from 1983 to 1986 in a small midwestern rural high school with about 80 students in each grade. By the time the students reached senior status, about 25% were enrolled in programs at the county joint vocational school. For the remainder, senior English stood between them and graduation, a clear problem for nearly half of the students who had no intention of continuing in any postsecondary school education. Few would have serious difficulties, but many would just endure the year and slide by on minimal efforts.

In facing this group of students, Jamie began rethinking the basic purpose of English instruction. Constructing an English curriculum that has appeal and utility to the entire population of students is not a problem localized to Jamie's experience, or to just the twelfth grade of school in 1985. Even more today than in the mid-1980s, inclusion and detracking initiatives have surfaced questions about the purpose of the English classroom in public education. The English curriculum has long been driven by the purpose of preparation for college English courses and academic writing. Literacy evaluations in English classrooms, perhaps more than any other component of the modern high school curriculum, have served the purpose of sorting students into academic or vocational tracks. And, unfortunately, this activity constructs a purpose for public school that is related more to workplace preparation than to participation in a democratic community. Even the curriculum of higher education today is driven largely by the demands of the workplace, rather than the demands of knowledge generation through inquiry and critique.

Given the fundamental question of the purpose of senior English in that small school, Jamie's solution was a bit surprising. He didn't throw out all the classic literature; in fact, the students read more literature than ever before—two novels and a play each 9 weeks. Nor did he abandon the traditional literary essay, with the inclusion of quotations from the text under examination. Instead, he reframed the whole experience of the English classroom as an implicit inquiry into students' collective and individual social lives. All of the students became engaged in a program that Jamie (Myers, 1988) defined at the time as: "Self-discovery through literature: Fluency not Lit. Crit., Every student should be in the novel."

In terms of curricular theory, the classroom structures were based on writing process theories, and, unknown to Jamie at the time, were also highly connected to reader response ideas. The students completed fluencies—"free-writing" in which the pen/pencil tries to keep up with the mind—in response to the characters and events of the texts. Jamie would prepare for class by searching for a statement, description, or interaction in the text that might generate some relevance for the students by connecting to their everyday lives with peers, family, or community. In *Cyrano de Bergerac*, for example, when Cyrano describes his soul in Act 1, Jamie asked, "Why does Cyrano carry adornments inside, on his soul? Is there a difference between our appearance and our inward soul? Should we be concerned with outward appearance? Is Cyrano vain? How do you deal with ego?" Or later, during the famous balcony scene, Jamie asked: "What is Cyrano realizing about this situation-opportunity? Is he speaking truthfully and/or honestly? Can he be honest in this situation? Does he have a right to pursue his dream? At all costs?"

The prompts attempted to put the student into the events of the play, and the ideas of the play into the events of students' everyday lives. The fluencies that ensued allowed the students' thoughts to flow beyond the questions posed. Students were encouraged to just let the mind run with the ideas without concern for grammar or spelling, and to keep going for at least a page if they could. When he collected the fluencies, Jamie would underline ideas that would be fun to talk about. Fluencies written by Lori, Kent, and Doug represent a range of students.

> LORI: Cyrano always said that people should not just look at the
>   beauty of a person. That what the person's personality is like is
>   more important. *Even though he preached this, he did the
>   opposite with Roxane.* When he is asked who he likes his reply is
>   the fairest girl who is out of his reach. Throughout the book he is
>   in love with Roxanne. Even though he helps Christian try to win
>   her. He didn't look at Roxanne's personality, or anyone else's. He
>   only said people should. That is because he knew that people
>   first looked at his nose and decided they didn't like *Cyrano. he
>   wanted people to look deeper but how could they when he
>   didn't.*
>
> KENT: The old, "I'll write it, you send," or "I'll tell you and you speak
>   it," routine. Cyrano and Christians' plan seems almost too perfect
>   for them. Too perfect to work I imagine. I've seen stories like this
>   on T.V. or have often dreamt of such things. The one writes all
>   these letters to the fair maiden (that the other guy doesn't even
>   know about) and tells him what to say to her & how to say it, and
>   what to say if and when she says this. Just when things are going
>   fine, the one with the girl messes up one of his lines and she
>   leaves him only to discover from the other guy that he was the
>   one who actually wrote her all the letters. The story usually ends
>   happily, but *I have a feeling this book will be a tragedy (oh no
>   another one!).* Possibly like Romeo and Juliet ending. Death
>   anyway because of all the sword language we've already been
>   exposed to. But I'd like to see Cyrano end up *with Roxanne
>   because* the author already *has me rooting for Cyrano.* I don't
>   think the *place has faith in it enough* from both gents and

> Christian doesn't seem too masculine of character so he'll end up failing. It should be interesting, but I already know the ending!
>
> DOUG: Doubt and Pride have to do with love. I don't *think that doubt has anything to do with love.* Doubt is something that you don't think so, how could anybody love some one if they doubt them, love is something that you really care for a lot and Pride to me is love like I love to play sports at Falcon and I think Pride is a big thing in this *story with pride you can go far. If you got pride in your life there's nothing that can stop you.*

Lori explores how Cyrano says one thing but does the opposite, revealing her understanding that people can be contradictory, and her desire for consistency. Kent dreams of such a love and roots for Cyrano, but he thinks things are too perfect to work out. He knows that everyday life isn't that simple. Doug connects pride and love through his own experience playing football for the school team. All three students connect the ideas in the novel to their own life experiences through the writing of fluencies.

However, for these fluencies really to be "free-writings," what happened with the papers was just as important. Most often students would exchange fluencies or read them aloud. The students' favorite activity involved passing them around in a circle and silently scribbling comments and questions on each paper, with one's original fluency arriving back by the end of the period full of notes and asides. With each novel or play, students would write three to five fluencies. Each received a "grade" of a fraction indicating the length in terms of pages. When they finished the novel or play, students would reread their fluencies and write a new one about the whole work in relation to their own lives. From this they would select an idea and build a catalog of quotes from the text related to that idea. The next draft integrated the quotes with their ideas about the work in terms of their own life experience with the ideas. Every 9 weeks students would rewrite one paper based on teacher and classmate responses.

While this version of senior English retained canonical texts and academic essay writing, the students constructed a different type of discourse in the classroom. This discourse invited all the students to participate in talk about the characters, their motivations and desires, their ideals and struggles, and their relationships and identities within their social worlds. Through these discussions, students were able to ponder the social construction of their own lives in response to each other and the stories' characters. Two conversations support the success of this English curriculum. The first conversation involved one of the most academically accomplished students. At the beginning of a class, Laura asked, "How come writing papers in here is so easy and totally impossible to do in college composition class?" In the second conversation, a mother of a student who had taken reading support classes throughout junior high and high school commented near the end of the school year when she caught Jamie leaving school one afternoon: "I want to thank you for getting my son to read all of those books." "Does he like them?" Jamie replied. "Oh, yes," she said. "He has read more this year than I have ever seen."

Before this chance meeting, it was questionable how many of the non-college-bound seniors kept up with reading two novels outside of class every 9 weeks. Most English teachers never would have handed some of the titles to these students from rural backgrounds who had little if any interest in academic achievement. However, because fluency writings were in response to key quotations, students did not need to read more than the page with the quote. Because discussions were focused on how story ideas played out in the lives of students, everyone always had plenty of life experience to share. And the nature of talk and writing in this classroom intrigued these traditionally resistant readers, pulling them into reading some, if not all, of the books. Within the discourse created in this classroom, the books became stories related to the students' lives, much more than classic books with specific authorized meanings that should be learned in order to secure a bright future. The seniors talked about the stories in the cafeteria, the library, and during after-school activities.

The seniors became highly engaged because the conversations in class about the stories explored possible social worlds. Although Jamie didn't fully realize it at the time, the discourse, or talk, created in senior English helped students inquire into what made life important, how social lives made sense, and what might be different in their relationships and identities. Class talk about the characters or plot events was always extended in comparison to what they would do if it happened to them, or what others would do if it happened in their community. While Jamie was just attempting to put "every student in the novel," the students put their social worlds into the classroom.

All of this wonderful exploration of ideas about self, others, and the world probably would not have developed if Jamie had graded students on each class contribution. Instead of quality grading students' work, students were guaranteed a C grade if they attempted every activity. This actually became an ongoing joke in class, when students read responses on returned papers and asked, "How did I do? . . . Oh yeah, it's worth a C, right?" While the fear of grading was reduced, the discussions were also invigorated because Jamie followed the students' lead in discussion and did not attempt to force talk to achieve predetermined ideas. Because teachers normally repeat the same content each period of the day, they often force class discussion to follow the same pattern or reach the same interpretation each period. Jamie deviated from this traditional practice. Since only a single class set of any of the books existed, 9-week units were shuffled across the periods of senior English, and because no one class read the same text at the same time, conversations were always fresh and unique. This also led to many reinforcing conversations outside of class between students who compared what they were reading or had read earlier in the year.

Although this reader response and writing process classroom succeeded, several revisions would strengthen its focus on inquiry into social worlds. First, the books read were Eurocentric classic literature. Inquiry into the social lives of students through literature is exploration into culture, both the culture constructed by characters in the text and the culture of the students constructed through their responses and made visible through discussion and critique. The English curriculum needs to involve the vast range of multicultural works by diverse authors that have been largely marginalized by the traditional canon.

Second, although the students read two books and a play connected thematically each 9 weeks, any inquiry into life-relevant ideas and issues cannot be narrowly confined to literature alone. Many other kinds of texts— movies, advertisements, sit-coms, newspapers, art, music, video games, the world wide web, sports, dance, even conversations at the dinner table—provide represented worlds that can furnish the basis for significant classroom inquiries into the language and literacy practices of lived social worlds.

Third, the traditional genre of an interpretive essay on literature constrained the knowledge that students produced and the teacher validated. Even the conversation in class depended mainly on the linguistic abilities of students. In our multimedia world, life is represented and our culture therefore is constructed through a vast array of texts that rely heavily on images and sounds, as well as words. To more fully participate in the creation of cultural meanings, students need to author their ideas in the same range of media as they encounter. Art, mixed-media, and technology tools for authoring multimedia texts also play an important role in conducting inquiry into lived and represented social worlds.

Perhaps the biggest change would make more explicit the purpose for inquiring into social worlds. With those seniors years ago, the explicit purpose went little further than the motto, "Every student should be in the novel." Jamie wanted the students to think about their own lives in terms of the characters, but this self-reflection was framed within a humanistic tradition in which great literature can enlighten one's personal life. Our culture values this individualistic ideal, yet our possible identities and relationships are constructed through social interaction, not individual desire and control. Literary texts have a role in the inquiry into social worlds, for through those works we struggle to represent our lives to each other in sensible narrative ways. But we represent our lives in every symbolic utterance, and social activity in our community, and we construct our possible identities, relationships, and values through the language and symbols we use in our everyday social interactions. The English classroom of the future needs to engage its students in inquiry into how we use language and symbol, text and artifact, to construct everyday social practices and discourses, and most important, into how these practices and discourses define our existence in social, rather than individual, terms. As English teachers, we can provide a context for students to develop and reflect on multiple literacy practices, to recognize how practices are constructed in and valued by different social worlds, and to critique the uses of these practices in order to entertain ways of transforming social worlds.

PART I

A Model for Inquiry-Based English Instruction

IN THE FIRST half of this book, we describe a model for inquiry-based English instruction about social worlds. As we describe this curricular model, we fuse the most recent developments in pedagogy, literacy, cultural studies, literary theory, sociolinguistics, and educational psychology. In Chapter 2, we present the inquiry model as a practice-oriented curriculum in contrast with content-focused and student-centered instruction. We then, in Chapter 3, illustrate the implementation of a social worlds inquiry unit in a ninth-grade English classroom. Building on this relatively complete description of a social worlds unit, Chapters 4, 5, and 6 explore in greater detail the inquiry strategies involved in conducting projects about social worlds. Chapter 4 examines several classroom examples of the three strategies of immersing; identifying concerns, issues, and dilemmas; and contextualizing social worlds. Chapter 5 examines classroom instances in which social worlds are critiqued and transformed. Finally, Chapter 6 explores the many ways in which students have represented social worlds in their inquiry projects. It is important to emphasize that the various inquiry strategies are employed simultaneously and recursively. As the strategies are introduced to students, a lockstep order or sequence should not be emphasized. As we work with students, we find that their inquiry projects may begin with immersion in some new social world through a text, or a sense that some lived social world has been forever transformed. And strategies involving the consumption and production of representations of social worlds are pervasive throughout the inquiry.

2

A Practice-Oriented Curriculum for Inquiry into Social Worlds

To BUILD greater agency in social worlds, students and teachers mutually engage in inquiry projects about how social worlds are constructed. We inquire into social worlds by examining the tools of language and symbol that humans use to construct those worlds. Social worlds share particular constructive processes in which social activities produce and use texts in systematic ways that create conventions, discourses, and codes, to accomplish valued identities and purposes for activity. We talk about these systematic ways of using symbols as literacy practices and discourses. When we engage in practices, or participate in discourses, with some conscious attention to the social world that we hope to construct with others, we can participate with a greater sense of belonging and shared power. We can critique the social worlds being realized and expand our possible relationships and identities by seeking different symbolic interactions (discourses) and social activities (practices). With such a sense of power, there is less chance for language, text, and activity to marginalize people, and a greater chance that a diversity of views will be considered as we, together, continually create and resolve our multiple social worlds.

THE SIX INQUIRY STRATEGIES

Six inquiry strategies form the basic framework for the various inquiries into social worlds described in this book. We briefly introduce the strategies in order to describe the curricular model for inquiry into social worlds. In Chapters 4, 5, and 6, we provide a detailed description of each these strategies:

1. *Immersing*. Entering into the activities of a social world, experiencing the social world as a participant, or observing a social world
2. *Identifying*. Defining concerns, issues, and dilemmas that arise in a social world, or from conflict across multiple social worlds

3. *Contextualizing*. Explaining how the activities, symbols, and texts used in one or more social worlds produce the components of a social world—identities, roles, relationships, expectations, norms, beliefs, and values

4. *Representing*. Using symbolic tools to create a text that represents a lived social world or responds to a represented social world

5. *Critiquing*. Analyzing how a representation of a social world privileges particular values and beliefs; analyzing how particular literacy practices within a social world promote certain meanings while marginalizing other possibilities

6. *Transforming*. Revising one's meanings for the components of a social world, changing one's actions and words within a social world to construct more desirable identities, relationships, and values

As illustrated in Figure 2.1, these inquiry strategies mutually support each other and revolve around various research techniques—wondering, question asking, observing, note taking, interviewing, and data analysis. Although most inquiries begin with the strategy of immersing oneself in the social world of study, a student might identify a concern in the midst of actions attempting to transform a relationship with another person in a social world. Or a student attempting to contextualize a statement in terms of the values it promotes, might decide she needs to immerse himself in that world for a longer period of time to better understand the common expectations and practices of that social world. While students may begin their projects with identifying and end with transforming a social world, they also may begin at other points in the circle, moving from any one strategy to another strategy. And the circle never stops. Once students have transformed a social world, they only encounter new issues, problems, conflicts, and tensions, requiring further inquiry.

MODELS OF INQUIRY FOR A SOCIAL WORLDS CURRICULUM

The six inquiry strategies of a social worlds curriculum engage the student in a "problem-based" English curriculum. In moving away from content-focused literacy instruction in which students learn what scholars have deemed the important content of literature and language convention, students spend their time inquiring into how social worlds are constructed and represented. All experiences and texts can support this inquiry. The object of instruction is not a list of skills or ideas, but the creation of an everyday thinking practice in which students use literacy tools to better understand how social worlds are constructed through words and actions, and how social worlds in turn construct possible identities, relationships, and values. Contextual teaching

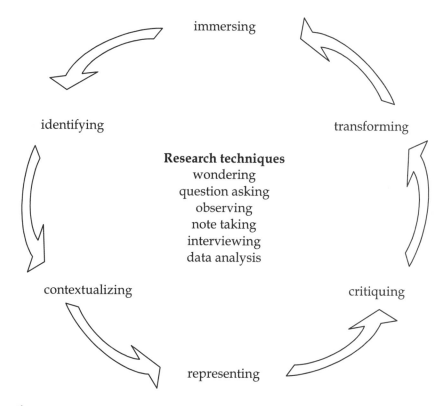

Figure 2.1. Inquiry strategies.

enables learning in which pupils employ their academic understandings and abilities in a variety of in-school and out-of-school contexts to solve simulated or real world problems, both alone and in various dyad and group structures. Activities in which teachers use contextual teaching strategies help students make connections with their roles and responsibilities as family members, citizens, students, and workers. (Howey, Sears, DeStefano, Berns, & Pritz, 1998, p. 2)

Contextual teaching and learning assume that the uses of literacy are situated within social contexts, as opposed to being language skills embedded in students' minds independent of contexts. They also assume that knowledge about these literacy practices is distributed across individuals, contexts, and tools, with learning a consequence of using tools within specific contexts (Salomon, 1993). Therefore, students will learn literacy practices primarily through active participation in purposeful social activities that use texts to experience and negotiate meaning in social worlds.

Within a social worlds curriculum, the primary purpose of engaging in inquiry is to help students gain an understanding of how we construct or author the social worlds we inhabit. Students conduct inquiry projects about their own everyday experiences in social worlds as well as social worlds portrayed in literature or the media. Understanding social worlds as constructed requires students to reflect systematically on their experiences in these worlds. In his model of "dialogic inquiry," Gordon Wells (1999) argues that constructing knowledge involves four intersecting processes: experience, information, knowledge building, and understanding. For Wells, *experience* involves "participation in the multiple communities of practice that constitute . . . [an individual's] life-world" (p. 84), a component related to our strategy of immersing in a social world. *Information* involves "people's interpretation of experiences and the meaning that they have made" (p. 84). *Knowledge building* involves "meaning making with others to attempt to extend and transform their collective understanding" (p. 84). Knowledge building often results in some final product in the form of a representation, model, or written summary. *Understanding* involves formulating a personal, intuitive, "interpretative framework in terms of which we make sense of new experiences and which guides effective and responsible action" (p. 85). Each of these four components feeds the others. As students construct their understanding, they revisit their experience and information. And as they engage in knowledge building, they negotiate their model against others' information or understanding.

Wells's model of inquiry was useful for us in perceiving inquiry as a constructivist process in which students move toward knowledge building and understanding of their social worlds. In social worlds inquiries, students go beyond the traditional student role of "information reporters" to explore dilemmas or issues requiring them to consider what is possible or what could or should be the case (Mosenthal, 1998). Rather than simply collecting information about a world, students study how they and other participants construct worlds, including imagined alternative worlds. Understanding how participants construct worlds involves what David Sumara (1996) describes as "hermeneutic inquiry" that focuses on the processes of constructing knowledge in worlds. For Sumara, this involves the following basic approaches:

1. "[Hermeneutic inquiry] seeks to locate sites for inquiry that situate interpreters in the middle of the activities related to some topic of mutual interest" (p. 127). That is, students select issues or topics in which they have access to participants as they experience certain social worlds, including themselves. For example, they may study the operation of a political campaign in which they are volunteer workers. In this position, they can observe the operations of the campaign,

as well as interview participants about their perceptions of the campaign. Or, if they are working in a large restaurant, they can talk to the manager, chefs, maître d', and waiters/waitresses as they are doing their work. It is important, then, for students to select a social world to which they have ready, easy access.

2. "[Hermeneutic inquiry] seeks to situate all participants in activities that allow the path of inquiry to be 'laid while walking.' . . . [This] method depends on interpretations given to questions that 'present themselves' rather than questions which are predetermined" (pp. 126–127). This suggests the importance of continually formulating and reformulating questions, concerns, problems, issues, or "wonderings" (Short & Harste, 1996) during the process of studying a world. As students discover new ideas through observing and talking to people, they formulate new questions. They are therefore not locked into prematurely defined questions that may turn out to be irrelevant to their study. Moreover, they continue to generate new concerns, issues, or dilemmas requiring further study.

3. "Hermeneutic inquiry does not seek comfortable situations or solutions" (pp. 127–128). Students also need to be willing to study difficult or controversial issues. And, in doing so, they need to be open to challenging the status quo. For example, students may be disturbed by the infusion of advertising in the school world through the Whittle Broadcasting Channel One or through paid sponsorship of sports or school activities. In studying this issue, they may discover that there are considerable financial benefits to the school in return for the willingness to accept advertising. In challenging this use of advertising, students may encounter resistance from administrators who must work within a limited budget. When any inquiry project involves a challenge to the status quo, teachers and students need to make preparations for coping with potential repercussions.

DEFINING A PRACTICE-ORIENTED ENGLISH CURRICULUM: TEACHERS AND STUDENTS AS CO-INQUIRERS

These models of hermeneutic, dialogic, and contextual inquiry emphasize a practice-oriented curriculum model. Traditionally, teachers organize activity in the English classroom around covering literary authors, works, or time periods; lists of test-driven vocabulary; or the need to write a literary analysis paper. This classroom activity is represented by the curricular metaphor of the content-focused approach to teaching English. An alternative metaphor is the student-centered approach. The models of inquiry above suggest the need to build problem-solving activities around students' perceptions of their own concerns, issues, or dilemmas. If teachers assign concerns, issues, or dilemmas, students may simply perceive them as "school" or "teacher" issues. Having both teachers and students mutually identify their own concerns, issues, or dilemmas engages them in a "problem-finding" process of discovering or unearthing matters they perceive as important to their own lives in social worlds. Engaging in co-inquiry means that both the teacher and student are motivated by a shared need to achieve some level of understanding. It also moves away from building inquiry simply around student-centered choices. Both the content-focused and student-centered metaphors revolve around a decision about the content of learning. While the content-focused metaphor emphasizes the great ideas of the world as determined by experts, the student-centered metaphor privileges whatever the student thinks is important about the world. Although classroom activities would be different with the two approaches, both make invisible the literacy practices through which we construct and interpret any idea about the world.

A third metaphor for curriculum—a practice-oriented classroom—is based on the following five assumptions:

1. Classroom practices are constructed by the participants.
2. Practices are multiple, cutting across and interpenetrating the different worlds of school, home, peer group, church, club, work.
3. Students can acquire and become conscious of practices through participation in activities.
4. The possible relationships, identities, activities, and products that practices construct can be critiqued in terms of underlying values, such as equity, agency, responsibility, and community.
5. Based on the values we collectively wish to promote, future practices can be simultaneously co-constructed and examined through a more reflective interaction.

As writers, drawers, readers, viewers, speakers, listeners, or photographers, we participate in social practices that use systems of signs such as language, music, or media to represent and communicate lived experience in a social world. Our skill in this participation is a consequence of our extended involvement over time in the particular textual activity or literacy practice. Although we would like to believe that we can be instructed in the skillful manipulation of symbols, we can learn to use the symbol system only through social interaction with other participants who value the activity. Thinking of skills as consequences of prolonged and engaged participation in symbolic activity, rather than as prerequisites or targets of instruction, supports a practice-oriented metaphor for literacy instruction in the English classroom. Table 2.1

summarizes distinctions between content-focused, student-centered, and practice-oriented conceptions of curricula.

In a practice-oriented curriculum, practices are ways of being and knowing, in which our language and activity construct social worlds that define everyday routines, relationships, and possible identities. We often are not consciously aware of our use of these practices, yet we know that we delib-

Table 2.1. Models of Curriculum and Assumptions About Learning

	Content Focused	Student Centered	Practice Oriented
Skills	Explained as demonstrated, then practiced until automatic	Embedded in an activity or problem and learned as needed to complete the activity or problem	Consequences of membership in a group working toward some valued object
Objectives	Acquiring ideas to gain access to knowledge communities and/or material/cultural capital	Personal development to achieve a more enlightened understanding	Increase participation in activities that create social practices and belonging
Activity	Sequenced ideas that gradually uncover and develop the best knowledge	Given problem or project narrowed by interests of learner to relevant purpose	Engage in valued activities of group and reflect on underlying beliefs
Knowledge	Resides in the world and is universal for all	Individual arrives at different amounts through different relevant experiences	Constructed through symbolic interaction and specific to community activity
Relationships	Expert-novice	Expert guide-explorer	Collaborative inquirers
Assessment	Comparison to predetermined standards for all learners	Developmental comparison to judge individual's progress on predetermined lines	Public reflection on activities in terms of desired community beliefs and values
Decision-making	Leadership	Ownership	Membership
Literacy practices	Reproduce conventions and genres of standard English	Question standard English and promote cultural dialect	Tools situated in purposeful activities of multiple worlds

erately employ certain practices to achieve certain objects of value in a social world. When, as members of a soccer team, students interact with each other on the field, they are employing a range of practices involved in working together as a team. They are using language to define their own and their opponents' strategies, for example, "laying back" and assuming a defensive mode in a soccer game. They are setting up plays involving intricate coordination between roles. And they are drawing on mistakes made in prior games to acquire new practices, continually improving their play.

These practices are newly created in each interaction, yet they are shaped by past interactions as social participants seek consistency and stability across time and space. A goalie may learn to anticipate on which side of the net a shooter is aiming the ball, but knows that she needs to be consistent in how she reacts to an incoming ball—she can't do something unique each time she's faced with a shot on goal.

Students learn these practices not as isolated, autonomous participants but through participation in a joint, collective activity motivated by a purpose or object (Cole, 1996; Engestrom, 1987). The team members perceive their practices as geared to achieving the purpose of winning the game. The practices they acquire in the world of their soccer team transfer for use in other worlds. What is transferred is the use of a practice that works well in one world, in the belief that it therefore may work well in other worlds.

These practices also reproduce underlying rules or value systems. The team members value working together as a team and their coordinating practices of passing off the ball and setting up plays. In school, students learn to value those practices that please the teacher or get a high grade, practices valued within the ideology of a competitive society. To seek to construct a different practice of literacy in school classrooms, a different school world of knowing, a different way of being and relating to others and the world, is to work against a significant cultural ideology played out in our everyday interactions with each other, the media, and the material objects of our social worlds. What is probably the biggest irony, is that although this ideology of school success is dominant, what we remember most throughout our lives are the relationships we established with the people we met in school and the knowledge we generated with them in valued activities within and beyond the classroom walls.

Part of learning to participate in a social worlds curriculum involves learning to employ the literacy practices that will best support active and collaborative inquiry. Rather than simply asking, "What do I want my students to know?" or "How can I help my students learn what they want to know?" the teacher and students consider, "Why do we want to explore this world?" "How are texts used in this social world?" "What inquiry strategies will we use to help us better understand how this social world is constructed?" and "What can literacy do for us and what do we want it to do in a social world?"

To build the inquiry-oriented approaches advocated in this book, we must conceptualize curriculum as a practice-oriented activity. Consciousness and reality are consequences of social and symbolic interaction, not the result of individual progress in learning content directed by teachers or self. Although social worlds seem to be "out there" as timeless institutions, they are being constructed continually through participation in the literacy practices of the valued social world. When we teachers think of the activity in English classrooms as the enactment of socially constructed literacy practices, we enable ourselves to transform the nature of those school literacy practices to better support the shared inquiry into the meanings of self, others, and the world.

3

A Social Worlds Unit in Ninth-Grade English

IN A PRACTICE-ORIENTED curriculum, the teacher's primary concern is with class-room activities. As we have described, it is through activity that participants construct a social world with its component values, identities, and relationships. Within instructional activities, various representational tools, such as literacy, art, or music, support sharing of life experience, responding to a text, negotiating different interpretations, and reflecting on how words, actions, and texts both generate and are shaped by social worlds (the dialectic in which critical thinking can occur). The skilled use of these representational tools is a consequence of participating over and over again in these interpretive activities with the purpose of creating a sense of community belonging.

However, for skilled use of literacy to develop, the sense of meaning must remain generative, negotiated, and reflective. Although classroom events in a practice-oriented curriculum rarely involve direct instruction, teachers use the traditional objectives in a language arts curriculum to certify that students have achieved the curriculum goals, and to develop future activities with a sense of what skills would be learned. But what remains critical to the success of an activity is an overwhelming sense that meanings are open for generation and negotiation by students through their engagement in the activity. This does not exclude the teacher from equal participation in the culture and meaning being constructed in the classroom by the social interactions and joint activities.

While we advocate the study of social worlds as a curricular framework, it is vitally important for the teacher to think about the classroom itself as the construction of a social world, separate from the larger social world of school and from other social worlds "outside" of school. An inquiry practice-oriented curriculum may require the teacher and students to construct identities and relationships that vary from the school norm. Given such "new" forms of activity, it requires time and negotiation to enact the curriculum we advocate.

In this chapter, we examine how, together with Carol Paul, Kelly Bertoty, and Amy Taylor, we designed and implemented a social worlds inquiry project in ninth-grade English at State College Area High School, State College, Pennsylvania. Carol was the mentor teacher, Kelly was an intern, Amy was a university associate supporting her year-long experience in a professional development collaboration, and one of us, Jamie Myers, was a co-planner and co-teacher during the unit. We did not directly teach the six inquiry strategies introduced in the previous chapter. However, the classroom activities established to interpret literature immersed the students into the social worlds represented in literature, media, and their own lived worlds. The activities helped them to identify and contextualize issues important within social worlds, required them to represent these ideas using a variety of literacy and media tools, and structured their responses to critique the aspects of a social world and consider how words and actions might transform a social world.

We developed classroom activities around an anthology of short stories about teen experiences entitled *Coming of Age* (Emra, 1994). In each of 4 weeks, students read three or more stories of their own choice from one section of the anthology, identified an idea connecting the stories, and represented that idea in a new text produced and shared by the students. We called the representations produced by students artifacts, and encouraged students to use a different media or genre each week. As students shared their artifacts, we discussed how the ideas fit various social worlds constructed through our readings of the stories. We identified several social worlds, including family, peer, romance, work, school, hobbies, and sports. As a culminating project, students identified a social world important in their own lives; researched the actions, language, and symbols involved in creating that social world; and then represented important ideas to critique the components of that social world in a final project. Throughout the unit, students shared thoughts on how social worlds might be transformed by changing participants' actions and symbols. A closer look at the classroom activities illustrates how we developed this particular instance of a social worlds curriculum.

ACTIVITIES IN THE SOCIAL WORLDS UNIT

The students began their study of social worlds by creating impromptu skits based on four characters: a popular student, a new student, and two best friends. With the characters' situation left undefined, small groups invented scenes common to school hallways, cafeterias, classrooms, and sports activities. After each scene, we recorded on the chalkboard a brief explanation of how the words and interactions created separation or belonging among the actors. Students explained how the identities and relationships they represented in their scenes arose out of ideas like popularity, fashion, body image, being true to self, loneliness, social class, cliques, and conflicting expectations and desires. In this first-day activity, students reflected on how a person's words and actions with others create feelings of belonging and separation, providing a foundation for understanding the construction of social worlds.

On the second day, we distributed the *Coming of Age* short story anthology (Emra, 1994) and performed a reader's theater of the selection "And Summer Is Gone" (Kretschmer, 1994). To build upon the prior day's analysis of impromptu scenes, students brainstormed ideas on the chalkboard about the following question: How do the words and actions of the characters in the story create separate worlds or belonging in the same world?

The students expressed little initial response to the story. As teachers, we wanted to avoid the common English classroom practice of reducing a story to the traditional analytic categories like plot, setting, character, language style, and theme. Too often a story dies within these categories. The meanings that this analytic approach intends to enlighten are better framed by exploring the social worlds being constructed by the characters' actions and words, the descriptions of surroundings and objects, and the interactions between them. Also, we certainly wanted to avoid the common literary analysis in which students attempted to guess the right answers to teacher questions. Therefore, we prompted discussion of the story by creating a variety of artifacts that represented our different responses as readers to the social worlds built by the characters.

Our artifacts used print, speech, music, and multimedia texts to represent an idea highly connected to the social worlds represented to us in the story. The variety of media used to create artifacts in response to the story illustrated how many different types of symbols and actions are used to construct a social world. Carol shared two artifacts: a collage with a poem about body image surrounded by magazine images of beauty, and imagined journal entries by the female character written 20 years later just before a class reunion. Kelly played an excerpt from the movie *The Breakfast Club* and presented a series of magazine ads connecting friendship with clothing. Amy played her guitar and sang new verses she wrote about the character's actions using a popular tune, and turned the story into a picture book for children. Jamie shared a minute-long quicktime video about romance by setting images and titles from a *YM* magazine to music about romance.

It took us a total of 2 days to share all these artifacts. After each artifact was presented, students were asked about connections between the story and artifact, and how the artifact might help them to think about the story in new ways. As the connecting ideas were recorded on the chalkboard, we pointed to actions or words in the story and/or the artifact that contributed to the construction of a social world in which that idea was important.

On the second day, we sought connections between all of the artifacts and the story to explore the lived worlds of students that made ideas significant. The ideas discussed in response to this story and the teachers' artifacts, ideas like self-image, the pressure of popularity, people changing, losing friends, body image, fitting in, and keeping memories, demonstrated for the students how values, identities, and relationships arise within social worlds. Most important, the use of response artifacts as the basis for discussing the story established a classroom practice in which meaning was a generative, negotiated, and reflective activity.

As described above, the entire first week of the social worlds unit introduced the foundational idea that our words and actions with others construct social worlds in which particular ideas about self, others, and the world are valued. These ideas then can be represented through artifacts that use images, music, and video, as well as print.

Handouts to Structure Class Activities

At the end of the week, we provided the students with handouts to support their own production of artifacts and their analysis of the social worlds represented in the short stories. Although the weekly schedule in Handout One below is unique to this particular unit, the overview of the experience and the explanations about social worlds are relevant to all English classrooms implementing a social worlds curricular approach.

HANDOUT ONE: NINTH-GRADE SOCIAL WORLDS UNIT
EXPLORING TEENAGE SOCIAL WORLDS

Overview of the Experience

The short stories in the anthology *Coming of Age* are about teenagers who live in many different worlds. The interactions between characters in these stories involve words, actions, and symbols that are used to create connected, separate, or even overlapping worlds. We will respond to these stories by making artifacts that connect the story to something we have experienced in our various everyday worlds. As we experience different social worlds, we have similar and different points of view about our own identity, our relationships with others, and the activities we most value in any one social world. Our artifacts should help us to think more about a story, more about how social worlds are created, and more about how media texts of all types use words, images, sounds, and actions to create and portray specific ideas and feelings about a social world.

Weekly Schedule

Each week we will focus on one section of *Coming of Age.*

- We will read at least three stories from each section of *Coming of Age*
  Week One (10/18–21): Do I Fit in?
  Week Two (10/25–29): Families and Friends
  Week Three (11/1–5): Falling in Love
  Week Four (11/8–12): Out in the World
- Thursday (of the prior week) is reading day: You will need to read more outside of class after each Thursday to prepare for the next week.
- Monday is workshop day: Each week, we will create an artifact that communicates a connection between the stories read for that week and some everyday life experience. Everyone will need to work on their artifact outside of class, bringing materials and ideas to class on Monday, and using that day in class to collaborate and finalize weekly artifacts.
- Tuesday and Wednesday are sharing days: As each artifact is shared, the presenter(s) will lead a discussion about connections. First, others will have a chance to share connections they find with the artifact, everyday experiences, stories, or even other artifacts. Exploring different points of view is a central activity. Then, the author(s) of the artifact should be ready to explain his/her own connections.

A social world begins in the symbols, words, and actions we use with others as we interact during any activity. Our language, dress, gestures, activities, habits, and clothing define the social world to which we belong at any one moment in time. Our interactions with others in these worlds will shape our dreams, desires, customs, norms, and traditions. These expectations for our actions and thoughts further shape who we might become (identity), how we relate to others (relationships and power), and our purposes for being alive (values). By exploring how social worlds are always being created by people as they interact, we might have more conscious control over the future worlds we create together.

Accompanying the overview handout were two other handouts. The first functioned as a worksheet for students to use to plan their weekly artifact. It had the following four headings and space for students to brainstorm and to reflect on their artifact/process: *Connecting Idea* asked the student to identify an idea connecting the stories they read with their own experiences; *Artifact Type* required the student to describe the artifact they planned to make; *Reflection About Making the Artifact* asked students to describe their thinking as they made the artifact; and *Reflection on Sharing the Artifact* encouraged students to describe ideas the class shared in response to their artifact and/or new ideas that occurred to them as they shared.

The third handout listed 45 different textual forms for artifacts. As teachers, our goal for the first week was to support the creation of artifacts in response to the stories. We wanted as many different types of media as possible in order to encourage the exploration of how social worlds are constructed through interactions with all symbolic forms of representation.

HANDOUT THREE: NINTH-GRADE SOCIAL WORLDS UNIT
TEXTUAL FORMS

Letters to or from a character	Family tree
Poem	Puppet show
Dance	Dialogue
Mime	Narrative or short story
Impersonation	Play/scene
Image	Impromptu
Video clip	Tableau (wax museum)
TV show	Board game
Music/instrument/song	Background research
Interview	Art
Picture book	Film
Web site	Poster
E-mail	Reader's theater
News broadcast	Costuming/clothing
Gravestone/eulogy	Cartoon
Sequel	Computer video
Siskel and Ebert review	Lost scene/chapter
Panel debate	Advertisement for the story
New character	Timeline
Painting	Collage
Mobile	Diorama
Party plan for the characters	Sculpture
	Journal entry of a character

In addition to helping students generate a response to the story through the creation of an artifact, we wanted to support the discussion of how each artifact represented, and therefore contextualized and critiqued, ideas about the social worlds constructed within the stories. As students shared their artifacts in small groups, or in front of the entire class, we posed questions like: "How do the symbols, words, and actions presented in the artifact create some meaning? Why is this idea important within a social world? How does the artifact help you to think about the social worlds in the stories in new ways?"

After students discussed their artifacts, they recorded the central idea represented by each artifact on a quarter sheet of colored paper. With each section of the anthology, we used a different color. As explained later, these idea slips were organized on large wall charts to help contextualize issues identified by students within various social worlds.

After the students completed the first sharing of their artifacts, we introduced a worksheet activity for the analysis of social worlds in a short story. For each of the four sections of the anthology, students completed between one and three analyses, depending on the grade they desired. The worksheet emphasized three steps to explain the social worlds constructed within a story: first, students quoted the story to identify some significant words, symbols, or actions; second, students described how these words, symbols, or actions created the common components of a social world—traditions, expectations, dreams, roles, relationships, desires, or identities; third, students explored issues about social worlds through a free-write prompted by four questions at the bottom of the worksheet:

1. How do the social worlds shape the characters' identities and relationships?
2. Does the story seem to value one type of social world over another?
3. How are the characters caught between different social worlds?
4. How do the characters resolve conflicts within and/or between social worlds?

Responding to Story Worlds and Naming Social Worlds

After the second week of stories, we generated a large wall chart in each English class by creating a web of the social worlds we had discussed. Although each class web was unique, they shared many of the same social world titles. The social worlds chart for Period 8 is shown in Figure 3.1.

After the few minutes it took to generate the chart, we distributed the yellow and green slips students had used to record the ideas represented by their artifacts in the first 2 sections of the anthology. Each student read a slip, then suggested a social world in which that idea would be created. Class members could make other suggestions and at times a vote helped to decide the social world in which the particular idea would be most important. Although this was a simple activity, it reinforced how the interactions within a social world produced the meaningful issues, dilemmas, and concerns that students had been representing in their artifacts. For the last two sections of the anthology, students taped their idea slips onto the wall chart immediately after discussing their artifacts with classmates in small groups. Because of the large number of artifacts produced each week, most students shared them in small groups, supported by the luxury of having four co-teachers in the room.

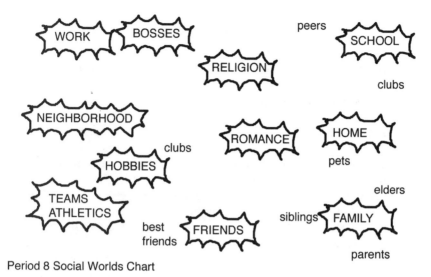

Period 8 Social Worlds Chart

Figure 3.1. Social worlds chart.

However, several students chose to share with the whole class when given the opportunity.

At this point it might be helpful to examine some of the artifacts students created in response to the stories and some of the writing they did on the analysis of social worlds worksheets. This work demonstrates how students began to think about how the words and actions of others—both the characters in stories and people they know in lived social worlds—created multiple social worlds with particular identities, relationships, and values. The artifacts and analyses below are organized roughly by particular social worlds.

Family Social Worlds

Ryan's analysis and artifact of social worlds in "A Private Talk with Holly" (Felsen, 1994) explored the values, identities, and relationships constructed within family social worlds:

QUOTE

And she won't know until some day in the future when her own child—with or without a word of warning—turns a back on home and walks out into the grown-up world forever.

SOCIAL WORLD CREATED

Shows the father–daughter tradition of going fishing, it also shows relationship while fishing—their dream of catching a big fish . . .

EXPLORE IN FREE-WRITE

Because of the father–daughter fishing trip there are many different social worlds created. One is the relationship between father and daughter. Their past fishing trips have brought them close together. Fishing has allowed them to communicate with each other, sharing secrets and deep thoughts—for example, Holly says that she wants to go to college now instead of going to a branch campus.

Another social world created is one of dreams. As a fisherman, of any skill, you always dream of catching that elusive "big one." Holly and her dad are no different. Holly's dad does finally catch the "big one," the biggest and most beautiful bass either of them had seen. But, to Holly's surprise, her dad lets it go. Holly is amazed and that was the one that would make a perfect addition mounted on the wall above the mantle. What was he thinking? He then explains that a mounted fish is a lifeless thing, saying: "Honey, I've always dreamed of having a fish like that mounted on my wall, where I could look at him whenever I wanted to. But a fish on a wall is a lifeless thing, no matter how much you prize it. That fish fought so hard for his freedom that I had to let him go back where he belonged, to live his own life." Holly understands what is meant by this comment. And also thinks of it as an answer from her father if it's okay with him that she goes to college . . .

Ryan's analysis demonstrates his understanding of how the social interaction between Holly and her dad, both their words and their highly symbolic actions with the bass, constructs shared values and a close relationship. In his artifact the same week, Ryan creates a dialogue between two characters from different stories that further demonstrates his understanding of how multiple overlapping social worlds are constructed.

Setting: Barry is sitting at a table in his new church social hall after the service. It is his first week of college, and he is looking gloomy, even though people around him are enjoying the coffee hour between services. Holly, a sophomore, is also at the coffee hour alone, but is much happier than Barry. Seeing Barry alone she decides to talk to him.

HOLLY: Hi! Mind if I join you?

BARRY: No, have a seat.

HOLLY: My name's Holly, what's yours?

BARRY: Pleased to meet you Holly, I'm Barry.

HOLLY: Are you new here?

BARRY: Yep, just moved here from Harrisburg. What about yourself?

HOLLY: I'm a sophomore, used to live in Des Moines, Iowa.

BARRY: Oh, so you're a Hawkeyes' fan?

HOLLY: I wouldn't say that, it's a little hard to be when you go to school here at Penn State. But my parents are, they went to school at Iowa. So you've been a Penn State fan since you were born I take it?

BARRY: That's correct, I've always liked Penn State, back in the days of John Cappelletti, I always wanted to be like him. He's the reason why I played football.

HOLLY: Do you play here at Penn State?

BARRY: Yeah, I'm a red-shirt this year, so I don't play. Hopefully next year I will get a few snaps at running back.

HOLLY: That's really cool! My little brother has always wanted to be a running back—I can't wait to tell him, he's 14. My parents are die-hard Iowa fans; in fact, last time we played them they came up to watch the game. We have pictures and everything. Here's one at the farmer's market. [Ryan has inserted a photo from a magazine that represents Holly and her father.] Do your parents come up to watch you play, being that Harrisburg is only a few hours away?

BARRY: I wish they did. But they can't.

HOLLY: Why not?

BARRY: 'Cause my dad is really sick, that's why I'm so depressed. I'm always thinking about him, how tomorrow may be his last day, and I won't even be there to say goodbye.

HOLLY: I'm sorry, it must be real hard with your dad the way he is. When was the last time you saw him?

BARRY: Right before I left to come here. I have a picture of him before he got real sick, that is, if you want to see it? [Ryan has inserted a picture of a man in a wheelchair with two sons behind him.]

HOLLY: Of course I do!

BARRY: That's him in the wheelchair, me on the right and my brother on the left. It's an old picture—about 3 years old. Do you and your dad do a lot together—I can guess that you two are real close.

HOLLY: Oh we are. I used to go fishing with him. Now I don't have the time. The last I spent "quality time" with him was before I left for

my freshman year. It was real nice; we went fishing together all
the time. He caught the biggest bass we had ever seen! I told him
to keep it—but he let it go.

BARRY: That's nice that you and your dad still have good times.

HOLLY: I'm really sorry about your dad. If there's anything I can do . . .

BARRY: No, thanks anyway. Look at the time, I need to leave. It was
nice meeting you, Holly.

HOLLY: Nice to meet you too, Barry, see you next week!

Holly and Barry begin to talk every Sunday, and they become pretty
good friends. Slowly Barry gets happier now that he has a friend in
Holly. He still remembers his dad, and visits him as much as possible,
because life is too short not to spend time with the ones you love.

In his dialogue artifact, Ryan invents many new aspects of the characters'
identities as he extends them beyond their stories into social interaction with
each other. Ryan's own love of sports becomes a social world overlapping
the social world of church in which their meeting is possible. In the closing
note, Ryan highlights a value for spending time with those one loves, and
recognizes how positive relationships in one's peer social world can have an
impact on one's identity in family social worlds.

Posters and collages were favorite artifacts of students. A small poster
by Emily was titled "Fathers," and included quotes from two stories and an
original poem superimposed on the image of a snowcapped mountain in front
of a large lake. The quotes, "Holly first became my fishing buddy when she
was about 6 . . . but when she reached her teens, she developed other interests," and "I felt like kissing him goodnight. But didn't, of course. Who kisses
his father at 16?" were juxtaposed with the poem.

TO DAD

Dad you came home kind of late last night
sorry I missed you
are you sorry you missed me too
what other things do you miss
a hello hug a goodnight kiss
what about the night mom was gone,
and you tucked me in instead
and the early Christmas mornings when
you'd wake up to me singing by your bed
how about the time at the park when

> we rode the roller coaster six times in a row
> and the time I made the team, and my
> face was magnificently aglow
> what about how easy it was to say I love you
> and now how the times are so few
> I told you in my head
> And I know exactly what you'd said
> And even though it's hard for me to
> Tell you in that way
> I think about it everyday
> And I'll just take this chance to say
> I love you dad

As the students connected artifacts like Emily's to the stories they read, they prompted a critique of the values, actions, and words of parents and teens in both the represented worlds of the stories and their own lived social worlds.

In their analysis papers the students often focused on how family social worlds conflicted with other social worlds within a story. Brett and Justin explore the relationships and values in their analyses of the short stories "Shaving" (Norris, 1994) and "Sucker" (McCullers, 1994):

> In this story, Barry is caught between social worlds. He is caught between the social world of his family and his school social world of his friends, classmates, and teammates. Barry does not seem to have trouble with that however. He handles the situation well, and decides to do what is best, spend time with his family. (Brett)

> The two characters are caught between social worlds because whenever Sucker looks at him, he gives him an odd stare. There is conflict in their present social world and they are caught between wanting to talk again, and staying mad at each other. . . . The story seems to value the social world that was created with Sucker and the main character when they used to talk late at night. This social world is valued because the main character tells us that he wishes that he and Sucker could have talks like that. . . . The characters do not resolve conflicts between social worlds at the end of the story. There is a "boundary" set. (Justin)

While Brett clearly identified how peer social worlds create pressure and tension within the family social world and test the values of a person, Justin focused on how a conflict between siblings within the family social world can force people into creating new separate social worlds to resolve the tension.

Several stories represented the family social world at a time when grandparents, parents, or siblings died. In Justin's analysis of "A Veil of Water" (Boesky, 1994), he interprets the actions and words of the uncle and niece in terms of their difficulty within unfamiliar social worlds that they must live in as a result of death:

> The characters resolve conflicts between social worlds by comforting one another, such as the uncle tried to do in the aquarium. Comforting someone brings them out of a confusing or painful social world, and into a more comfortable one, especially when something bad has happened.

Justin recognizes how death presents people with difficulty within any social world because it removes the everyday interactions that constructed the familiar experience of the world. His observation that people can help others into a more comfortable world shows that students easily can grasp how words and actions can transform a social world.

Two very different artifacts in response to a grandfather's death in another story illustrate the power of students' representations as a response strategy for discussion. Debbie sewed a small panel of cloth with symbols to represent the significant people, objects, and events of the story. Diana wrote a letter to her own grandmother, who died recently, saying things she wished she could have said beforehand; this paralleled the experience of the main character who regretted being mean to her grandfather before he died.

> Dear Grandma,
> Hi. I really really miss you a lot. It is so weird not having you around anymore sometimes when I'm on the phone with Dad I almost ask if I can talk to you. Even though you were always sick for as long as I can remember I never thought that you would die. I know it sounds weird but when we went to dad's house while we were in Long Island for the funeral the house was so empty. I got kind of nervous when I went into your room. I really wish that I could have seen you before you died so I could have talked to you and hugged you.

Especially important about these artifacts is how they allowed the students to bring into the classroom experience their lived experiences and their personal talents at representing ideas about the world.

Responding to School Social Worlds in the Stories

Many of the stories in the anthology represented teen experiences in school with peers, romance, and teachers. Artifacts and analyses of stories often emphasized the confusion teens experienced as they sought to define their own identities within the school social world. An ingenious artifact by Chris, using different colored fall leaves, generated discussion about how different people have trouble fitting in (see Figure 3.2).

Katie's analysis of the social world represented in "Eleven" (Cisneros, 1994) contextualizes how the actions and words in the classroom confuse the character Rachel's own sense of identity and force her to desire the identity she experiences in her family social world:

> Her relationships with her teacher and other classmates is not very good at all during this story. The way that a few of her classmates, one being Sylvia Saldvidar, were acting toward her was unintentionally

Figure 3.2. Fall colors fitting in.

rude. This story, in my opinion, seems to value the social world of the "home environment" over school. The wall that Rachel periodically talks about, her birthday cake, her mother and father, and just the basic atmosphere of being back in her own home, suggests that that is where she would prefer to be. Rachel probably feels more needed at home. She probably feels as though her input really counts there as opposed to her classroom. . . . She's feeling only 3 years old and surely wishes that instead of a cold, hard desk which the school provides for her to cry on, she could just hop into her mother's warm inviting lap, which is part of "home." She needs to feel the protection of one atmosphere (home), while in another (school).

The students often identified issues related to the existence of cliques formed around academic tracks in school social worlds. In fact, they clearly saw students as belonging to different social worlds within the school based on academic subjects, sports, and clothing. Students analyzed these multiple social worlds in different ways, considering them as flexible boundaries that students could move beyond to establish relationships, or definitive divisions that kept students well separated. In response to the story "I Go Along" (Peck, 1994), Abby and Candice made the following analyses about the social worlds constructed in the story:

The two main characters, Sharon and Gene, are both in two different social words. Sharon is one of the girls in school that most of the guys are after, and who is very popular; even more popular than the cheerleaders. . . . Sharon compliments Gene, and says that he should be in the advanced class because he is smart and he should try. I think that makes Gene feel good coming from a girl like Sharon. . . . I don't know if Gene and Sharon are "falling in love," but I do sense some sort of friendly relationship. (Candice)

I like the quote I chose, because it sort of talks about social worlds within social worlds. Like there are slackers in the advanced classes, overachievers in the regular classes, etc. I think the boy in the story changed his opinion about the advanced group. He thought they were stuck up and too "smart" but he found out that they were kind of like the regular group. I think this shows that sometimes we stereotype and prejudge people from other social worlds. (Abby)

When the students describe how the story seems to favor one social world over another, they reveal their ability to critique how specific language and symbols construct particular social worlds. They understand how authors intend to construct specific identities, relationships, and values by representing particular actions and symbols in a story. When students can critique the author's craft, they can grasp how their own identities are constructed through social interaction in which participants invent their actions and words at the same time the social world provides valued conventions to enact.

Peer and Romance Social Worlds

The wide variety of artifacts and analyses students created to represent ideas about relationships and identities in peer and romantic social worlds often emphasized a value of being true to oneself.

> I think in this story especially it was saying that who you have a relationship with classifies if you are cool or not. . . . [Tossie] dated guys her friends would think are cool rather than who she thought were cool inside. (Stephanie)

> I think Millicent originally wasn't very popular, and suddenly she was introduced to this new group, they wanted HER. This was her chance. She could be known by everyone. People would now look up to her, and they'd want to be friends with her. She would now have connections. . . . I think finally reality hit her. These people that she was associating with came from two completely different social groups. They may never accept Tracey so why should she cut herself away, and lose her closest friend . . . she shouldn't brush her hair to fit in, she should do it because that's what she wants. That would be what makes her, her. (Steph)

Students expressed strong critiques about how characters sought romantic relationships as represented across the short stories and other media texts. Elise used the computer to digitize and edit the scenes in which Aladdin is reconstructed into the Prince in order to win the love of Jasmine in the Disney movie. She juxtaposed quotes from two different stories with scenes from the movie *Aladdin*, to conclude, in her own words, that "the places you go and the way you are dressed can totally change you and place you in a different world, and change people's perceptions of you." Abby excerpted lyrics from five different songs to represent different kinds of love: crushes, loving someone who doesn't love you, jealousy (fighting for someone else's love), true love, exciting love, and love within families. Elyse created a poster titled "Sucker" to present the cycle of relationship between boys and girls that repeats itself over and over again. The subtitle asks, "Who's the real sucker?" At each stage of the cycle she included a quote from the story "Sucker"

(McCullers, 1994), juxtaposed with an image from a magazine that represented the appropriate emotion for that stage. The recognition of a pattern for romance required her to contextualize how actions and words of participants frame possible identities and relationships, and her work to select just the right image for each stage required her to critique the potential ideas portrayed in each image.

Community Social Worlds

The students' artifacts and analyses identified issues of class and race, supporting a critique of the values, identities, and relationships in various community and neighborhood social worlds. Katie contextualizes the actions and words of Lizabeth in the story "Marigolds" (Collier, 1994) within a race/class dilemma that limits possibilities and creates strained community relationships that force Lizabeth to examine her own values in an unfair world:

> The social world that Lizabeth was living in shaped her into believing that she was less of a person when compared to Whites and other superior races. She thought that the only way she would ever be able to make a living would be to work for a wealthy family or another job closely related to this. She believed that her family would never be treated with the respect and the love that every human being deserves and this probably hurt her plenty. This story definitely values the social world of "living in a higher-class society" as opposed to "working for those living in a higher-class society." . . . Although this reading shows that the higher class was indeed valued over the lower class, most of the people living as one in the lower class were the real hard workers who cared so much for their families.

Katie critiques the values of the social worlds represented in the stories and likely reveals her own values for hardworking and caring families. She continues her analysis by exploring how Lizabeth hoped to transform the lives of her family through her own actions:

> Lizabeth is caught between these two worlds which society had created. She was a part of the poorer side while her parents and relatives longed to be a part of the richer side. She probably wished very much to have the advantages that other children received and just took for granted. She wanted for her family to not have to work so hard. She especially wished that she would be able to be with her mother during the days when she was at work all day. These are only a couple of examples of her being caught between social worlds. They

all relate to each other because they all show how much Lizabeth
probably wanted for she and her family to be together all of the time
and live a fruitful life without working their hands to the bone. I don't
think that Lizabeth ever really resolves the conflict these two worlds
create. She does try though. All of the tension is being built up inside
of her each time she is annoyed by her siblings or when she hears her
father crying and her mother trying to comfort him. She needs a way
to feel some control, a way to feel like she is superior to somebody. So
she decides to take advantage of dear old Miss Lottie. She needs to
find some way to get out all of her anger and frustration, and she
chooses to destroy. Yet, the conflict is never settled because as soon
as she gets out all of her anger, she realizes that she did it in the
wrong way and that Miss Lottie never did anything to deserve what
happened to her precious marigolds. She then feels terrible about
something new and so the conflict is never gone. Nobody will really
ever make all of it between the different races go away in this world
even today.

Katie extends the relationships represented in the social worlds of the story
into her own lived social worlds, concluding that people will not be able to
transform the racist social interactions that construct separate conflicting
social worlds. Although she contextualizes Lizabeth's destruction of the marigolds in a neighbor's lawn as an act of attempting to take control of her own
possible identity, she suggests that part of growing up is realizing that you
have to have certain values even when social worlds control you.

Unlike many of the analyses and artifacts representing family, peer, and
romance social worlds, the students often represented the issues of class and
race as strong forces of community beyond their control. In the other social
worlds, they were more likely to express a belief in one's ability to transform
relationships and identities through different actions and words. For example,
Nilu wrote:

The social worlds or environment teaches the children about its
values and what is expected of them. In many ways it teaches the
children what the "social world" wants them to learn: . . . If, for
example, they wanted the children to be racist about another group of
people, they would only teach them the bad things about the group,
and turn any good things that they would do into bad things.

Nathan explained how the upper-class values and desires embedded in the
fancy ball clothing and dancing exerted tremendous control over the young
girl at her first ball:

But the ball obviously has more power and quickly sweeps her off her feet. The characters don't actually resolve the conflict, the social world does. It does it by drawing the girl back and making her happy again.

A similar, but more impassable, divide was expressed in an artifact, a collage, responding to "Adjo Means Good-bye" (Young, 1994). The collage segregated White girls from Black girls and left a gulf between them (see Figure 3.3).

In an analysis of the same story, Debbie concluded that even though a Black and a White girl wanted to be friends, the social world of the community was too strongly against the friendship:

> In this story the two girls are torn between three worlds. The world of their friendship, the world of the White people, and the world of the Black people. Marget, the little White girl, is forced into her new world (the world of the White people) after no one came to her party because her Black friend was there. Her mother pushes her into this

Figure 3.3. The racist divide.

world by saying her Black friend is not to come to her house anymore. Marget also wants to be in her world of their friendship. This is shown because she cries when she has to tell her friend what her mother said. Marget's friend is also forced back into the world of Black people. She is not allowed to see Marget anymore and no one comes when they know she'll be there. She also wants to be in the world of the friendship. She shows this by going over to Marget's house uninvited. This is how the two girls are torn between the three worlds. The two formed by their difference and the one made by their similarities.

Another artifact carried a similar tone of young people coming to realize that they have little control over the reality of adult social worlds. This multimedia artifact in pencil consisted of a first-person narrative titled "Coming of Age" surrounded by symbols and drawings. Down the left side of the page ran unhappy faces, and down the right side ran a series of small hearts. At the top of the page were two black clouds with raindrops coming out. Two thought bubbles came from a person holding suitcases, one with a rainbow and butterflies and the other with a ballerina and the words *twinkle, twinkle*. In the midst of the background were two stern eyes with the eyebrows tilted inward. Alongside the girl was one small photocopied image of a man facing a fire-breathing dragon. The accompanying narrative read:

> I step outside into a brand-new world. I am away from what I know and what I am used to. Away from my "security blanket." Away from all the rainbows and butterflies away from "Mommy" and "Daddy." Now I see that the world is not happy smiling people holding hands. Now I see guns, and bombs, and rats and roaches. Now I see cold, Now I see dirt. Now I see me. I see that things are not what they seem. Now I hear rumors, and gossip. Not twinkle, twinkle from the pink jewelry box which once dwelled upon my miniature makeup kit. Now I have Truth, and lies, and now I know the difference. Now I see, hear, smell, feel, and taste truth. Now I see, I am coming of age.

This was among the most powerful artifacts created by the students. The juxtaposition of images and words to represent the student's own lived experiences in response to the stories created the feeling of a child full of twinkling power smacking into a world full of social interactions that work against, shut down, and limit one's own agency and identity. But there is hope in the narrator's sense of truth that suggests students can be conscious of how their own words and actions with others can construct good and truthful social worlds.

SUGGESTIONS FOR DEVISING AND
IMPLEMENTING INQUIRY PROJECTS

On the basis of our work with teachers in the ninth-grade project as well as teachers working on other inquiry projects, we conclude this chapter with some suggestions for devising and implementing inquiry projects.

Letting Students Select the Inquiry Topic

We have discovered advantages and disadvantages to having students select their own inquiry topics. By selecting their own topics, students are more likely to be invested in or motivated to study a social world. On the other hand, having students select from a menu of choices allows teachers to ensure a curriculum that exposes the entire class to a range of social worlds relevant to a particular novel or class project that may be the springboard for inquiries. One compromise alternative is for both teachers and students to initially explore the same topic together, followed by students generating subtopics or relevant new topics.

Defining an Overview of the Project

Students need a big-picture overview of their inquiry project in order to understand and plan how specific tasks contribute to the project's larger purpose. They then can understand how various research activities can help them to construct a representation of a social world. The following overview was used for the final project for the ninth-grade social worlds unit:

THE WEEK FIVE FINAL PROJECT

> The final project is a written or media text that represents a social world important to teens. You could author a short story, a play, a collection of poems or songs, a portfolio of drawings, a photo essay, a video documentary, an analysis of television shows, a web site, a large mural, etc. Think bigger and more complex than the weekly response artifacts. The project has two layers: (1) the text/media you create, and (2) your written explanation of how the text/media portrays ideas about one or more social worlds.

Specifying Inquiry Tasks

It is helpful to provide students with a list of the specific tasks involved in completing a project. For her students' inquiry projects on social worlds,

Brenda Robertson of North High School, North St. Paul, Minnesota, specified the following inquiry tasks for beginning their projects:

- Brainstorm possible topics.
- Explore several topics for viability and interest.
- Choose your topic.
- Develop a research proposal that provides a rationale for the topic. (Why did you choose your topic? What importance does it have for you? What importance does it have for the rest of us? Who will be the primary readers?)
- Describe prior knowledge of the topic (personal experience, personal biases, factual information, vocabulary).
- List focusing questions.
- Formulate a research plan. (How do you plan to gather information? Where will you find sources of information? Whom will you interview? What assistance will you need in order to complete your research?)
- State a working gloss: In one sentence, state your topic and purpose (what you hope to accomplish by completing this project).

Teachers also need to provide students with a detailed schedule, along with deadlines for completing these tasks. While this may be interpreted by students within the traditional evaluation discourse practice of school, teachers should emphasize how the production of all representations involves a series of activities and deadlines.

Providing Models for Tools, Inquiry Strategies, and Research Techniques

The six strategies and the different research techniques described in more detail in the following three chapters are difficult for many students, particularly early adolescents. Teachers must use as many tools as possible to demonstrate ways to represent ideas about social worlds. In the ninth-grade unit, the teachers created various artifacts using different tools, and throughout the unit consistently demonstrated ways of connecting quotes from the stories to representations of social worlds ideas.

Providing Time for Students to Learn to Employ Different Tools and Inquiry Strategies

Students need ample time to study a social world, especially in their first experience of inquiry. In reflecting on a project involving the study of rebels in society with ninth through twelfth graders at the St. Paul Open School, St. Paul, Minnesota, Leo Bickelhaupt noted that it was difficult for his students to learn to use all of the strategies effectively, particularly the strategies of critiquing and transforming. As a result, many of his students reverted to a more traditional research report format. In the future, he will focus instead on each of the different strategies in more depth so that students become accustomed to an inquiry orientation over a longer period of time.

Providing Criteria for Evaluation

Evaluative practices require the greatest amount of change to construct a discourse practice of inquiry into social worlds. Teachers often have used more reflective forms of self-evaluation to invite students to participate in assigning their own grades. To help students assess drafts of their research report, Brenda Robertson provided students with a checklist for assessing their drafts:

- Focus is clear and sustained.
- Relevant background information is presented clearly, concisely, and accurately.
- Organization is clear and appropriate for audience and subject matter.
- Language/vocabulary is clear, concise, consistent, and appropriate for audience.

Students also need criteria for how their final project report or presentation will be evaluated. To evaluate students' work on the social worlds project, Carol, Kelly, Amy, and Jamie provided students with the following checklist criteria:

- Own point of view expressed about a social world (originality)
- Creative use of text/media to portray social worlds
- Thoughts and decisions while making project detailed in project journal
- Written explanation of ideas presented in the project about social worlds
- Evidence of time and effort
- In-class workshop time used effectively to develop project

Contract forms for grading final projects establish threshold levels for the amount of work students wish to complete to achieve each grade. For example, the following contract-grading form was used with the ninth-grade unit:

FOR A C

- Effective use of time during in-class workshop week
- The project reflects complexity, time, and effort
- The written explanation fully explains your point of view on a social world

FOR A B

- All of the above plus a project journal that documents your daily thinking and creating process

FOR AN A

- All of the above plus originality and creativity

These forms of evaluation can help shift the classroom discourse practice; however, the underlying issue involves a shift in beliefs about knowledge and conventions central to the whole concept of social worlds. By this point in the book we hope it is evident that within a social worlds curriculum, knowledge and conventions are constructed through social interaction as participants negotiate shared meaning about experience. It is antithetical to a social worlds orientation to convey the purpose for an activity as the achievement of predetermined conventions and knowledge. Instead, teachers must encourage students to engage in an ongoing critique of the conventions and knowledge of a social world, and to consider how their participation in those worlds can transform possible values, identities, and relationships to make a better world.

SUMMARY

Additional examples of how these ninth graders used the six inquiry strategies to negotiate meaning about various represented and lived social worlds appear elsewhere in this book. Several of the larger final project inquiries are shared in the chapters in Part II on particular social worlds, and issues related to the evaluation of students in the unit are discussed in Chapter 6.

It is helpful to note that the weekly analyses, artifacts, and discussions generated by the students in the particular unit described in this chapter helped them to far exceed the critical thinking generated by traditional categories of literary analysis. By exploring how interactions, language, and objects constructed identities, relationships, and values in conflict across multiple contesting social worlds, the students became deeply involved in the characters, the plot, the setting, and even the style of language in the text. The classroom practice created by the interpretive activities supported the sharing and negotiating of meaning through multimedia texts that tapped into the students' diverse abilities to represent meaning with a range of symbolic tools. And, the social world constructed in the classroom community itself opened up the possible identities and relationships that the students experienced, and thus vastly increased the value of participating in the critical thinking that occurred. Many students came out of their shell, so to speak; of the approximately 120 students involved in five periods of English, only one or two remained somewhat resistant to the activities at the end of the social worlds inquiry unit.

4

Inquiry Strategies: Immersing; Identifying Concerns, Issues, and Dilemmas; and Contextualizing

HAVING DESCRIBED in general terms the inquiry strategies involved in a social worlds curriculum, we now look more closely at three inquiry strategies: immersing in a social world; identifying concerns, issues, and dilemmas to focus inquiry into social worlds; and contextualizing components constituting social worlds. While we discuss these three strategies separately, they are intimately linked to the activities of representing, critiquing, and transforming social worlds.

IMMERSING IN A SOCIAL WORLD

In order to identify a focus for an inquiry project, students usually must first immerse themselves in a particular world—their family, a sports team, a novel—and intentionally reflect on aspects of the relationships, identities, or values that concern or interest them or that are problematic. In immersing themselves in either a lived or represented world, students need to consciously attend to their own reactions to that world, because these reactions often suggest those aspects a person would find urgent or significant enough to study. By attending to and reflecting on difficulties or problems in their experience in a social world, students can identify concerns, issues, or dilemmas.

One characteristic function of print literacy is the reflective distance it can provide from one's moment-to-moment participation in a social world. Students may be more likely to reflect on their social interactions and the material conditions of their social worlds by recording their reactions to experiences in a dual-entry journal format. On the left side of the page, they may describe observations of particular objects, symbols, activities, interactions, or practices in a world. Then, next to each of these observations, they note specific thoughts and feelings evoked by the practices and material conditions of the social world. This is similar to the social worlds analysis worksheet described in the previous chapter, on which students noted a quote from the story, then explained the kind of social world created by the words, actions, or objects portrayed in the quote.

Another research technique for immersing oneself in a social world is the "I-Search" research paper proposed by Ken Macrorie (1988). To begin an I-Search project, students study how they learn some new activity, or how people already engage in some activity valued in a social world. In contrast to the traditional, objective research report in which students simply rehash information, inquirers make explicit their own processes of how they conducted their research in a first-person point of view. By delineating how they conducted their research, inquirers move from descriptions of being immersed in the activities of a social world, to identifying issues relative to the construction of their participation in that world, to contextualizing and critiquing the values, identities, and relationships important in that world. Writing an I-Search paper is similar to keeping a journal or diary that documents everyday experiences and provides space for observations and reflections. Concluding activities involve re-examining the descriptions to construct overall patterns that describe and explain a social world.

Students should choose an appropriate social world in which to immerse themselves. If they hope to study a lived social world, they must have ready access to it so they can gather sufficient evidence. Students who have a limited amount of time or access to a site may examine a social world as represented in literature and the media. Or, they may study a virtual world in the electronic environment of the computer or video game. Richard's university students have studied sites such as a 3-day country western festival, tattoo parlor, triathlon, coffee shop, parent-education organization, small-town celebration, church choir, group of baseball fans, nightclub in the Mall of America, co-op apartment club, gay bar, and school classroom. For each of these sites, students had ready access because they were participants in or worked at the site. For example, one of Richard's students, Joshua Coval (1999), conducted a study of the world of snowboarding. He was interested in what practices were involved in learning to snowboard. Already immersed in the world of snowboarding as an experienced snowboarder and instructor himself, Joshua more closely observed and interviewed various snowboarders at a local ski slope, Buck Hill, located outside of Minneapolis. He also studied representations of snowboarding in snowboarding magazines and videos.

Joshua found that learning to snowboard involves acquiring both skills and language. As he notes:

> Learning the language is the first lesson students get at Buck Hill. They learn basic terminology. It makes them feel like they are entering into a secret world. They feel that they have the key to the first door in the labyrinth. . . . A person

with a background in either skateboarding or surfing will have an easier time learning the language and the tricks because the moves are all related. This is not to say that others cannot learn; they just have to pay more attention to the details of the language. A frontside 180 is different from a backside 180. An indy grab differs from a stale fish, and a nose grind is different from a tail grind. A McTwist isn't a frozen treat from McDonalds. It is a front flip with a 180-degree spin. (pp. 3, 12)

Joshua identified five different groups of people in terms of differences in their learning about snowboarding. He envisioned these "five groups of people as operating in different rings, with the 'professional riders' at a central core, along with the 'market departments' [who] have their fingers on the pulse of the snowboarding world. As with the professional riders, the marketing people dictate what the outer ring inhabitants see as the images and style to imitate" (p. 2). He argued that much of the marketing of snowboarding builds on representations from the worlds of surfing and skateboarding. He critiqued a magazine advertisement for snowboarding from *Transworld* (1995) picturing a snowboarder doing a turn on a hill: "25 years ago . . . this move set the standard for bottom turns. Snowboarding is a world of surf-inspired power bottom turns all day long . . . everyday" (p. 35).

Joshua contextualized the perceptions of the sport in "television commercials for Mountain Dew and other 'extreme' products," as well as experiences in the virtual worlds of video games. By discovering links between lived, represented, and virtual worlds, Joshua explained some beginners' perceptions of belonging and alienation: "They feel that snowboarding will come as easily to them as it did on the video game; at least that is what one beginner told me when he sat frustrated and crying with his brand new top-of-the-line gear" (p. 3).

Immersion in the Medieval World of *Catherine Called Birdy*

To illustrate the process of immersion in the classroom, we turn to an example of a middle school inquiry project conducted by a group of 15 seventh-grade females who volunteered to meet in an after-school group called The Girls' Book Club organized by Sarah Gohman, a teacher at Wayzata Middle School, Wayzata, Minnesota. These students conducted their project on the medieval world in preparation for responding to the novel *Catherine Called Birdy* (Cushman, 1994), which portrays the life of an adolescent female coping with a controlling father and the patriarchic world of the Middle Ages. Working in pairs, they studied a specific aspect of medieval life, such as the feudal system, the life of lords and peasants, the church, education, and so on, and taught what they learned to their classmates. Then they immersed themselves in the text of *Catherine Called Birdy*, recording and sharing their dialogue-journal responses with partners. As they read the novel, Sarah shared some of her own questions in response to the novel, questions such as, "How do you feel about the way Catherine is treated by her father? Would you enjoy living in this society? Why not? Is there anything that Catherine could have done to have changed her situation?"

In their journals, the girls responded to Sarah's prompts. They also asked questions of one another such as, "I wonder why anyone would ever hit someone they are supposed to love? Why would someone use another person to increase their wealth?" (Chelsea), "I wonder what the old woman meant by, 'You little Birdy must learn how to fly.' Do you know?" and, "Chelsea, what do you think of Catherine's relationship with Perkin? Do you think that it would be shunned now?" (Brook).

IDENTIFYING CONCERNS, ISSUES, AND DILEMMAS

Based on or as part of their initial immersion, students then identify those primary concerns, issues, and dilemmas that will serve as the basis of their further investigation of a social world. To frame such an inquiry project, students may list questions, or what Short and Hartse (1996) describe as "wonderings," about their experiences. In the I-Search approach, students ask questions throughout the process regarding what and how they are learning, questions such as

- What do/don't I already know?
- Why am I studying a certain topic; what is my purpose?
- How am I studying this topic; what methods am I using and are they working?
- What am I learning from my research? What is its value or significance? (Macrorie, 1988)

The focus of an inquiry must be open to continual revision as students discover new information. It is common for students to begin with a rather large topic and to need to refine the scope to some specific aspect of a social world. Attempting to study all aspects of peer worlds, for example, will likely result in a superficial set of conclusions, as opposed to studying just one concern, issue, or dilemma in interactions with peers.

Identifying Concerns

Students are often overwhelmed by a wide range of concerns, creating high levels of stress. They often become concerned when things do not work as they hoped or when they perceive inequities or do not perceive solutions, creating high levels of uncertainty, distrust, and anxiety. Rather than throwing up their hands in despair, students need to learn how to step back and identify reasons why they have certain concerns.

In sharing their journal responses in small-group discussions, students in The Girls' Book Club verified each other's concerns and anger about Catherine's plight as shaped by the forces of her social world. They were particularly perplexed by the power that religion played in politics. They were baffled that people were physically punished for not believing in Roman Catholicism. The girls were also surprised by the methods of warfare that were utilized during this time. One pair reported on the spillage of hot oil onto people over the castle walls. This seemed particularly horrific to the students.

Through her questioning in discussion, Sarah helped the students to focus their inquiries around their concerns about the treatment of Catherine in the novel. She asked them, "Given what we know about society in the Middle Ages, why do you think women were treated unfairly?" Andrea noted: "They were not allowed very much freedom at all and could be abused by men. The roles they played were those of not very smart or talented people, although they might have been as smart or smarter as the men, given the chance to learn . . . they didn't get educated because it was considered a waste because they were women." Ann noted that "they were called too 'expensive' to go to school. So they didn't get their education that they needed . . . women were also considered weak and fragile." And, Julia noted, "I don't think they had many opportunities to voice their own opinion . . . [or] chances to do a job or activity that they *wanted* to do . . . everyone, including the women, was stuck." As Sarah's students moved beyond their emotional reactions to consider the reasons for those reactions, their concerns led to critiques.

Identifying Issues

Issues differ from concerns in that they revolve around contentious phenomena on which participants disagree, as with the issue of gun control or abortion. In identifying issues, students note aspects that strike them as debatable or problematic in terms of ethical or social implications, for example, issues of fairness, equity, justice, and truthfulness. In framing issues, students define both the specific micro-level experience in a lived or represented world, as well as the larger, macro-level implications for social agencies, laws, and procedures through which values are enacted.

In her written log about The Girls' Book Club, Sarah reported on how the students identified several issues of the medieval world in terms of the values, identities, and relationships important to that world. Her journal also hints at how the students began to critique aspects of the medieval social world as they contextualized the issues within their own social worlds:

> I asked them to reflect on what they had learned in determining how women were treated in general during this time in history (in Britain). All of the girls felt that the treatment of women during this time was terrible. They were appalled that girls were told who they must marry. They were also disturbed by the fact that Catherine's father beat her regularly. In addition, they thought that life for females at that time was boring. Several commented on the fact that women spent much of their time indoors embroidering and cooking. They were upset by the lack of opportunity for women during this time period. (I am finding it very interesting to hear their reactions to such topics. I am not surprised by their views, however.) One girl commented about how lucky we are today compared to women back then.
>
> The girls didn't seem to understand that Roman Catholicism was THE religion in Britain during this time period. . . . All of the girls seemed surprised by the lack of modern conveniences during the Middle Ages. They have been particularly focused on the differences in personal hygiene. Some of my students reported that they shower twice a day—thus, they were astounded that during the winter months people during the M.A. might not shower at all! I must admit, I found that a bit disgusting myself. . . . Our society seems a bit over-the-top about cleanliness, but there are many places in today's world where people bathe much less often than we do. Also, this came up when we were talking about treatment of females in today's society. Life for women in the U.S. is much different than life for women in other parts of the world. This is something that we will come back to when gleaning ideas for the inquiry projects. It would be interesting to have some students do research on treatment of Muslim women, for example.
>
> We also discussed why women and men had the roles that they did during this time period. The girls talked about the issue of men being stronger and therefore more able to succeed in fighting in the Crusades. This didn't go over very smoothly. What I mean is that the girls had a hard time agreeing that men make better fighters. This also makes me think about the inquiry projects. Some girls might want to look at women's roles in the military (there's an unusual "society"). We also talked about how some women did fight in the

Crusades and discussed how this might have led to change for women in general.

Through journal writing, peer research projects on the Middle Ages, and discussion of reading, the students identified many aspects about their social worlds for further inquiry.

Identifying Dilemmas

Students also experience various dilemmas in their lives to which they have no easy answers or solutions. They may be caught in the dilemma of wanting to maintain friendships with peers but being uneasy about doing something illegal with those peers. Or, they may face the dilemma of being in love with someone of whom their parents disapprove. For Mosenthal (1998), a traditional problem-solving approach fails to provide much help in coping with these dilemmas. He argues that a problem-solving approach assumes that there is some "ideal goal to be achieved or a desirable outcome to be attained" (p. 334). Often, solving problems only leads to discovery and creation of new problems. And, a problem-solving approach assumes that problems can be easily defined and readily solved. However, the dilemmas faced by adolescents caught between the values of multiple social worlds, or in contest with co-participants within one social world, are "often messy, lacking in structure, and intractable to routine solutions" (p. 336). Mosenthal suggests having students study dilemmas as defined by competing social agendas. He breaks these competing social agendas down into specific aspects:

- The goals or purposes for an agenda
- Who defines and who benefits from an agenda
- The material resources and tools available
- The actions prescribed and taken
- The outcomes and evaluation of the success of the outcomes

Dilemmas can occur when people adopt competing short-term versus long-term goals—"do drugs now and be part of the peer group with the risk of being caught; don't do drugs, avoid the risk of being caught, but be scorned by peers" (p. 340). Dilemmas also arise when students' agendas conflict with agendas of parents, teachers, or employers. While parents or teachers want students to be successful in a science class, they may perceive themselves as having little interest in science. Students may frame an inquiry project around dilemmas associated with these competing agendas, or what we often refer to in this book as values contextualized within and between multiple social worlds.

CONTEXTUALIZING SOCIAL WORLDS

As students develop their inquiry of a particular concern, issue, or dilemma, they generate explanations that connect the actions and words typical within a social practice to the consequent identities, relationships, and values possible in a social world. In "contextualizing," students actively construct versions of a social world in terms of the purposes, roles, rules, beliefs, and history operating in that world (Engestrom, 1987). James Gee (2000) provides an example of how contextualizing works:

> If I come up to a female colleague and in "everyday talk" say, "you look great this morning," this means little or nothing until that colleague has actively constructed the context in a certain way. It may be taken in the context of "friendly banter between colleagues"; or as "intended or unintended sexual harassment"; or as "joking with someone who cares too much about her looks"; or perhaps as "irony meant to defuse a 'politically correct' environment." That colleague will consult what they know about me and about themselves, our mutual histories, where we are and what it means to be there here and now, and a myriad of other factors, in order to actively construe the context as being a certain way. (p. 64)

The variety of possible meanings for the greeting in Gee's illustration are framed, or contextualized, by the components of a social world, such as purposes, roles, beliefs, rules, and history—and others like expectations, desires, and dreams. If one thinks of a social world as a system, it would be composed mainly of these components. The components frame the meanings for words and actions and shape the possible identities, relationships, and values within a social world. The components work to extend a social world across ongoing social interaction by using conventionalized words, symbols, objects, and activities. Yet, as participants interact in their multiple social worlds, the specific meaning for each component is continually negotiated. Different social worlds have different purposes, different roles and relationships, and different rules. As students inquire into various social worlds, determining the meaning of these components in a social world can help them examine and represent that world, how it is constructed, and how it might be transformed.

Purpose

Activities are driven primarily by purpose or motive—they are designed to achieve some outcome (Engestrom, 1987). Understanding a social world therefore involves understanding an activity's raison d'être. The activity of meeting and interacting with others at an annual block party held in Richard's neighborhood serves the purpose of having neighbors, some of whom may not know each other, become acquainted with each other. This activity serves the larger purpose of building a sense of living in a shared space in which everyone knows everyone else and is concerned about their well-being.

In trying to make sense out of people's participation in an activity, students may ask, "Why are people doing what they are doing?" or "What are they trying to accomplish?" In studying the organizing meetings of a neighborhood's protest against its destruction in order to build a bridge, Stillwater (Minnesota) Junior High students noted that a primary purpose for these meetings was the residents' need to preserve a sense of dignity and self-respect in the face of the loss of their neighborhood.

As students conduct inquiries into concerns, issues, and dilemmas, the following questions may help them to represent the purposes held by participants for their language and activity:

- Why are people doing what they are doing?
- What are people trying to accomplish?
- What is driving this activity?
- Are multiple, and possibly conflicting, purposes at work in the activity?

Roles

Within a social world, participants or characters adopt roles or identities that reflect their commitment or allegiance to the social world. Participants make sense of a world in ways that are consistent with attempts to maintain that identity. A student who perceives herself as a "competent waitress" in a restaurant enacts practices with customers to maintain her sense of being "competent." As Lave and Wenger (1991) note, "Learning . . . is a process of becoming a member of a sustained community of practice. Developing an identity as a member of a community and becoming knowledgeably skillful are part of the same process" (p. 65). For example, in the activity of the small-town Minnesota summer festival, assuming the role of a festival queen entails confirming a commitment to the beliefs and values of the small town (Lavenda, 1997). Lavenda describes the queen competitions as "about fitting in, doing well, and demonstrating poise, confidence, and capacity" (p. 32). Being crowned a queen is therefore part of assuming the role of a representative of the town's idealized expectations for young people. And it represents the fact that the town successfully initiated the queen into its prevailing value system:

> Some expecting to see a young person taking his or her place in the community through the performance of a community-defined set of activities that stand for long training and a willingness to accept commitment will be pleased to see

that child's growth to adulthood. It does not matter how well he or she does it, what matters is that they do it. (Lavenda, 1997, p. 32)

Participants vary in the roles they adopt across different worlds. Within the world of her peer group, because she listens to problems without criticizing, an adolescent female may assume the role of "loyal friend"; within the world of her family, because she helps without being asked, she may be a "dutiful daughter"; within the world of school, because she raises her hand before speaking, she may be a "good student" (Dillon & Moje, 1998). Given the similarity between these practices across the different social worlds, her identity may readily transfer across different worlds. However, for many students, this transfer is not easily accomplished because the roles they have in one world do not fit well within other worlds. When students from non-middle-class homes enter the social world of school, they must cope with the disparities or borders between practices valued in their home and those valued in the school (Phelan, Davidson, & Yu, 1998). Frequently, students who have difficulty negotiating or resist these borders experience failure in school, leading many to give up and drop out.

In another example of contextualizing the roles within social worlds, the members of The Girls' Book Club compared females in the contemporary world with those in the medieval context represented in *Catherine Called Birdy*. They constructed a "Comparison Chart," listing activities, symbols, and texts of the medieval world on one side, and pairing these up with comparable aspects of the modern world on the other side. Pairings included: "rarely bathed/bathed often," "one main religion/variety of religions," and "father finds a husband for daughter/father's approval is not necessary, but nice."

After finishing work on *Catherine Called Birdy*, the girls began an inquiry by contextualizing the identities of women in present-day societies, both their own society and other societies throughout the world. The projects explored single-sex classrooms; women in the military; ERA, girls, sports and Title 9; mail order brides; comparing women in different cultures; historical women; women during war; the media and females; the glass ceiling; and super mom. Based on these social worlds of women, the students conducted inquiries and presented their findings to a group of sixth-grade females for the purpose of helping transform these sixth graders' beliefs about women's roles in society. Making these presentations bolstered the inquirers' own sense of self-efficacy and expertise about how women's roles are constructed in social worlds.

In studying the negotiation of roles/identities within and across worlds, students could ask:

- What roles/identities do participants or characters enact in an activity or a world?

- How do these roles/identities vary across different worlds?
- What practices or language do they employ to enact a role or an identity?
- How do they align themselves in relationship to alternative identities within a world?
- What are their feelings about being in a role/identity?

Rules

In constructing social worlds, people also apply their knowledge of rules or norms to understanding what are considered to be appropriate, significant, or valid actions and words within a social practice. In studying the school's annual prom within the larger context of the school social world, students may note that certain behaviors are considered to be appropriate, while others, such as wearing casual clothes, getting intoxicated, or dancing in a "strange" manner, are inappropriate. Students acquire these rules and norms through participation in their own local social worlds of peer group, family, school, community, workplace, or social organization (Ianni, 1989).

Students typically identify concerns, issues, or dilemmas associated with conforming to the rules or expectations in peer, school, family, or community worlds. In a peer group, students may establish certain norms as constituting the exclusive nature of their group identity. In the novel *The Chocolate War* (Cormier, 1986), gang members create certain rules designed to maintain a strong sense of group loyalty. Members who violate those rules, including the key member who narrates the story, are punished or excluded from the gang.

The following questions may help students describe how rules and norms are constructed in a social world and represent the tensions that may develop when a norm becomes contextualized by conflicting purposes and agendas within or across social worlds:

- What are the rules/norms operating in a social world?
- Who establishes or defines these rules/norms?
- What are the cues or violations of rules/norms suggesting inappropriate behavior in a world?
- What are the consequences for not following these rules/norms?
- How might a rule/norm be both good and bad at the same time?

Beliefs

Participants also contextualize words, objects, and actions in terms of the beliefs operating in a world. Systems of interconnected beliefs about self, others, and the world often have been called discourses—highly patterned ways of knowing typical to activities like law, medicine, business, religion, science, and so on (Fairclough, 1989, 1995; Foucault, 1980; Gee, 1996; Lankshear, 1997). When newcomers first encounter a social world, they note a typical manner of speaking and style of interaction that support, even produce, a system of beliefs and values called a discourse. Part of the socialization into a new world involves acquiring the practices and discourses that constitute that world. Acquiring that discourse serves to define one's role or identity in that world. The largely male sports talk show is constituted by a discourse of masculine gender identity that values the sharing of technical expertise about players, rules, and "stats." Participants also celebrate the value of competitiveness and hard work, and generally avoid topics related to emotional, interpersonal matters associated with "feminine" television talk shows. Adopting these practices serves to define program participants and their audiences as allied to a discourse of masculinity.

The worlds of romance novels, romantic comedies, soap operas, and song lyrics often are created through a discourse of romance, or what Linda Christian-Smith (1990) describes as a "discourse of desire." The language of this discourse is typically that of an idealized, often hyperbolic description of the desired partner or lover. Song lyrics often contain males' use of a "sweet-talk" language of flirtation that plays on the idea of females' desirability. Underlying all of this is a belief that "love triumphs over all," a belief that could be challenged with counter examples from lived experience.

The following questions may help students explain how a social world is constructed through the beliefs and values of its participants:

- What must a person believe to have said or done something?
- How do different beliefs connect to form a system or discourse that frames the meanings of words, objects, and actions?
- When meaning is contested, what underlying beliefs are in opposition?
- How do different discourses shape meaning within a social practice?

History

Participants in a social world know the history or traditions associated with the practices and discourses of the world. Contextualizing a world in terms of its past history helps to establish the material conditions that influence current values, identities, and relationships. As Kathleen McCormick (1999) notes:

> This recognition of historical difference helps us in the present to question the apparent naturalness or universality of our own points of view: We come to

see that there are changing beliefs and assumptions behind even such everyday activities as wearing jeans to class. Why, for example, does our manner of dress differ so dramatically from the dress of only one hundred years ago? What larger values and beliefs are revealed by the clothing that we wear? (p. 4)

McCormick (1999) encourages an analysis of how the meaning of texts or images changes over time due to various social and cultural forces. For example, students may study the image of men in lace, such as a picture of King Louis XV and how people reacted to that image in the past and in the present. While lace was associated with masculine power in the eighteenth century, it is now associated with femininity.

Students also may explore the traditions operating in social world, traditions that shape practices in a world. In studying a family world, they may examine traditions of celebrating holidays or taking vacation trips. In studying a school world, they may examine traditions of the prom, graduation/ awards ceremony, pep-fest, orientations for new students, and so on. In many cases, these traditions involve ritualistic practices. In William Golding's *Lord of the Flies*, Jack and the "beasties" become a tribe engaged in frenzied rituals in which they hunt down and kill other boys stranded on an island. Or, in *The Crucible*, townspeople in a Puritan village stage ritual-like trials of women accused of witchery as a symbolical act of purifying the village from evil. In the represented worlds of many texts, the social construction and deconstruction of traditions and rituals consume the protagonist's mind and action as he or she seeks to transform a social world or reconstruct a social world that has gone awry.

RESEARCH ACTIVITIES TO SUPPORT IMMERSING, IDENTIFYING, AND CONTEXTUALIZING

Various research activities can help students produce the information that reveals the nature of a social world's components and the social interactions that construct that world. These research activities can support any of the six inquiry strategies of a social worlds curriculum.

Observing

One primary research activity involves observing people's social practices in a specific world. For example, in observing conversations in the school cafeteria, a coach's training session, or a classroom discussion, students can record which participants do or do not talk and for how long, what topics are discussed, the types of speech acts employed (requesting, questioning, asserting, ordering, criticizing), the style or register of the talk (informal, formal, rehearsed, spontaneous), and the effects of language use on audiences. To study language use, students may tape-record conversations, or, if recorders are obtrusive or a violation of participants' privacy, they could record the talk on laptops or in longhand.

Note Taking/Mapping

An essential part of observing involves note taking or taking field notes in which students record their specific observations about a certain world. In recording their observations, it is important that students describe specific practices and artifacts, as opposed to general impressions. For example, in describing observations of students in a cafeteria, students need to record unique details such as dress, talk, behaviors, gestures, and uses of artifacts, among others.

Students also could draw maps or sketches that portray their perceptions of a site or world. In a study of college students' experiences of university life at Rutgers University, Michael Moffatt (1989) asked students to draw maps of the campus. Their maps reflected quite different attitudes toward the university experience. In some cases, students included drawings of local restaurants, bars, stores, sorority and fraternity houses, social clubs, and routes to nearby towns. In other cases, students drew detailed descriptions of classroom buildings, the library, and computer center. The former maps reflect the high value the students placed on having a good time, while the latter reflect an allegiance to going to classes and studying. Students then can analyze these maps as visual portrayals of participants' beliefs and attitudes about a world.

Relying on Cultural Brokers

Students who are unfamiliar with a site may want to rely on a cultural broker—an insider member of a world who can provide students with behind-the-scenes perspectives on or interpretations of a world. For example, a group of high school students decided to study a local comedy club. To gain access to the club, they worked with a cultural broker who was an actor at the club as well as a teacher in their school. This cultural broker provided them with a lot of useful background information about the operation of the club.

Interviewing

Another central research activity involves interviewing participants in a world about their experiences in and perceptions of that world. By interviewing participants, students gain information to help contextualize participants' language, important objects, and activities. For example, one of Richard's students, Cheryl Reinertsen (1993), analyzed a group of her daughter's female friends viewing two television programs, *Beverly Hills 90210* and *Melrose Place*, programs that focus primarily on issues having to do with male/female relationships. The group, composed of high school junior and senior females, met weekly to share their reactions to the television programs. Cheryl observed the group discussions of the programs and interviewed various group members about their perceptions of the group meetings. She posed questions designed to elicit group members' perceptions of both the programs and their own social experiences of sharing responses to the programs.

To prepare for interviews, students formulate a set of questions beforehand, questions that are consistent with the concerns, issues, or dilemmas they are investigating. In some cases, they may want to ask broad questions, having participants describe their overall experience in a world. In other cases, they may ask about specific components of a world.

Categorizing, Analyzing, and Generalizing from Data

Once students have gathered information, they need to sift through and make sense out of the data collected. In reviewing her interview data, Cheryl developed several patterns about the social world connecting the girls and the television dramas. She found that the members developed a backlog of shared knowledge about the different characters that served to unite the group. For example, group members enjoyed predicting how characters would act based on their previous behaviors. Members also used their responses to the programs to vicariously discuss concerns and problems associated with their own male/female relationships.

Group members frequently judged the characters according to what Cheryl characterized as middle-class assumptions about family, work, and sexual behavior. For example, in one episode of *90210*, a female college student becomes engaged to an older man. The group shared their displeasure with her decision to become engaged: "'She likes him just because he's rich.' 'She should stay in college.' 'She's too young.' and 'Wait until her parents find out. They will really be mad.'" For Cheryl, these comments reflect a cultural world in which "college age students should not be engaged because they are too young. If they do get engaged, they will drop out. Education is important, love can wait" (Reinertsen, 1993, p. 8). For Cheryl, these responses reflected a belief in achieving success through working hard and going to college, as constituted by a discourse of middle-class values.

In conducting this study, Cheryl noted that these students exhibited little critical analysis of their own social worlds in their discussions or interviews.

She speculated that they are so immersed within a consumer world that they have difficulty stepping outside that world to examine its limitations. The activity of contextualizing data from a social worlds inquiry must begin with a descriptive level of analysis, but hopefully can support the reflective strategies of critiquing and transforming social worlds, as discussed in the next chapter.

SUMMARY

As students immerse themselves in the everyday experiences of lived, represented, or virtual social worlds, they identify concerns, issues, and dilemmas. They explain how particular acts, objects, and words are contextualized with specific or multiple meanings within the purposes, roles, rules, beliefs, and history of overlapping social worlds. All of this sets the stage for students to represent social worlds in order to critique the practices and discourses that construct participants' values, identities, and relationships, and to transform their conscious participation in the components that contextualize future possible meaning within a social world.

5

Critiquing and Transforming Social Worlds

As a result of the three inquiry strategies laid out in the previous chapter, we hope that students will go beyond simply describing the practices and components of social worlds, to generate ways to critique and ultimately transform relationships, identities, and values within a world, and to resolve conflicts within and between overlapping social worlds. Students may be more motivated to engage in inquiry once they connect their critiques of significant activities in their everyday lives to a sense of power to transform a social world through their own social interactions. In The Girls' Book Club study of medieval worlds, Sarah noted that her middle school girls' group was more engaged in their study of gender-role issues because they could both critique beliefs about gender roles and entertain ways of changing those roles. As she noted in an interview about her project, "Being able to propose change makes it more real for students" than traditional research reports.

In discussing critiquing and transforming in this chapter, we are delaying until the next chapter a discussion of various strategies and tools for representing meaning. We do so because while our model places representing before critiquing, we believe that representing through tools recursively pervades all aspects of inquiry and therefore should be discussed as the final strategy.

METHODS FOR CRITIQUING SOCIAL WORLDS

In critiquing social worlds, students challenge or interrogate the commonsense, taken-for-granted assumptions underlying the construction and representation of a social world. In transforming social worlds, students envision and test out new, alternative versions of that social world in ways that address issues, dilemmas, or concerns. Yrjo Engestrom (1999) proposes seven phases that encompass both critiquing and transforming social worlds:

1. *questioning*, criticizing, or rejecting the status quo operation of a social world

2. *analyzing* the social world to explain why the status quo is inadequate or dysfunctional, often in terms of examining the historical development or the operations of a social world
3. *modeling* new, alternative ideas, representations, tools, or models that address problems in the status quo
4. *examining* or testing out the model to determine its potential limitations
5. *implementing* the model to entertain further applications
6. *reflecting* on and evaluating the process of implementing the model
7. *consolidating* the model to create a new set of social practices (pp. 383–384)

These seven phases are driven by the need to find some alternative to a status quo social world that is not working. A sports team wants to win more games, but knows that its current game strategy is not achieving that purpose. So coaches and players devise an alternative strategy. Teachers in the Montclair, New Jersey, school system were concerned about the negative influence of tracking on high school students. They proposed the creation of a special "detracked" literature class with students from different tracks. As demonstrated in a videotape portraying interviews with students, teachers, administrators, and school board members (Fine, Anand, Jordan, & Sherman, 1998), there was considerable controversy over the proposal for changing the system. However, once the class was approved and taught, "low-ability" students who otherwise would languish in low-tracked English classes, flourished in the class. And "high-ability" students, who often have little interaction with the more diverse population in the lower tracks, benefited from relationships with a diverse population.

Perceiving the Familiar as Strange

One means of questioning what is considered to be "normal" or "real" in a social world involves perceiving the familiar as strange. Perceiving the familiar as strange involves suspending one's usual ways of perceiving or contextualizing a world and adopting an outsider, "Martian" perspective. The Martian visitor knows nothing about the usual, accepted practices in a social world and is therefore in a position to question or challenge those conventions. Adopting the perspective of a naive outsider means that a student would be more likely to ask questions such as, "Why are people doing this?" or "What is the purpose of this practice?"

Adopting the stance of an outsider also involves bracketing and critiquing one's own preconceptions about the world being represented. An important step for students conducting ethnography studies in Brenda Robertson's class at North High School involves reflecting on their preconceptions about a world. In studying a local auto-repair shop, Mike's Amoco, Jessica Nieuwboer,

Molly Chermak, and Chrissy Mann described their own preconceptions of auto mechanics:

> Our previous ignorant beliefs put the mechanics in a poor light. In our minds, we made them out to be greasy pigs who never wash their hands or clothes. We envisioned them as middle-aged men with receding hairlines who weren't overly concerned with their appearance. They were more interested in making money than in satisfying the customer. I mean, how much education could it possibly take to look under someone's hood and tell them that everything needs to be replaced and it will cost thousands and thousands of dollars.

Contrary to their expectations, the office was "neat and tidy, unlike the stereotype of a mechanic." And, when asked, "What do you think about mechanics who cheat people," one of the mechanics felt that such mechanics "give guys like us bad names. You cheat people once, they're not going to give you a second chance, and after working at Mike's Amoco for 21 years, I know that repeat business makes a thriving business."

After their visit, the three students recognized that "a day in the life of a mechanic wasn't anything like any of us thought it would be. There is a lot more to their job than dirt and grease. . . . In a sense, mechanics are 'car doctors.' It takes a lot of knowledge to diagnose and heal the ailments of a car."

Analyzing Worlds as Systems

Critiquing also involves going beyond a focus on individuals' actions to contextualize those actions as shaped by larger institutional systems. As Carole Edelsky (1999) notes, "Studying systems—how they work and to what end—focusing on systems of influence, systems of culture, systems of gender relations . . . means questioning against the frame of a system, seeing individuals as always within systems, as perpetuating or resisting systems. Being noncritical . . . means seeing individuals as outside of . . . [and] separate from systems and therefore separate from culture and history" (p. 28). Sarah's students were able to critique the patriarchy of the medieval world because they went beyond being sympathetic toward Catherine to examine the religious and political forces shaping her actions. They analyzed her as operating within a larger cultural and historical system, which has parallels to contemporary systems perpetuating patriarchy. Critiquing therefore draws heavily on contextualizing a world in terms of the components constituting that world as a system, especially juxtaposing how the meaning for the component would differ in another social world to deconstruct conventional understanding and open up new critical possibilities.

CRITIQUING REPRESENTATIONS OF SOCIAL WORLDS:
ANALYZING THE AMERICAN WEST

Students also may critique distorted, misleading representations of social worlds. In an inquiry project revolving around the world of the American West, twelfth graders in Kim Van Voorhees's class at Osseo Senior High, Osseo, Minnesota, explored the world of the American West as portrayed in the novel *Montana, 1948* by Larry Watson (1993). The novel, set in a small Montana town in 1948, portrays the conflicts between a family as told through the eyes of a 12-year-old boy, David. The main character, the town's sheriff and the boy's father, faces the dilemma of having to put his own ne'er-do-well brother in jail for the rape of a Native American female. The father of the sheriff and his brother tries to protect the brother, creating tension between the sheriff and his father.

Kim wanted students to understand how their perceptions of the contemporary West portrayed in the novel are shaped by various myths about the "old West." To immerse the students in the world of the West, she began by having them brainstorm a list of all of their associations with the West. Sample responses included: cowboys, Indians, 10-gallon hats, saloons, guns, horses, frontier, ghost towns, tumbleweeds, ranches, sheriff, dirt, wind, dreams coming true, glitter and gold, Hollywood, movie stars, the pull of California, and so on. The class then discussed likely differences between these associations and the contemporary West. Kim then showed students a clip from a modern western movie, *Tombstone*—a scene in which the "retired law man" is beckoned out of retirement to defeat the villain cowboys assailing a village. One student noted that the big showdown at the O.K. Corral took 5 minutes in the film, but may have lasted only 30 seconds in reality.

The students then discussed their responses to the novel, comparing the portrayal of the contemporary West with Hollywood versions of the West. Students noted that Watson was trying to debunk various myths about the West by portraying Davy as being disappointed that his sheriff father doesn't carry a gun, doesn't wear a badge or cowboy hat or boots, has a law degree, wears a shirt and tie, and only seems to lock up the occasional town drunk.

Working in groups, the students identified other myths deconstructed by Watson in the novel, myths named by the students as "the model family," "the small town," "law and order," "Native American," "the 1950s," and "gender roles." Then students returned to the novel to find quotes about the myth they researched, and analyzed these quotes to explain the difference between the identities, relationships, and values represented in the novel and the myth in the social world of the West they had chosen to study. This act of analysis required the students to contextualize the actions, language, symbols, and material objects located in the novel in terms of the problematic values, identities, or relationships represented in the novel or their own lived world. One example of this analysis comes from a group who examined and critiqued the dysfunctional aspects of the family in the novel in relationship to idealized versions of the family in the media:

QUOTE

In the 1950s we had the Andersons on *Father Knows Best*, the Stones on the *Donna Reed Show*, and the real-life Nelson family on *The Adventures of Ozzie and Harriet*. Over the next 3 decades, the model stretched to include single parents, second marriages, and interracial adoptions on *My Three Sons*, *The Brady Bunch*, and *Different Strokes*, but the underlying ideal of wise, loving parents and harmonious, happy families remained unchanged.

STUDENT ANALYSIS

These are all great examples of television shows, model or not. Throughout the years since the 1950s, television shows have become more and more realistic with the second marriages, etc., but the happiness and love never changed.

QUOTE

Then I knew. She saw him now, as she hadn't before. He was not only her husband; he was a brother, and brother to a man who used his profession to take advantage of women, brother to a pervert!

STUDENT ANALYSIS

This is a very nonmodel-like family situation. We would never expect to see our family members in this situation or any others like it.

In identifying other myths deconstructed by Watson, students were also simultaneously engaged in the critique of social worlds, especially those in which myths are constructed.

Based on their study of the West as portrayed in *Montana, 1948*, Kim's students examined various media representations of the West, the family, small towns, gender roles, and Native Americans that perpetuate various myths about these worlds. Nermina, Stacy, and Nancy conducted a study of media representations of the small town portrayed as a "safe, good environment [with] acres and acres of land, green trees, fresh air, and peace [in which] everyone lives in a home with a white picket fence." They critiqued these myths by examining the portrayal of crime in *Montana, 1948*, in which the townspeople deliberately admitted to various crimes, quoting David, the narrator of the novel: "From the eccentric to the unusual to the aberrant. From Scott and her palominos to Mrs. Russell, who was a kleptomaniac, to Arne Olsen, a farmer, who never bathed . . . to my Uncle Frank who molested his patient. How many secrets had our town agreed to keep?" (p. 46). They concluded their report by noting that "there are many secrets that people don't know about because some people like to keep the bad stuff to themselves because they are afraid of gossip and ruining the family name."

Sarah Vallez, Mandy Statz, Allyson Bros, and Molly Swaser studied idealized representations of the model family on television programs such as *Father Knows Best* and *The Brady Bunch*. They then contrasted these idealized representations with more conflicted versions of the family portrayed in *Home Improvement*, *Married with Children*, and the novel. They raised the concern that "the majority of television watchers are kids, and most of the shows on television portray happy, model families. Then kids relate those families to their own, and think that they are doing something wrong."

Matt Dallin, Mike Olsonoski, and Eric Sobraske studied the stereotyped representation of Native Americans in the film, *Dances with Wolves*, which portrays Native Americans "smelling the smoke that comes out of a pipe before battle . . . their faces painted, holding weapons, and making Indian war cries. Right at the end of the scene, you hear the Indian make a war cry right before he knows he's going to die. Most people in that situation would try to do anything to stay alive." They explore how these myths shape the narrator David's perspective in *Montana, 1948* after his uncle kills Mary, a Native American female. "In a dream, David sees all of the Indians he knows on top of Circle Hill in normal clothes walking around. But in the dream, he is wondering why they are not coming down the hill and attacking everything they see to somehow avenge Mary's death. . . . He also wonders why the Indians aren't lined up in battle formation streaked with war paint and holding onto weapons. This part of the book tells us what people are brought up to believe Indians are like."

Through critiquing these various representations of the American West, Kim's students ultimately grappled with tensions between myths versus reality associated with historical understanding, particularly in terms of understanding the decades of the 1950s and 1960s. They grappled with the issue of determining the "truth" in history given their experiences in classes in which history is treated as facts. As Kim noted:

> They showed interest in talking about the 1960s—another decade that would be good to explore in terms of myth versus reality. The idea of history being anything other than chronological, factual, and "true"

seemed to be too much of a contradiction for them. Even though the novel shows us how history is skewed by cover-ups and taboos, the students were unwilling to tackle that dilemma. History is fact in school.

CRITICAL INQUIRY IN CLASSROOM DISCUSSIONS: COLLABORATIVE CRITIQUING OF *THE GREAT GATSBY*

Students are often more likely to engage in critical inquiry when they collaboratively share alternative explanations, critiquing each other's beliefs and assumptions. To illustrate this process, we cite the example of discussions about F. Scott Fitzgerald's *The Great Gatsby* (1925/1980) in Sharon Eddleston's contemporary American literature class at Armstrong High School in Robbinsdale, Minnesota. In this class, students wrote informal responses in which they posed questions and generated hypotheses; individual students then volunteered to begin discussions by reading aloud their writing.

In one discussion of *The Great Gatsby*, students engaged in a critical analysis of the role of Nick, the narrator. They disagreed about the role of Nick as simply a neutral commentator versus a participant in Gatsby's nefarious actions. Most of the students believed that, in his role of narrator, he should refrain from asserting his opinions and remain a neutral observer. A smaller group of students argued that he had a moral obligation to openly challenge the other characters. The students framed this debate in terms of their own experience in balancing the need to be discreet versus the need to challenge others.

The discussion begins with a student, Berke, reading aloud his writing about Nick:

> I think that this Nick guy is the most perfect guy in this book because . . . he respects everybody to a certain extent. . . . He supposedly sees Gatsby like 50 yards in his yard, away. And he's like, should I go talk to him? He's like, no, no. He just lets the guy be alone with his thoughts, you know. He doesn't want to bother him. I mean, that's just a respectable gentleman. I know if I see somebody, and nobody lives around me really, you know, and there's somebody in my yard, I'm going to approach him late at night, you know, what are you doing? This guy, I don't know, he's just . . . yeah, he's just the kind of guy anybody could talk to and he keeps his own opinions in his head and his actions so far haven't shown much to what he really is. I think he's just a perfect gentleman. That's what I feel.

Berke argues that Nick is the "perfect gentleman" in that he "keeps his own opinions in his head" and does not challenge others. He draws a connection to his own experience of being ambivalent about confronting an intruder. However, his position is then challenged by Tom.

KYLE: I think . . .

TOM: Keeping your opinions to yourself is not a good quality . . .

TEACHER: Tom, just a minute. You interrupted Kyle.

TOM: That's my opinion, see? [laughter]

TEACHER: Let's let Kyle speak for a minute.

KYLE: What Berke was saying stems back to, on page 4, ". . . he was going to become that most limited of all specialists, the well-rounded man," and then he says that it's more successfully looked at from a single window, after all. Which I tend to agree with, but the well-rounded man . . . I think that definitely characterizes Nick and he didn't, maybe he's just kind of soaking things up rather than giving his opinions. Like about the book, and I think that's a very important part of his character.

SARAH: That makes sense.

TOM: I'll say what I was saying again, in case anyone didn't catch it. I interrupted . . . [laughter] I don't think keeping your opinions to yourself is a good quality at all. [laughter]

SARAH: It's is not necessarily a good quality, but it's true to Nick's character.

In this exchange, Tom argues that the failure to assert opinions is "not a good quality." Kyle counters that Nick is a "well-rounded man" who is "soaking things up rather than giving his opinions." In stating that "keeping your opinions to yourself" is "not necessarily a good quality, but it's true to Nick's character," Sarah argues that being discreet is consistent with Nick's role as narrator in the novel.

MATT: I think that being able to keep things to yourself is a virtue . . . it's something very few people can do. People who tend not to keep finding themselves in situations that they shouldn't be in; I mean when someone opens their mouth at the wrong time in the wrong place.

TOM: Yeah, but see, if people who didn't state their opinions are going to stay in the position that they are in, I mean, if no one were ever to state their opinion about slavery, there would still be slavery.

In this exchange, the students discuss the moral implications of asserting opinions, as well as the fact that issues often are framed by "closed-minded specialists" who may not perceive larger moral implications. Tom argues that without open critiques of slavery, "there would still be slavery." His historical contextualizing serves to introduce a larger moral dimension into the discussion that other students pick up on later in the discussion regarding the consequences of silencing. As Kyle notes:

> The people who have changed history throughout the world, who have changed history I think tend to have been stubborn in some way with their beliefs and, you kind of have to be, you kind of have to close your mind to what's going on around you like Tom said, the slavery thing . . . I think if you bought into the ideals of the time . . . it's kind of a paradox.

The group later concludes their discussion by reflecting on the value of openly arguing as opposed to reserving judgment and not challenging others.

MATT: If everyone agreed on one subject, on one certain point, it wouldn't be worth discussing and it wouldn't be worth it.
JOHN: Why should you always go out of your way to make arguments with someone?
TOM: You learn a lot from arguing.
JOHN: But you don't have to go out of your way. I mean, to be the devil's advocate is cool sometimes, but not always.
STEPHANIE: If you believe it, it's not going out of your way.
MARK: If you go out of your way, a lot of times you're going too far and you're going to look obnoxious and give a bad representation of yourself.

This exchange demonstrates that students engage in critical analysis by noting and challenging disparities between each other's positions, and drawing analogies to their own real-world experiences. They therefore were stimulating each other to adopt critical stances. They also were willing to challenge each other because they perceived their positions as representing tentative, negotiable ones, as opposed to definitive, hard-line positions. Through critiquing the representations, explanations, and assumptions operating in the social world constructed in literary works and other media text-stories, students can critique the limitations of practices and discourses in a social world, creating the basis for future action to transform lived social worlds.

TRANSFORMING SOCIAL WORLDS

Transforming a social world requires participants to interact in new ways, to disrupt the conventional practices and discourses that construct inequity or injustice, to negotiate the taken-for-granted meanings of common words and actions, to contextualize activity with different purposes and roles, and to construct new, alternative representations both in the lived world and about that world. For example, a group of female musicians, producers, and fans produced the female zine magazine, "riot grrrl," which served to transform the music industry. Marion Leonard (1998) describes the evolution of this activity as part of an expanding network of activities:

> Riot grrrl is a feminist network which developed in the underground music communities of Olympia, Washington, and Washington, D.C. The initiative was promoted by members of the bands Bratmobile and Bikini Kill who sought to challenge sexism in the underground music scene and encourage girls and women to assert themselves. . . . As women and girls began to identify with this idea, riot grrrl networks spread across the USA and Britain. The realization of this initiative took several forms. Female audience members began by challenging the traditional division of the gig environment into gendered spaces, where women were largely absent from front of stage. Other grrrls formed bands, wrote zines, arranged meetings and organized events to introduce girls to music making. . . . Riot grrrl zines employ small scale production, with issues sometimes numbering only twenty copies. . . . Acquiring the addresses of zines involves tapping into the informal friendship networks active within riot grrrl. (pp. 102, 103, 106)

Within this riot grrrl activity, members defined their roles and allegiances in terms of acquiring expertise in composing music, writing articles, and publishing zines, actions driven by the need to assert their own brand of music. Once riot grrrl established a stronger foothold in the music industry, and attendance at riot grrrl concerts increased, members perceived their purpose as broadening their audience to include a range of different groups. They used their music to espouse feminist beliefs/attitudes about the need for more women's voices within the music industry. At the same time, as they gained in popularity and became more a part of the mainstream music industry, they lost their sense of being resistant outsiders, creating new problems in terms of appeal to their audiences.

Through participation in riot grrrl publications and music production, members transformed their world, adopting new uses of tools—new forms of music, ways of communicating, and ideas about women's role in the music industry. In the process, they also were transformed, adopting new identities associated with new purposes and responsibilities. As their numbers grew, they constructed new and expanded versions of their zines. And, as they gained more power and status within the music world, they continually reformulated their purposes.

These transformations arise from the need to address problems in the status quo through the construction of new ways of interacting and representing in a world, often through the use of new tools for representing self, others, and the world. Van Oers (1998) cites the example of young children engaged in operating a play shoe store:

> In the context of their play in a shoe store, constructed by the children in a corner of a classroom, the children encountered the problem of measuring the size of shoes. How could you know which size you have? Some children knew that sometimes you could read it from the bottom of a shoe, but this was not always possible. In one situation, the teacher introduced a new measuring device, a measuring mat with drawings of soles, and indications of the different sizes. The children immediately started measuring their own feet on the mat and reading their sizes. They started guessing and predicting which size babies or the teacher would have. (p. 140)

In this example, using the measuring mat as a new tool stimulated the children to adopt a new set of practices for running the store. Constructing new tools leads to new ways of contextualizing or representing a social world. Martin Luther King's "I Have a Dream" speech provided the civil rights movement of the 1960s with a sense of possibility and hope for the development of a more integrated, equal society. His dream of a world in which "all men are created equal" provided a sense of purpose and moral principle that motivated both Blacks and Whites to challenge forces attempting to maintain segregation. Civil rights groups continue to evoke his vision, while at the same time defining new, alternative perspectives on issues of economic inequality, poverty, racism, and discrimination.

As part of contextualizing or "recontextualizing" (Van Oers, 1998) their worlds, participants adopt new roles or identities associated with employing new tools for new purposes. For example, in the novel *Huckleberry Finn*, Huck Finn is caught between an allegiance to a bourgeois liberalism associated with Tom Sawyer and a moral anarchism associated with Jim (Engestrom, 1987). Huck must choose between conforming to the social world of middle-class life in his small segregated town and challenging the conventional assumptions of that world. Given this choice, he adopts a new role as vagabond. As a vagabond, he defines a new purpose of resisting conventional middle-class life and creating a new mode of existence with Jim on the raft, employing the tools of parody and storytelling to outsmart his opponents. At the same time, he continues to operate as a member of his segregated community, a constraint that creates a felt need for change. Through his adventures with

Jim, he transforms himself, Jim, and his multiple social worlds (Engestrom, 1987).

Students Engaged in Transforming Worlds

Challenging the Bridge Construction. Students may use their inquiry projects to effect change in their local institutions and community. For example, a group of students at Stillwater Junior High School, Stillwater, Minnesota, worked with their social studies teacher for several years on a project related to the issue of the destruction of a neighborhood located on the banks of the St. Croix River. These students were upset about the fact that an entire neighborhood of homes was displaced in order to build a new bridge to replace an older bridge. While there was considerable support in the town for building the new bridge, necessitating the destruction of the neighborhood, the students perceived this displacement as an issue of the rights of individual citizens versus the imposition of the government to destroy the neighborhood simply for the need to build a new bridge. They were concerned about the proposed bridge's environmental effect on the area and the displacement of the people whose neighborhood was destroyed. They were also concerned about the fact that there was growing political opposition from environmentalists, and the U.S. Park Service that managed the river, against building the bridge, leading to the possibility that the bridge might not be built, in which case the destruction of the homes would have been for naught.

The students therefore participated in a project in which they interviewed the neighborhood residents about their experience of losing their homes. They then used these interviews to write essays and articles about the displacement of the residents. They also took photos before and after the neighborhood's destruction. In all of this, they were interested in more than simply studying this event. They also wanted to influence public opinion related to the bridge construction. They therefore mounted a public exhibition in a local Stillwater gallery to display their photos and writing. The exhibition received a lot of publicity in the local news media and also won an award. Through their efforts, and those of others opposed to the bridge construction, the construction site was changed, but not until after the neighborhood had been destroyed.

The Rebel in Literature and Film. In studying the history of a social world, students might identify challenges that precipitated a change in the dominant social world's perspectives. In some cases, a particular individual may have articulated an emergent perspective that led to change—Galileo, Newton, Martin Luther, Marx, Freud, Darwin, Sojourner Truth, Martin Luther King. These innovators or rebels formulated a new, alternative version of reality that led to changes in the everyday social interactions in their worlds.

In one inquiry unit, students in Leo Bickelhaupt's English class in the St. Paul Open School, St. Paul, Minnesota, studied examples of rebel characters in literature and film. Leo provided the following inquiry strategies to guide student work:

- *Identifying.* What were some of the concerns, issues, and dilemmas that helped shape the rebellion?
- *Contextualizing.* What types of assumptions, conventions, values, traditions, and so on, dictated the two sides of this rebellion?
- *Representing.* What tools were used to facilitate the rebellion?
- *Critiquing.* What was known about how the mainstream responded to the rebellion? Were there winners and losers?
- *Transforming.* What was the lasting influence of the rebellion?

Leo asked the students to consider not only the rebel's emergent perspective, but also the dominant perspective under challenge, as well as reasons for these competing perspectives. Students selected from among several options to represent their findings:

- An I-Search paper that described their research process
- A narrative about the rebel character's experience, in some cases adopting that character's perspective
- A speech to the class, with visual prompts
- A museum board with sketches and illustrations
- A multimedia presentation—a web site or use of computer technology

In his report, Andy examined the rebellion of Michael Collins and the IRA against the British. He contextualized the rebellion by providing the historical events leading up to it, as well as Collins's specific purposes, role, beliefs, and tools. He also critiqued the rebellion as involving tensions within the anti-British forces and as not leading to the successful transformation of Ireland into a free state. In reflecting on what he learned, he noted a change in his attitude toward the IRA. While he was initially sympathetic toward the IRA, he noted that "now I know that the IRA do not stand for the people of Ireland, only a small percentage. When the IRA split, had I been there, my allegiance would have unquestionably turned to the free state." Thus, in studying transforming, students may discover that in some cases the transformation benefits a world, while in other cases it does not.

TRANSFORMING SCHOOL WORLDS

The thought of transforming the world can be daunting. It is commonplace to look at the world as a fixed system with correct ways of doing things that are beyond anyone's individual control. This may especially be the case for adolescents as they begin to more fully participate in peer, family, school, and community social worlds. A key location in which adolescents can experience their constructive power in shaping social worlds is the school classroom. When the class, as an interacting group of members in a social world, can transform the traditional patterns of school activity, students can extend this agency to their participation in the many social worlds outside the classroom. The practice-oriented curriculum we advocate in this book, focused on inquiry into our social worlds, can lead to the transformation of experience in the English classroom.

Mark is one example of this classroom transformation. As the social worlds unit began in October, Mark was quiet and seldom lifted his eyes from his desk. During the third round of artifact creation and sharing to explore the social world of romance represented in the short stories, Mark surprised the class with a live performance, playing his guitar and singing the Led Zepplin song "Going to California." His risk taking extended to the other students in the class and created an atmosphere of great excitement and interest in the ideas about romance highlighted by the music. Mark's level of engagement in class interactions was high for the rest of the school year. In his final inquiry project, he explored the world of romance by recording his own band playing original songs, then pressing a CD release. The opportunity for Mark to express meanings about the world in a symbolic form or genre significant to him, but rarely validated in the academic classroom, gave him access to the classroom dialogue, and thus success. The classroom structure supported his transformation as a student and the social construction of a positive self-identity.

As the social worlds unit developed and more and more students found ways to express their ideas about social worlds, the social interaction among class members increasingly supported inquiry into ideas about social worlds. Students' evaluations of the unit supported this claim:

> I liked how everyone got to interact with each other and how we got to see how everyone felt about a particular social world. (Tim)

> [The unit got] us thinking about real-life situations and to learn to work together with other students in a group. (Kim)

> It was more expressive. Not confined to one thing that everyone in

the class would do. There was a lot more sharing of ideas to the classmates than in previous classes. (Anonymous)

I liked it. More class participation than most classes when we are told to shut up when we voice our opinions. (Elyse)

I think that telling the way you felt about the story and what you got out of it was probably the best thing about the social worlds unit. (Jon)

As the experience of literacy in the English classroom is transformed through activities and interactions, the participants also begin to extend their sense of agency and control into their social worlds beyond the classroom. Rachel B.'s inquiry project was similar to many that explored peer social worlds to categorize the many different types of relationships. She represented and critiqued common interactions between peers as the basis for her categories of good friend, best friend, friend, enemy, acquaintance, bothersome friend, boyfriend, and meanie. In her writing reflecting on her inquiry, one sensed her ability to actively transform her future peer worlds, although she did not provide any direct evidence that her inquiries had already transformed a social world:

The social world of peers has a lot of microcosms, and they are all very important, because if you are having problems with one person, then that might affect the way you would act or talk to another person. This idea is important to me because I can experience this firsthand, and actually everyone has peers, so they can as well. . . . If you don't have good relationships with peers you could become lonely and sad for a majority of your life. You should try to make relationships with them as positive as possible to get along well in life.

In separate inquiry projects, Matt, Curtis, and Chris J. photographed various scenes around school and created posters that defined the different social groups in school and focused on the issues of popularity, dress, and movement between groups, especially based on sports and gender differences. Again, although the students did not document any actions to transform unjust social interactions between or within peer groups, their representation of boundaries and memberships is a significant base for future critique and transformation.

Weekly artifacts by Zach F. and Elise further emphasized the agency one has in constructing social worlds. Zach shared a poem from the Internet that created an analogy between the concentric circles of a pebble dropped in a pond and the words and actions between people. For Zach, the poem represented the idea that you "don't say what you don't mean because once you say it you can't take it back." In that short thought, Zach demonstrates his consciousness about how social worlds are constructed, even transformed for good or bad, through symbolic interaction. Elise created a collage that juxtaposed images and words of disaster, death, and grief surrounding a poem that expresses hope if people work together to make the world a better place.

It has taken lifetimes of struggle to transform social worlds, so it may be too extreme to hope that students will become transforming agents in their social worlds after a 2-month unit, or even a whole year, in English class. We believe a social worlds curriculum is successful if students at least demonstrate a new awareness of social worlds as multiple, overlapping, emergent, constructed, and negotiated through social interaction with language, symbols, objects, and activities. Many students claimed such a new awareness:

> We never talked about things like friendship and love in any of my other English classes. (Laura)

> I think the goals of the unit were to help us to understand how to work between different social worlds. You could say, to help us manage it all. (Chris J.)

> To get you to think about social worlds. I didn't even pay attention to them before. (Nathan)

> I think the goals were to help us look at the world and to see how many social groups that there really are and to see how they connected to one another. (Candace)

> I think I was supposed to learn how different influences have an impact on my life. (Rick)

> I've never spent so much time studying ideas and the social aspects of people. In the past we've always studied literature and other concrete and tangible things instead of ideas. I think the goals of the unit were to teach us how to examine the way we interact with people and how it affects us and others. (Elise)

> I liked seeing a certain social world from another person's viewpoint, and also seeing how many different types of social worlds there are. (Justin)

What these students didn't know how to say was that the curricular structures for inquiry into social worlds experienced in the classroom enabled them to negotiate their different representations of their worlds in order to negotiate and construct more just and shared social worlds. The development of such consciousness about language, symbol, object, and action is the basis for transforming social interaction.

When students first begin to study texts and their own lived experiences within a social worlds framework, they may not be very successful at pushing their analyses beyond description to critique and transformation. We have found it helpful to focus students on the concrete words and actions within a social world to support thinking about how these words and actions limit possible identities and relationships, and how different words and actions might generate change. We have used the following simple guide to help move students from description to activities of critique and transformation:

- Explain how the words, sounds, images, and actions illustrate important ideas in the social world.
- Explain how we create belonging to a social world by using typical or specific words, sounds, images, and actions.
- Explain how conflicts between or within a social world are created and/or resolved by specific words, sounds, images, and actions.
- Explain how people might change aspects of a social world by using different words, sounds, images, and actions.

From this examination of the concrete aspect of participation in a social world, students often are able to identify and represent more abstract values, assumptions, and conventions to critique and transform.

6

Tools for Representing Social Worlds

To THINK, we represent our experience of the world, others, and self. Through these representations we create a consciousness that allows us to exist both in the world and alongside the world. Freire (1973) asserts that the human ability to live "with" the world, beyond living moment by moment "in" the world, distinguishes our humanity from other creatures. Langer (1957) also believes that the human ability to create symbols allows us to remove objects of experience from their immediate space and time context and use them as tools in other future contexts. Our acts of representing meaning through our language, actions, and material objects establish both the interactions that construct our social worlds, and our consciousness of the world.

In this chapter, we explore many of the symbolic tools that allow us to represent and construct our social worlds. We learn to use these tools through ongoing social interaction in which new tools and meanings are invented, negotiated, and conventionalized over time and space. We define our patterned uses of language as discourses, our systems of activity as practices, and the material objects that are both natural and the products of discourses and practices as texts and artifacts. Texts metaphorically encompass everything that can be read and interpreted, including a tree, a piece of clothing, or a person, as well as a book, a song, or a photograph.

TOOLS AS MEDIATING ACTIONS

As described in the previous chapter, the Stillwater Junior High School students used their photos and writing as tools to change the townspeople's attitudes toward the bridge construction project. The curricular purpose for this book is to enable students to better understand how representational tools are used to contest, negotiate, and construct a social world. This helps to achieve our twofold purpose that students critique the use of representational tools, and ultimately employ them with more agency and control in an effort to transform their social worlds.

How then are tools used to create and represent worlds? In his book, *Mind as Action*, James Wertsch (1998) argues that rather than focusing on students as agents isolated from tools, and tools as isolated from agents, we need to consider how the two interact in mediating agents' achievement of a certain purpose or object. In a similar way, in Vygotsky's (1978) triangle of agent, tool, and purpose, a tool is defined by how it functions to mediate or link the agent to an activity's purpose. Wertsch (1998) cites pole vaulting as an example. A fiberglass pole has no intrinsic meaning in and of itself, but is indispensable to the pole vaulter, who cannot perform the action of pole vaulting without it. The action of pole vaulting therefore is mediated by the pole as a tool used to achieve the purpose of vaulting over the bar. The meaning of a tool is constituted by the actions performed when people use the tools with others (Wertsch, 1998). While students learn to use tools to study social worlds, they also study how tools connect participants with valued purposes in the activity of a social world (Vygotsky, 1978).

All of this points to the primary theme of this chapter—*that tools are employed to simultaneously produce meanings and purposes within social activities.* Without an understanding of their purpose, tools are meaningless. Helping students learn to use tools therefore means helping them learn to use discourses, practices, and texts to achieve specific purposes with others in a desired social world. For example, within the world of Girl Scouts, the activity of selling Girl Scout cookies involves a range of specific actions—assigning roles to troop members, targeting potential customers, approaching customers in house-to-house campaigns, and keeping track of finances (Rogoff, 1995). To perform these actions, Girl Scouts learn to employ tools such as the sales pitch designed to establish rapport with customers and persuading them to buy cookies. To keep track of sales and customers, they use charts or ledgers to organize information. They learn to use these tools through participation in the cookie-sales campaign, evaluating the extent to which the tools achieve certain purposes. If their sales pitch isn't convincing to customers, they may improve it. The meaning of these tools is defined by how they are used to achieve the object of the campaign—selling cookies.

DISCOURSE PRACTICES AS TOOLS

Tools are understood more easily as text-producing actions like speaking, writing, reading, listening, drawing, viewing, sculpting, and photographing. Artifacts like clothing, and the other objects with which we surround ourselves, also are understood easily as tools we use to signify meanings that solidify our membership in social worlds and achieve our valued purposes. It is more difficult to understand tools as discourse practices because they form the almost invisible patterns of our everyday social interaction.

In the classroom, when our attention is focused primarily on the forms of texts and artifacts, we construct a type of discourse practice common to school classrooms. Based on a formalist approach, students are taught *about* the features and forms of narratives, poetry, images, or drama. They are taught the five-paragraph theme, the types of figurative language in poems, the features of the short story, or elements of persuasion in a speech. In this school social world, the purpose of producing texts is framed within a discourse practice of evaluation in which the primary value is the criteria and score for formulaic reproduction. Within this school discourse practice, students learn to perceive literacy tools simply as an end in themselves.

As we hope is clear by now, the curriculum we propose helps to construct a different school discourse practice in which literacy tools serve the primary purpose of negotiating shared meaning and value, as well as a sense of agency to transform possible identities and relationships in one's social worlds. However, simply giving students access to different tools for text production does not mean that the students will know how to use them for new purposes in different discourse practices. When Short and Kauffman (2000) gave elementary students a range of different tools to use as part of their inquiry projects, they observed that the students often could not perceive their play with these tools as linked to the purpose of their inquiry projects:

> Students' play often seemed purposeless. They did not connect their play with sign systems to either personal or class inquiries—it was just a time to "mess around." . . . The heart of the issue appeared to be that they didn't know *why* they were being given time to play with these sign systems—the play was not connected to the curriculum or their lives. (p. 47)

Students perceive the value and use of certain tools based on their understanding of the purposes the tools might serve to construct their identities, relationships, and values in some social world.

As students progress in their inquiries, they continually should ask themselves: "What tools are we using to achieve our purposes and how well are these tools working?" The examination of tools is embedded in the inquiry activity, not as abstract classroom content taught as formalistic knowledge. Rather than simply studying different types of video shots, angles, or editing techniques, for example, students learn about these characteristics of film as they use video-production tools to best represent significant ideas from their inquiries into various social worlds. In the ninth-grade social worlds unit described in Chapter 3, several students used the computer-based, video-editing program Adobe Premiere to create quicktime videos as their final inquiry project. Garrett illustrates how learning a tool's capabilities to represent the world is best embedded in a project representing one's interpretations about some social world:

> My artifact was a video that I created by cutting parts of the movie *Days of Thunder* and pasting them together. I then played the movie to the song "The Distance" by Cake. While I was watching the movie to find clips, I was mostly looking for scenes that involved two people who were romantically involved. I was also looking for action scenes because I was trying to relate the social worlds of sports and romance. The video part of the artifact turned out great. It contained scenes that I felt showed a direct relationship between sports and romance. The clips included many shots of race cars whizzing by. There were also many shots of the two main characters separated. What I was trying to do was show how the two worlds related to each other. I felt that I was successful in doing so, because I thought that my artifact showed how athletics can play a big role in romantic relationships.

Although Garrett doesn't state explicitly that he learned how to determine the best moment to cut from scene to scene, or how to best juxtapose the sound track with the video image, or how to best juggle the different scenes to build toward some idea or emotion, he does indicate an engagement in all of those aspects of using the video tool. Similar to the multitude of findings that emphasize the importance of writing to reading or process writing, knowledge about media likewise is developed through the activity of creating and critiquing media.

TYPES OF TOOLS: DISCOURSE TOOLS

We now turn to a description of a number of different types of tools, drawn once again from the ninth-grade class described in Chapter 3. We've arbitrarily categorized these descriptions into discourse tools and audiovisual tools.

Narratives

Narratives are probably the most common discourse tool we use to represent our everyday experiences and social interactions. The stories we share with each other invite belonging as we compare and confirm individual experiences and perspectives. Family members share the stories of key events in their history to construct a family world. Or, members of a soccer team in the locker room use stories highlighting moments in a game to create shared purpose and value as a team. By dramatizing what was unusual or extraordinary about an event, these narratives go beyond simply describing what happened to convey beliefs about the significance of the events in shaping lives (Labov, 1972). For example, Molly has just passed her driving test. When she describes the test to her peers, she dramatizes the fact that she just missed hitting the cones in the curb-parking part of the test. Because she just missed the failure cutoff score by one point, she plays up the fact that had she hit one of the cones, she probably would have failed. Molly dramatizes this near-miss by repeating words—"I came really, really close to hitting the cone," or by adding asides in describing actions, such as, "I was really nervous then," or, "You won't believe what happened next." Thus, *how* students tell their stories conveys *what* they believe about the event.

In listening to these stories, students adopt a "point-driven stance" that helps them attend to cues that dramatize or convey the point of a story (Hunt & Vipond, 1991). When listening to Molly's story about passing the test, her friends sense that she's doing more than simply describing her experience. The point of the story is not "in" the story; it is socially constructed within the context of the peer world. Understanding the point involves contextualizing the purposes, roles, rules, beliefs, and history constituting that peer world. In this case, a primary purpose within a peer world is to assert one's own independence and autonomy from an adult world.

Narratives also can function to critique or transform the interactions and practices common to a particular social world. Emily's final project in her inquiry of family social worlds was a short story about one family. Her explanation of her story shows how she used the tool of narrative to achieve the purpose of critiquing family communication:

> Communication is a key aspect of the social world of families. If there is no communication between a family's members, and there's no feeling of trust, the members of the family may have very unhealthy relationships with each other. In my story when Rick would talk to [his brother] Erik about how he felt, it still wasn't what he needed. He needed to tell his father what he told Erik. He wrote in his [suicide] letter to Erik that he couldn't live up to his father's expectations anymore. He talked about how their dad wouldn't let him go after his own dreams, but he should have tried to explain it to the father. I think that this is true a lot of times in families. Many things go unsaid, and feelings are kept hidden inside of them. When people do this many conflicts are left unresolved. . . . But in the end [of my story] he (Erik) and his father have a fight, and Erik says what he's been feeling. His father even reveals some of his feelings about the death of his son (Rick).

Emily's narrative also represents how the family members in her story began to transform their relationships through different words and actions.

Signs and Codes

Signs and codes define the conventions that contextualize the meaning of individual words or actions. Within these discourse tools, signs may consist of an image, a word, an object, or even a certain type of practice (Maasik & Solomon, 1994). One's identity is a sign in continual construction within the whole system of signs that constitute the activity of a social world. In much of this book we have discussed words, actions, symbols, and material objects as signs with meanings that are negotiated or contested within and between social worlds. For example, in the novel *The Outsiders,* "the word Cool, the cars that the Socs drive, the imagery of sunsets, and the way that Ponyboy Curtis slouches, his body language, are signs with which these two gangs socially construct themselves" (Moore, 1998, p. 212).

A sign stands for a meaning only within a cultural discourse practice, in which that meaning has been conventionalized, or coded, through ongoing interaction between people using the sign. A sign can have multiple meanings depending on the different codes used to interpret it. Codes therefore serve as systems for deciphering the cultural meaning of signs (Barthes, 1974). While female beauty in the nineteenth century was associated with largesse, during the twentieth century beauty was increasingly associated with slimness (Rubinstein, 1995). The meaning of images of beauty as portrayed in romance novels, soap operas, romantic comedies, or song lyrics is constituted by what Linda Christian-Smith (1990) describes as "codes of beautification"— that a woman's physical attractiveness contributes to building relationships. These codes specify what it means for a woman to be beautiful as defined by the cosmetics, fashion, and hair-product "beauty industry" and as represented in teenage magazine advice columns and articles on how to attract men (McRobbie, 1991).

Decoding a sign means unpacking the meanings operating within a sign system using a set of codes (Maasik & Solomon, 1994). In John's study of the school social world, he chose to represent his findings through the voice of an alien coming to learn the codes that shaped meanings for words and actions in school:

> At the beginning he thinks that humans are cannibalistic because of the signs in the halls saying "What's Cooking" and "We are." We don't prove him wrong by eating the strange meat in the cafeteria. . . .
> (From the alien's journal:) On my fourth day here I examined one of the rooms which the students spend their time in. I chose the room

with the snake, as I learned it was called, the fish and the insects. One of the female students did a male student a favor during the second time slot. She made a deal with the teacher that if she held one of the "cockroaches" the teacher would remove a bad behavior mark, the consequence of which is unknown to me. She held the cockroach and even showed it to all the other class members. She then was completely unreluctant to deposit the cockroach in its glass box. I then made my most important discovery. I discovered that the teachers are there not only for supervision, but for educational purposes as well.

It is important for students to explore contested meanings or multiple meanings for a particular word or action as the consequence of different codes based in different discourse practices. Students most often understand different meanings as the result of different personal experiences. Questions like, "What must a person believe or value to have this meaning?" can help students locate their understanding of codes with a social rather than an individual context.

Genres

Another discourse tool worth examining is what commonly is known as genres. Genres traditionally have been defined as formulaic text/media forms such as mystery, romance, science fiction, horror, comedy, adventure, and so on. More recently, the concept of genre has been expanded to include conventional discourse practices such as greetings, interviews, jokes, sales pitches, speeches, recitations, sermons, parodies, songs, and even classroom "show and tell" (Bakhtin, 1981; Berkenkotter & Huckin, 1995). These genres are "forms of life, ways of being, frames for social action. They are environments for learning" (Bazerman, 1994, p. 1). Defined as such, genres are very similar to the description of discourse practices we have presented in this book. As familiar patterns of social interaction, genres function as tools to organize activity, identity, and relationships within a social world. For example, within the world of a religious ceremony, participants use recitations, songs, and sermons to represent their roles and beliefs as consistent with the traditions of their own denomination or sect. Likewise, a group of African-American students may employ "signifying" or "he-say/she-say" gossip exchanges to construct their belonging within a shared social world (van Dijk, Ting-Toomey, Smitherman, & Troutman, 1997).

Because they are familiar, predictable ways of framing action, genres can act as social glue for dealing with stressful events or violations of the norm. For example, when a family member dies, the surviving relatives employ the genres of grieving or funerals that help them cope with a family death. Or, a blues singer may use the genre of the blues song to lament the loss of a girl-friend or boyfriend.

Genres are generally larger sets of related activities and codes that organize social interaction over longer periods of time. For example, in working as an order clerk behind the counter at a fast-food restaurant, workers learn to use the genre of the "fast-food order." A person approaching the counter of a MacDonald's may say, "Big Mac and fries to go," without ever being asked, "What would you like to order?" "What size hamburger?" "Do you want fries with your order?" "Here or to go?" because the customer is familiar with the "fast-food order" genre.

In studying characters' or people's use of genres as tools, students can examine their adherence to certain rules or conventions. For example, in responding to the story "Bernice Bobs Her Hair," by F. Scott Fitzgerald (1951/1996), one of the main characters, Bernice, learns the genre of flirting as a tool for female characters to attract men. In this story, set in the 1920s, Bernice, who lives in a small Wisconsin town, goes to visit her cousin, Marjory, who lives in St. Paul, for the summer. Marjory is proud of her reputation as popular with men. When she observes that Bernice has difficulty socializing with men, she offers to teach her techniques for being flirtatious and "feminine." These strategies include flattering males and appearing helpless—techniques that bolster a presumed masculine sense of authority. As the summer progresses and Bernice begins to employ Marjory's techniques, the local men begin to spend more time with Bernice than with Marjory. Marjory becomes jealous of Bernice and seeks revenge. She dares Bernice to bob her hair on a bet, which represents losing her "feminine" hair. Bernice does so and Marjory regains her position as the center of males' attention. At the end of the story, Bernice completes her own revenge by cutting off Marjory's hair in the middle of the night and returning home. For Marjory, appropriate behavior consists of creating a pose of feminine flattery when talking with men, whereas inappropriate behavior consists of not aggressively pursuing men. In the story, flirting practices associated with being "feminine" are perceived as positive in the peer world of the 1920s. While such genres of feminine interaction with males might be evident today, the practice discourse may be layered with more negative value in current social worlds.

Similarly, many adolescents view romance as a cycle of events or genre. Several artifacts and inquiry projects represented romance beginning with crushes, then communication and flirting, a change of heart or hooking up, then cheating or fighting, making up or breaking up, making up again, or heartbreak and moving on. When students represent their own lived social worlds as patterns of activity, then locate these patterns in various texts, they connect a discourse practice with a genre. It is important to explore how different genres like poetry, historical fiction, essays, letters, or plays help authors and readers achieve different purposes. But it is also necessary to explore how these text genres are experienced in lived social worlds as discourse practices for social interaction. Once this connection is made, students can employ genres with greater control as they represent their lived worlds, critique others' representations, and negotiate meaning for experiences, identities, and relationships.

Survey/Questionnaire/Poll/Focus Group

A frequently used discourse tool to study social worlds is the survey, questionnaire, poll, or focus group. As a discourse practice, the tool often is used to establish the valued purposes, identities, and relationships of a social world in order to construct a representation of that world for a documentary or commercial purpose. In an inquiry project on the diversity of their school world, students at Crosswinds Interdistrict Arts and Sciences Middle School, St. Paul, Minnesota, used a survey to determine the interests, practices, and fads associated with their study of the "typical Crosswinds student." One group of students asked students about their future, posing questions such as, "What are your goals? What do you want to be? Where do you want to live? Do you want to get married?" One Crosswinds student, Theo, found that 25% of students indicated that their favorite type of music was rap music, a higher percentage than pop, R&B, rock, soul, Christian, jazz, and classical. In his analysis of these results, Theo noted that "people like rap because of the message it brings to the people. The lyrics are very strong and tell the truth but at the same time they're funny." In many cases, the students found that they had such a range of different answers to these questions that it was difficult to generalize about students' future as a composite group.

The effectiveness of the survey or interview ultimately depends on students' ability to analyze the results, in some cases recognizing the need to follow up an initial survey or response with further questions. Given the finding that 23% of Crosswinds students were the oldest children in their families, Onoma asked these students "what they liked and what they didn't like about being the oldest." She found that

> all of them liked being the oldest . . . they believe they get more
> privileges than their younger siblings. One thing that most older
> children don't like is that sometimes they get blamed for stuff because
> sometimes parents can't believe that their younger children could ever
> do something really bad (yeah right).

Survey or interview data provide students with a sense of practices, beliefs, or attitudes across different members of a social world. However, in using the data to make generalizations, students need to be cautious about over-generalizing from a sample to an entire population.

Drama

Another useful tool is drama—using role-play or simulations for dramatizing "what if" perceptions of a concern, issue, or dilemma. As Wilhelm and Edmiston (1998) posit, "Drama is a powerful tool for thinking about what we 'ought to do' and uncovering some of the moral complexities of situations" (p. 59). In these dramatizations, students "not only adopt positions; they encounter situations and points of view that challenge and change them and their views of whatever they are studying" (p. 6). In studying castles, a group of students in Wilhelm's university class decided to create a "living history" museum exhibit about castles. They assumed the roles of museum trustees, archaeologists, historians, and "experts" about different aspects of castles. The students then created slide shows, artifacts, narratives, and a prose poem for choral readings.

Students also may build a role-play around a particular issue or dilemma. For example, in a small-town school district, a group of parents objected to the use of a controversial novel in a high school English course, filing a complaint with the high school principal and the school board. The students in one class created a role-play around the issue of censorship, adopting the roles of school board members, parents, community members, teachers, administrators, librarians, literary critics, the media, and so on (Beach & Marshall, 1991). In the drama, a minister brandished his Bible, and members of a local, conservative group waved small American flags. Proponents of censorship employed narratives, depicting instances of innocent students who were negatively influenced or "corrupted" by reading books. At the end of the role-play, students stepped out of their characters and reflected on their use of tools to construct their roles and the world of the small-town school board meeting. For example, a student who assumed the role of the mother described her awkwardness in having to defend the need for censorship. By writing about their feelings, students grappled with differences between their own attitudes and those associated with their roles.

Rather than conducting an oral role-play, students may exchange written messages (Beach & Anson, 1988). Students exchange memos with each other in order to influence others' beliefs about the issue. At various points in the role-play, students stop and read aloud their memos. At the conclusion of the role-play, students reflect on the social strategies employed in their memos. For example, they may note that in some cases students introduced the memo by describing their relationship to their audience, as in, "As a voter in your district. . . ." In one long-term simulation of a censorship case over several weeks, students kept "simulation logs" reflecting on their experiences in the role-play (Brown, 2000).

TYPES OF TOOLS: AUDIOVISUAL TOOLS

Students also may represent their interpretations of worlds through audio or visual tools.

Music and Audio

Many students play instruments, sing, belong to garage bands, or just listen to a lot of music. Both the lyrics and the music can represent ideas important to a social world. Rich was one of many students who explored the social world of love through the lyrics of songs. In his project he printed the song lyrics, organized them on a poster with explanations, and made a CD. He shared some of his analysis in the project essay:

> People are willing to change their behavior and in some ways who they are to find love. . . . In the song "Walk This Way" by Aerosmith, a boy changes his behavior to try to make a girl love him. . . . In "Come Monday," by Jimmy Buffett, Jimmy's behavior was altered because he loved someone.

Beyond music performed by students and selected from popular culture to represent experiences in social worlds, audio recordings of interviews provide an important tool for the study of social worlds. Simply recording interviews can help students listen for patterns in participants' descriptions as they talk about life experiences. Students also can edit cassette tapes using a dual deck recorder to construct a shortened version of voices about a social world. In his study of the world of drug users, one of the ninth-grade students, Jamie, explains:

> For my project, I interviewed and constructed an audio documentary about the drug culture. Although not on purpose, the documentary specialized on users of marijuana. The final draft was about 10 minutes long, and included audio clips from interviews with three different individuals and of myself questioning them. (12/1/99)

The editing of recorded interviews can be facilitated through computer tools, as explained later.

Given the ways in which adolescents use music and audiotapes to both experience and represent their perceptions of different worlds (McCarthy, Hudak, Miklaucic, & Saukko, 1999), students can use these tools effectively to analyze the significant values, identities, and relationships constructed within a social world.

Cameras

An important tool for representing worlds is the photo, digital, or video camera. One advantage of video is that students can interview participants, capturing their talk about and perceptions of a social world. The documentary can inform people about specific aspects of or alternative perspectives on a social world. For example, a group of high school students produced a video tour for incoming high school freshmen, featuring a day in the life of a student at their high school. They showed the student being engaged in some classes and being bored in other classes, including interviews as to reasons for differences in her engagement.

Several of the State College Area High School students used digital and video cameras to document everyday interactions, interviews, and constructed scenes. Colleen explains her photos:

> It is a tradition that all my friends come over before the dance and get ready together. Then we take a group picture of all of us on my porch and go to the dance. . . . I also have included pictures of friends in the hallway. The hallway in school is where most of the socializing gets done, either before homeroom, during classes, or after school. It is noticeable that the two girls are friends because they have their arms around each other. . . . The other picture that I have is at Hi-Way Pizza. The two girls look like they are good friends to me because they have chosen to come out together and spend time with one another. The two girls also have matching coats in the background of the picture which could suggest that they went shopping together before.

Organizing and analyzing photos of their own past experiences often can evoke memories that help an inquirer describe the valued activities, identities, and relationships of a social world. Lauren identified an important connection between identities and relationships when she created a photo scrapbook for her final project on the social world of friends:

> In each of my pictures, I tried to convey the message that every one of my friends has their own personality and style. I think that when

friends are together at a party or something, they can act like themselves and be crazier than normal, and nobody will care that much. When you don't care how crazy you are in front of friends you know you have good friends.

Many students have video cameras at home and can film scripts they write to enact different social worlds. Amanda B., Alyssa, Kim, and Audra edited a 15-minute video on successful and less successful love relationships, using their home camera and video tape player. The characters and situations they represented in their video displayed how discourse practices construct personal relationships. While the form of editing they used in their final social worlds unit project was not as precise as computer editing tools or a professional videotape editor, more students have access to cameras and VCR equipment. As television and computer merge and the industry moves to digital formats by 2010, creating videos at home will become more and more common.

Art and Sculpture

Students also use artwork to visually represent their interpretations of social worlds. Many students in the social worlds unit described in Chapter 3 created art projects that used the entire range of media from pencil, to crayon, marker, clay, foil, yarn, colored paper, and cardboard. As they shared artifacts, we asked them how their selection of media fit the idea they were seeking to represent; many had not considered that issue, but it was central to our goals that they learn how tools achieve purposes. Some projects and artifacts did, however, use their form and media to support idea construction. Lindsay used specific materials to represent the various relationships between friends in her project on peer social worlds:

> In my project an easily broken and brittle relationship is represented by a strand of uncooked spaghetti. An example might be acquaintances, friends who have grown apart or don't know each other very well. A band aid represents a healing relationship. An example of a healing relationship is a relationship broken or almost broken by a fight or friends who are separated and have become friends again.

Across the 4 weeks of artifact creation, many students constructed dioramas and sculptures. Kayelyn's use of folded paper to create springs that held different emotions created in the social world of friends generated a lot of discussion about form and function. Liz created a scrapbook entirely from construction paper cutouts; each page represented a significant symbol from several stories about losing a friend or loved one.

Smagorinsky and O'Donnell-Allen (1998) studied how high school students responded to *Hamlet* by drawing large figures on butcher paper representing their perceptions of different characters in the play, using "body biographies." Students divided the figures into sections and listed character traits or added images depicting their perceptions of the characters. They used this tool to mediate their shared discussion of the characters, talking about their interpretations of the play as they constructed the figures.

In responding to literary texts or films, middle school students may use cutout figures representing different characters, the setting, ideas, themes, feelings, or themselves as readers (Ensico, 1998). By positioning the cutouts on a table or desk in relationship to each other, as they talk about the text, they move the figures around to portray connections between different aspects of the text. For example, as readers, they may move the "reader" figure closer to the main character, representing their increasing identification with that character. And, as with the "body biographies," these cutouts serve to stimulate shared responses to texts as students move the figures.

Collage techniques, montage, and dioramas are also extremely popular tools for representing ideas about a social world. The artist Robert Rauschenburg created a 50-foot collage of newspaper clips representing the conflicts and tensions of the world of the late 1960s. Collages were perhaps the most popular form for representing ideas used by the students in the ninth-grade unit as they juxtaposed images and words to generate intertextual links between the experiences of characters in the represented story worlds and their own experiences in lived social worlds.

Computer Multimedia Tools

With the increase of multimedia power in the desktop computer, students can bring together image, sound, and word to create dynamic textual experiences. As a variety of texts are juxtaposed, their sequence and arrangement generate new layers of meaning for each text as part of larger ideas about a social world.

Students easily transfer collage art techniques from paper and glue to the electronic environment, which has even more flexibility and power to combine various media texts. Students have used various multimedia software tools such as Adobe Premiere and Avid Cinema for video editing; Adobe Photoshop for image editing; SoundEdit for sound editing; Adobe Pagemill, Claris HomePage, and Netscape Navigator/Composer for web site authoring; and Microsoft Powerpoint, Hyperstudio, Authorware, or Storyspace for hypermedia presentations (McKillop & Myers, 1999). These tools can be used for larger projects in which students collect, store, edit, and construct links among many images, sounds, texts, or video. Single texts also can be experienced, and often analyzed more easily, by projecting a digitized excerpt. For example, during the exploration of the social worlds of peer groups in response to the story "And Summer Is Gone"(Kretschmer, 1994), Kelly presented a short scene from the movie *The Breakfast Club* in which the characters discuss why their membership in different cliques prevents them from being friendly during school. The computer gave her the power to edit out language that typically is considered inappropriate in a public school classroom. Perhaps most important, digitized files provide instant replay of scenes that students and teachers find significant for close analysis. The same is true for sound files.

Students become very excited as they see larger projects coming together on the computer. In the ninth-grade social worlds unit, Abby's inquiry into what makes teens simultaneously fit into several overlapping groups required several computer tools. First, she took many digital pictures of teens around school. She next edited these pictures by turning them into gray scale photos and colorizing single elements of a photo, such as the tennis shoes, shirt, or drink bottle—objects that signified belonging or not belonging to a group. Then she sequenced these images, chose unique transitions between them, and set them to music in a quicktime video (see project excerpts in Chapter 7).

Shawn, Doug, and Stephanie also created quicktime videos but used different tools. Shawn and Doug videotaped interviews of peers about their hobbies through a camera directly connected to a computer so the footage was instantly digitized. They edited this digital video file to rearrange the interviews, insert graphics representing different hobbies, and add underlying sound tracks and relevant transitions between the various images. Stephanie built her video with scanned images and music. She explained how her quicktime video emphasized what she believed was important about the social world of sports:

> For my final project I used the computer and scanned in pictures and
> added music to it. The social world I was portraying was sports teams
> while linking it to the social world of friends. In my final project I
> chose all the images from magazines for a purpose. I went through
> tons of magazines before I found them. . . . When you play on a sports
> team one thing you should expect is for people to cheer for you and
> give you team spirit at your games. The very first image of the fans in
> the crowd was chosen because not only do you become friends with
> your team but you become friends with the fans as well. Everyone's
> dream and desire is to win their game they are playing. One of my

pictures fitted this thought. This picture was of a baseball player sitting on the shoulders of his teammates because he won the game.

These students' work with computer tools also demonstrates that significant blocks of time away from the computer are needed to collect the necessary texts. This need can help balance the use of a few classroom computers by multiple project groups. In the ninth-grade social worlds unit, all of the videos were created on one computer, while some image editing and sound editing were done on two other computers.

As with creating a video, students can excerpt small sections of music and paste them together into a new sequence to emphasize important ideas about a social world. Sandy explains:

> For my final project I did a bunch of different songs that are about love, relationships, and romance. I did my project by using technology. I used the computers in the back of the English room to do my project. It was very hard doing my project on technology and I did not like it too much.

Technology tools offer new space and time possibilities to students who want to use multimedia texts to represent experiences in a social world. Movement between different texts is almost instantaneous, and the linear characteristics of print, music, and speech can be layered with the immediate sense of the image. But technology is not always easier than traditional poster collage, videotape, or cassette recorders. The first use of these tools almost always requires extra time, energy, and motivation.

SUMMARY

In using the various tools described in this chapter to represent social worlds, students learn how tools fulfill different purposes. By reflecting on their uses of tools as they employ them through tool-talk, as was the case with the "body biographies" and cutouts, students explicitly describe the ways in which tools mediate themselves and their purposes. As they develop proficiency in using these tools over time, they are perceived as having expertise and status within the classroom world, enhancing their engagement with school.

PART II

Resources for Studying Social Worlds

IN THE SECOND half of this book, we provide specific examples of student inquiries, resources, and sample activities for use in studying a number of different types of social worlds that are especially relevant to young people—peer, family, romance, school, sports, community, workplace, and virtual worlds. These particular worlds represent only a sampling of the worlds that could be studied. Students also could study the worlds of certain historical periods or events (the Holocaust, Depression, Vietnam War, Industrial Revolution), literary genres (mystery, comedy, romance, science fiction, horror, adventure), and institutional worlds not included in the community chapter—the military, hospitals, churches, religious organizations, prisons.

Each of the chapters devoted to these different worlds is organized around the basic framework of the six inquiry strategies, with illustrations of how students used the strategies in classroom projects. Chapter 7 explores peer worlds, Chapter 8 school and sports worlds, Chapter 9 family and romance worlds, Chapter 10 community and workplace worlds, and Chapter 11 the virtual worlds enabled largely through new electronic multimedia technologies.

7

Peer Worlds

ADOLESCENTS DEVOTE a considerable amount of their time to activities with their peers. Of all the social worlds in this book, they most prefer spending time with peers (Brown & Theobold, 1998). In this chapter, we describe how students might conduct inquiry projects about peer worlds, addressing questions such as

- How do peers perceive language, dress, gestures, or social practices as markers of allegiance to a peer group?
- What does it mean to have a "good" or "close" relationship with a peer?
- What practices serve to build positive relationships?
- What practices keep people from building positive relationships?
- Why do peer relationships last or fall apart?
- How do peers establish certain reputations in peer worlds?
- How do certain practices gain popularity in a peer world?

IMMERSING IN PEER WORLDS

Students immerse themselves in peer worlds by observing the practices of a peer group and interviewing peer-group members about their regular activities, shared interests, beliefs, and uses of certain tools associated with building peer relationships. Or, they could study the peer interactions between characters of a novel to identify how these characters construct friendships. For example, in reading the novel *The Outsiders*, by S. E. Hinton (1980), which portrays the relationships within and between the members of two gangs, students may discuss the development and unraveling of Ponyboy's and Cherry's relationship. Or, in *Roll of Thunder, Hear My Cry*, by Mildred Taylor (1976), students might examine how private and public relationships are constructed between the Black and White children of the 1930s "Jim Crow" south.

In immersing themselves in peer worlds, students may experience difficulty entering into others' peer worlds. In many cases, they will be perceived as outside intruders into another's peer-world "territory." Jennifer, Stephanie, and Amanda of North High School, North St. Paul, Minnesota, studied a group called "The Stargazers," an extracurricular astronomy club in their school. The students assumed that the stargazers would be "a crowd of math club wizards—intelligent, plastic glasses, jeans that were way too short, uncombed hair, and some free time that was spent observing the stars." After attending several meetings, the inquirers wrote: "We failed to develop any type of relationship between the club members and ourselves. Unfortunately, we concluded that we were not accepted into this group." To solve the communication problem, they provided refreshments at one of the meetings and openly expressed an interest in the club's activities. "We were finally included and asked of our perceptions of stargazing." They also recognized the need to change their stereotypical assumptions about the stargazers.

Even if the immersion into a peer social world is relatively easy, the members of that world may balk at the thought of being studied and represented to nonmembers. The ninth grader Jamie experienced this in his social worlds inquiry into the drug culture:

> During my search for members of the drug culture, I found it easy to find people who were very willing (sometimes almost eager) to tell me they used drugs. However, the people's openness to tell diminished upon my request for them to admit to it (anonymously) on tape. One college student even got worried that I was an undercover police officer trying to trap him.

IDENTIFYING CONCERNS, ISSUES, AND DILEMMAS

A major concern for adolescents is how to affiliate with peers. Despite the perception that adolescents have a lot of friends, many teens often have difficulty establishing and maintaining friendships, resulting in feelings of loneliness and rejection. A study conducted by the Sloan Institute of some 6,000 adolescents found that

> closed peer groups in the 1950s have been replaced by fluid friendship groups. Students often move from one group to another, and friendships change over a period of a few weeks or months. Best friends are few, and students frequently refer to peers as "acquaintances" or "associates." Building close, intimate ties with a special boyfriend or girlfriend that could lead to long-term commitment

or marriage is viewed as undesirable. Few teenagers "date"; instead, they "go out" with someone, which can mean anything from spending time together to a casual relationship that is recognized by the peer group as some form of special emotional attachment. (Schneider & Stevenson, 1999, pp. 190–191)

Several of the ninth graders' social worlds inquiries coincide with these findings. Steph interviewed her friends using several questions, including the following:

- Do you prefer to have one best friend, or do you like having eight?
- Do you get along most of the time with all eight friends, or do you have trouble with the same ones over and over again?
- Is it hard to find time for all eight best friends?
- When do you single yourself off to just you and your best friend?
- Do you feel like you need to open up your group of eight to a larger number (or minimize it) at all? At certain times? Why?

In her explanation of the interview results, she draws conclusions very similar to the published study of Schneider and Stevenson (1999). Steph received only one survey that indicated that a girl's boyfriend was her best friend, and while all the girls indicated that they had large groups of different friends, when relationships became strained they had only one or two really close friends.

> Not all of my best friends always get along with each other. This seems to be one of the hardest things to deal with and I got a lot of agreement on that when I sent my survey out. When our friends start to fight, sides are usually taken. It's difficult to deal with this because you sometimes agree with one friend's view on something. I've learned from past experience that not taking sides all together is usually the best way to go. We usually try to stay mutual, but that's almost impossible because when it comes down to it (especially in big fights) everyone sides with their best friends.

Steinberg, Brown, and Dornbusch (1996) describe three different forms of peer affiliations: "cliques," "crowds," and "activity groups." Cliques consist of a close, cohesive, often exclusive group of friends. Outsiders often have difficulty breaking into cliques because they may lack the social practices valued in a clique. In the story "I Go Along" (Peck, 1994), about students in different ability groups, Gene is tongue-tied in Sharon's presence because she is among the most popular girls in school and he belongs to a different "low-track" marginal group of students. Fehnja's analysis of the social worlds in this story highlights how it is only when Gene begins to talk on the bus, that they establish a relationship:

> He's not real popular at school so he is kinda shy and won't speak up much. The social world that I think is valued is friends. Even though him and Sharon were not really friends before she sat with him on the bus. They start acting like friends, cause they sit together at the poetry reading and on the way home on the bus.

Crowds consist of larger, more amorphous groups: "brains," "rednecks," "burnouts," "jocks," "druggies," and so on. Through momentary allegiances with these crowds, students experiment with "provisional identities" based on practices related to crowd membership in terms of class, race, or orientation toward school (Schneider & Stevenson, 1999).

Activity groups revolve around activities such as organizing for the high school prom, going on a camping trip, practicing for a "battle-of-the-bands" contest, or playing on a sports team (Schneider & Stevenson, 1999). In these activities, each member contributes his or her own skills and expertise, for example, as drummer, lead guitar, bass guitar, or singer. They work together collaboratively to achieve shared purposes, for example, winning a "battle-of-the-bands" contest.

Ian's inquiry on cliques identified grouping practices similar to those of Schneider and Stevenson (1999). He described teens' concern for belonging and the formation of cliques around social-class boundaries:

> For a high school student, feeling accepted by a group of peers is very important. Often high school students find acceptance in cliques. A clique is a small group of friends that usually act, dress and talk alike. The members in these groups are almost always from the same social class and share goals, dreams and beliefs. You see cliques everywhere you look. All over the school groups of friends gather and talk. And at lunch time most people will sit with the same group every day. Cliques can even be present to some extent with adults. An adult at work might tend to talk to co-workers who have similar interests and hobbies while they might not talk to others as much. . . . Cliques tend to be made up of people that are not best friends and have not known each other all of their lives. Most clique members have one or two close friends and the rest of the members are people that they might have met at the beginning of the year or the last year sometime. This creates a problem for some people because the friendships are easily broken. If you disagree with your friends or get in a fight with someone in the clique they won't hesitate to throw you out of the clique.

Ian highlights a tension between conforming to peer pressure in order to be perceived as "cool," "with it," or "awesome," versus asserting one's independence consistent with one's own beliefs. Given a desire for peer-group popularity, when students attempt to demonstrate their loyalty to the peer group, they often must compromise their values.

In the story "Initiation," by Sylvia Plath (1994), a high school student, Millicent, undergoes initiation rites involved in joining a high school sorority during the 1950s. As part of her initiation, she must not talk to men and must comply with all of her "big sister's" requests for favors. Just as she completes her final test, Millicent withdraws from the rush, recognizing that being a member of the sorority ironically means losing her ability to develop friendships with others. As she notes, "'So many people were shut up tight inside themselves like boxes . . . and really, you don't have to be in a club to feel related to other human beings'" (p. 249). Amanda analyzed the social worlds represented in this story in terms of the dilemma Millicent faced and the values required to solve it:

> Millicent has to make a hard decision between the added popularity and her and Tracie's relationship. On her way to deciding she asks a man on the bus what he ate for breakfast. When he replies heather bird's eyebrows on toast, she bursts out laughing. She realizes that being an individual can be fun as being in a group. In the end, she chooses to stay with Tracie, but still try to be friends with everyone in the sorority, if possible. I think that was the right choice. You should be who you are, not who someone wants you to be.

As students analyze peer pressure in their inquiries, they identify dilemmas in which they must make a decision about what's the right thing to do. On the one hand, they want to maintain their loyalty to peers. On the other hand, maintaining that loyalty may involve an unethical action. The similarity between the analysis of peer worlds by ninth-grade students and that by published scholars reflects adolescents' ability to produce thoughtful results, and should encourage teachers to give students the opportunity to study their social worlds.

CONTEXTUALIZING PEER WORLDS

In inquiry projects on peer worlds, students contextualize concerns, issues, or dilemmas in terms of purposes, rules, roles, beliefs, or histories being constructed within their peer social worlds.

Purpose

Participants in peer worlds are driven by certain purposes, sometimes defined in terms of opposing other groups. In Margaret Finders's (1997) study of two early adolescent female groups, the "social queens" and the "tough cookies," group members solidified their allegiance to their own group by deliberately responding in ways opposed to social practices of members of the other group. The "social queens" were actively engaged in social matters within and outside of school. They also defined their identities in opposition to the "tough cookies"—girls who were less socially involved in the school—through the use of exclusionary categories: "woof-woofs" [meaning not physically attractive], "babies," "dogs," "little girls," and "kids."

Finders cites the following example of the "social queens" responding to some teen magazines:

> LAUREN: What do [the "woof-woofs"] read? They probably just read books. They have nothing better to do.
> ANGIE: They probably don't even read these [holds up a copy of *Sassy*]
> TIFFANY: Did you guys see this? God, I'm gonna get some of these [holds open a page from *YM* and points to a pair of pants]. Isn't this so cool? (p. 58)

This group also referred to the fact that their teachers and parents disapproved of their reading teen magazines. "[My mother] wants me to read books, but I read *Sassy*" (p. 58). The very fact that they read these magazines serves to display their defiance of adult authority. As Finders notes, this magazine "reading serves adolescents to unite particular groups of peers and exclude others, serving as a powerful tool to mark insiders and outsiders" (p. 58). In themselves, the magazines have no meaning. As markers of social status, however, they serve to fulfill the group's objective of establishing their collective group identity. The "social queens" were using their responses to establish a set of conventions and codes associated with popularity in their peer-group world.

In other cases, members of peer worlds may perceive little sense of purpose, particularly poor adolescents with little prospect of a viable economic future. Writing about adolescents in Bergenfield, New Jersey, Donna Gaines (1991) finds little idealism and considerable division between youth groups:

> Face-to-face, young people in Bergenfield as elsewhere appear rather sober about life, less inflated by ideals, less encouraged to dream. They work hard for anything they've got—money, dignity, serenity, morality. Racial and ethnic lines of difference keep them apart. The variety of youth subcults reflects and reinforces this distance. Turf wars in neighborhoods, at shows, and in schools

divided them, as the future seems grim: no jobs, no security, no world, no future. (p. 242)

Without a sense of purpose or viable future, these adolescents perceive little value in activities designed to fulfill long-term goals. Peer groups provide some of the most powerful purposes for life activity, often in place of or conflict with the purposes constructed in family or community social worlds. For example, Mindy, a young woman from a working-class suburban area north of Los Angeles, initially joined a racist skinhead gang, but then became disenchanted with their violent treatment of some of her friends (Finnegan, 1998). She then joined an antiracist skinhead gang, a rival gang against the racist gang. Given her conflicting allegiances to these different gangs, she became caught in the middle of fights between the two gangs. Subsequently, she turned to drugs and alcohol, and narrowly escaped being killed in a gang fight. As Finnegan (1998) notes, "I met few teenagers in the valley who seemed able to see much beyond the immediate world of their peers" (p. 306). As students inquire into various peer social worlds, their analyses of the purposes for activities can support a critique of the values being constructed and contested across or within social worlds.

Roles

In conducting inquiry projects, students also may study how group members assume different roles within and across different peer worlds. In his study of "The Strange, Super-Fantastic Social World of Vinyl," Geoff described the roles fulfilled by his peers in his band Vinyl, and then represented his findings on a web site he created.

> In my artifact, I have each member and his role (drummer, guitarist, etc. . . .) and then a picture. The picture of the member with their instrument creates their identity. On the web site, Jon's picture is him stomping on his guitar. Most people would see this as being funny, so it creates Jon's identity as being one with a sense of humor.

To study roles in peer worlds, students could observe group interactions in various school or community activities. Using field notes, students describe particular features of other students—dress, hair, size, skin color, jewelry, physical behaviors, language, and so on, as well as their social practices and the ways in which they interact with each other. They also could draw maps of the classroom or lunchroom, indicating which types of students sit in which locations according to common characteristics they note as important to the social worlds being constructed.

Rules

Members of peer worlds also construct and adhere to certain rules constituting appropriate practices within a peer world. Geoff's study of his band Vinyl included observations about rules:

> First of all, I think every group . . . has expectations, or rules. For instance, I expect my band mates to practice the songs we chose to cover, or our originals, and we expect each other to cooperate so we can get things done. In other words, organization is a key aspect of being in a band.

Becoming a member of a peer world entails learning to judge what is considered appropriate or normal in that world. In describing his initiation into the Crips gang in South Central Los Angeles, Sanyika Shakur, AKA Monster Kody (1993), describes a series of initiations involving car theft and gun battles with rival gangs in which he had to demonstrate his prowess associated with his new name "Monster."

Students also learn various rules constituting appropriate gender-role practices from advice columns or quizzes in teen magazines. One study of quizzes in magazines for females found that practices associated with being a "good" versus "bad" girl were equated with females adopting traditional heterosexual, feminine norms (Ostermann & Keller-Cohen, 1998). In her study of female adolescents' responses to the popular television program *Beverly Hills, 90210*, McKinley (1997) found that the females identified various rules associated with the activity of dating: "Don't date your best friend's boyfriend, don't cheat on your boyfriend, don't go after a man, don't want sex. It is the man's prerogative to do the 'picking,' and a man may 'pick' where he pleases" (p. 215).

Beliefs

Students also could analyze the beliefs regarding the appropriateness of certain practices in a peer world. For example, a group of fifth/sixth-grade female students judged the characters in a *Sweet Valley High* romance novel in a manner that reflected their judgments of each other's practices as "good" and "bad" females (Ensico, 1998). In that novel, one of the main characters, Elizabeth, is assumed to be "good," while her identical twin, Jessica, is assumed to be "bad." Similarly, in the group studying the novel, two of the females perceive themselves as "bad," while the other members perceive themselves as being "good." Their responses to the characters reflected their beliefs about what constituted falling into one of these two categories. During one of the group discussions in the school library, two of the females who described themselves as "mean" openly flouted beliefs about public behavior by walking across the tops of chairs in the library. Through their actions, these females were mutually positioning themselves within their peer world according to shared beliefs. In their inquiries, students need to compare and contrast multiple social interactions in a world to establish patterns of activity that might contextualize the beliefs, or assumptions, that support one particular act or word in a social interaction.

History

Examining peer worlds in terms of the historical evolution of adolescence (Austin & Willard, 1998; Gelder & Thornton, 1997; Palladino, 1996) by studying portrayals of adolescents in literature or media from different historical periods offers further means of contextualizing. Prior to World War II, most young people moved from secondary school to work, particularly to support their families, so that there was no extended transition period between childhood and adulthood. After World War II, when families experienced more affluence, adolescents were afforded more leisure time and money for spending on themselves. As a result, the clothing, cosmetics, and entertainment industries targeted adolescents as a new market, a move that served to define or constitute adolescents as a group. During the 1950s, listening to rock music emerged as a new pastime activity. Adolescents responded to rock music as a tool for defining their own identity in terms of resisting conventional adult values operating in the 1950s and early 1960s.

During the 1960s, the social and political unrest revolving around protests against the Vietnam War, the civil rights movement, feminist challenges to patriarchy, and race riots in cities led adolescents to resist what they perceived to be the conservative lifestyles of the 1950s. Adolescent peer worlds revolved around social and political activities: the hippie movement, the emergence of "Black power" groups, the evolution of the women's rights movement, experimentation with drugs, new forms of rock music, and increased political activism (Palladino, 1996).

With the increasing globalization and corporate consolidation in the economy, the 1980s and 1990s brought a shift from factory work to white-collar work, and stagnating wages for the lower half of the workforce. Adolescents became more concerned with economic survival and success, moving away from political activism. With the increasing diversity of the population, issues of racial conflict surfaced more frequently, creating, in some cases, peer groups segregated according to race (Fine & Weiss, 1998).

Students could investigate these historical developments through interviewing parents and grandparents about their recollections of being an adolescent in past decades. Textual representations of characters' experiences during historical time periods also provide evidence of the purposes, beliefs, identities, and relationships that contextualized individual and social activity. Through researching these historical developments, students may discover that they share similar perceptions with youth from other generations, for example, the fact that they often resisted adult authority.

REPRESENTING PEER WORLDS

Central to the study of peer worlds is understanding how these worlds are constructed through various tools. Language is a dominant tool; however, we also use gestures, objects, and even clothing to represent significant meanings in our social worlds. Clothing is a significant aspect of peer social worlds and helps to define various aspects of membership within a group related to possible identities and desired relationships with peers. As students study their peer social worlds, they may find it helpful to represent aspects such as clothing and explain how that tool functions to construct a social world. Zach explains how clothing often is used to establish peer relationships:

> George is one of my best friends and we both wear velcro shoes. We don't do it because we think they look good or they're the first thing that we would want ever; we wear them mainly for attention I suppose. But we both wear the shoes because we think it's funny and we identify with each other because of that.

Representing the common activities of a peer social world also can support inquiry. Peer social worlds often are constituted through gender-specific activities. Male peer relationships, as stereotypically portrayed in the media, typically revolve around engaging in sports (*Hoop Dreams, Hoosiers, Mighty Ducks*), cars/hanging out (*American Graffiti*), playing hooky (*Ferris Bueller's Day Off*), or drugs (*Fast Times at Ridgemont High, The Kids*). In contrast, female peer relationships often revolve around aspects of physical appearance and establishing relationships with males, as in the films *Clueless, Some Kind of Wonderful, Say Anything, Sixteen Candles*, and *The Blue Lagoon*.

In Zach's study of the social world of friends, he also noted a gender difference in the activities that peers might partake in together:

> People that are friends usually become friends because they have something in common. . . . Especially girls, because they usually like to go shopping, they may just shop with each other all the time.

In her inquiry, Helen represented a difference between genders constructed through different styles of interaction, or what we have called discourse practices. She selected photos of her friends to portray how girls and boys exhibit different actions in their peer relationships:

> I thought the pictures with the girls' best friends showed how they were best friends by how they are close, but in the picture with the guys' best friends they show attitude, it showed how they are cool best friends trying to act cool. This describes how girl and guy best friends are different in little ways.

Students also employ text-publishing tools to represent their peer world to a larger media audience. For example, peer groups produce zines as a tool to communicate with a regional or even national audience. As Stephen Duncombe (1998) notes:

> Filled with highly personalized editorial "rants," "comix," stories, poems, material appropriated from the mass press, hand-drawn pictures, and cut-and-paste collages, the zine world is vast. . . . The print runs of these zines are small, averaging about 250, though the phenomenon, while hidden, is much larger. Anywhere from 10,000 to 50,000 different titles circulate in the United States at any moment. They are produced by individuals—primarily young people, raised with the "privileges" of the white, middle class—who feel at odds with mainstream society and feel that their interests, voice, and creativity are unrepresented in the commercial media. (pp. 427–428)

Students also can construct skits, plays, or video dramas to represent their concerns, issues, and dilemmas in peer relationships (Heath & McLaughlin, 1993). In working with seventh- and eighth-grade students as a writer in residence in a New York City junior high school, Stephen O'Connor (1996) provided students with a description of the gang murder of an African-American adolescent, Yusuf Hawkins, from the book *For the Color of His Skin* by John DeSantis (1991). This murder occurred when Gina invited her 16-year-old friend, Keith, to a party in Bensonhurst; she told him that some Black and Latina peers would be attending and that if he created any "trouble," these peers would "get" him. Keith then organized a large group of his White friends, who, in the street in front of Gina's house, attacked and killed Hawkins, who had come to the neighborhood to inquire about a used car. Students discussed the complex set of misperceptions associated with this murder and then wrote monologues in which they adopted the voices of different participants in this murder. Students then wrote letters to Hawkins expressing their feelings about the event. In one letter, an eighth-grade student, assuming the voice of Gina, expressed her sense of guilt over her role in causing Keith to organize what amounted to mob violence:

> Dear Yusuf,
>
> As I begin to write this letter I begin to think about what happened to you. Its to bad that I didn't get to know you and I'm sure that you were a wonderful person and I feel I'm the one to blame but lets not get into that now. As I watched the news that night I saw your Mother being interviewed and she was crying and saying what, why did this have to happen to my baby and she brought tears into my eyes. I could see the pain and anger she was feeling and I could see how much she loves you and all I could tell my self is why, why do we have to live in such a racist world why so much violence and why you. (O'Connor, 1996, pp. 122-123)

O'Connor then wrote a play based on these monologues and letters, which the students later produced for the entire school.

In constructing their own skits about peer relationships and conflicts, students working in small groups:

- Selected specific incidents or experience in their own lives, as did O'Connor with the Hawkins murder
- Discussed the different participants' actions and perspectives on those actions, for example, a student inviting someone to the prom and then, a week before the prom, telling the person that he or she had decided not to attend
- Wrote out a script, dramatizing the conflict, and performed the skit for the class
- Elicited class response based on their own related concerns, issues, and dilemmas

Students also can make use of various multimedia texts to represent their ideas about peer social worlds. Television and film provide abundant sources for inquiries into how peer social worlds are represented. By analyzing these texts, students can select segments to reorganize in their own representations and critiques of peer social worlds. Katie and Kaley created a quicktime video by using a sequence of clips from popular movies and television shows, with superimposed text to highlight various qualities of friends:

> Friends are always there for you: buzzards cheer up a sad Mowgli in a barbershop quartet song from "The Jungle Book."

Friends share surprises: surprise birthday party on the TV show "Friends."

Friends accept you unconditionally: Bugs Bunny accepts the bugs from space at the end of "Space Jam."

Friends play together: friends and their families playing football in the pouring down rain from the movie "The Big Green."

In her essay explaining the video clips, Katie stresses that "one of the major roles a friend has is to always be there for the other and try to cheer the other up. After helping a friend get through a problem, your relationship will get better because you'll know more about one another and trust each other more."

CRITIQUING PEER WORLDS

As part of their inquiry projects, students can critique the various forces shaping their peer-world experiences, as well as the representations of those experiences. Given their concern about how peer groups mark others according to dress, Neda collected pictures of clothing from as many sources as she could find and created a gigantic poster that organized dress into categories. As she analyzed the dress of teens, Neda began to question why girls choose to wear clothing just to belong to a certain group. Her critique ultimately valued individual choice in dress to support the practice of making one's image a unique work of art:

The way one looks and dresses is a big thing to most teens in this generation. Teens—mostly females, have categories of the way people dress. . . . It goes from tight, provocative clothing to baggy and super baggy clothing. . . . Usually if a teen wants to join a certain group he/she has to, in a way, dress similar to that group or in some way be similar to that group. Why?, because belonging to a certain group sometimes means meeting their expectations. There are also those type of teens who don't really care what others wear and choose their own unique style of clothing to wear because they are confident in themselves or maybe want to stand out and be different. Personally to me I think that is in a way a work of art.

Students also may critique their own and the media's uses of stereotypical perceptions of peer relationships by posing questions such as, What's missing in or what's left out of these portrayals of relationships? Peer groups, particularly urban adolescent males of color, often are portrayed on television news or documentary programs as unruly and even potentially dangerous. For example, African-American adolescent males often are linked with certain neighborhoods or streets in which youth gangs congregate and that are described as "violent," "crime-ridden," "dangerous," or "gang-infested," characterizations that stigmatize these spaces as immoral (Lucas, 1998).

Students also could critique media that represents peer-world popularity as gained primarily through consuming or shopping (Beach & Freedman, 1992). For example, a beer ad shows a young couple shopping in the women's dress department of a store. When the female member of the couple goes off to look at dresses, the male is summoned to join a group of males hiding within a rack of dresses. The males are watching football, drinking beer, and assuming the attitude that shopping is for women. These ads convey the message that shopping is primarily a female consumer practice, while watching football and drinking beer are male practices valued in male peer worlds.

TRANSFORMING PEER WORLDS

Based on their critiques of peer-world practices, students often consider ways of changing or transforming discourse practices to improve the quality of their lives. They also consider the degree to which their proposed transformations adequately address their concerns, issues, or dilemmas. By studying social worlds, they construct a consciousness that has an expanded sense of possibility for agency, identities, and relationships.

In discussing ways of changing peer relationships, students have formulated some ethical principles constituting appropriate practices in peer relationships. Zach explains that changes in peer worlds naturally happen as people try new symbols or activities associated with new friends: "The changes can be for the good or bad. People meet new people and start to try new stuff that is spreading away from their original friend. The only way these are resolved are if friends stick together and talk it out." Zach has a clear understanding of how peer relationships can be transformed as a consequence of "new stuff" in the discourse practices that create belonging to new friends and separation from old friends.

Abby also evidenced a keen insight into the multiple overlapping social worlds of peer relationships, and how the texts and artifacts people use, create belonging and exclusion from various multiple groups at the same time. In her social worlds project she photographed many of her friends, then colorized specific sections of the gray scale photos.

In one of my photographs there are a bunch of bottles sitting on a table in the cafeteria. One bottle is differently shaped and colored than the rest. This is meant to show that there is one girl at my lunch table who doesn't fit with our group. She doesn't drink Snapple like the rest of the girls, which capitalizes on the fact that she doesn't fit in. One of the most striking pictures is one of four girls all wearing the same style of Old Navy Tech Vest in the hallway outside of the bathroom. They are talking and laughing, and are obviously very comfortable together. . . . My favorite picture is one of a group of girls standing together in the bathroom. This represents something that I call "the bathroom group." The bathroom group is an objective group that consists of pretty much anyone who comes into the bathroom to socialize. Every girl in there is from a different group, and yet the girls all mingle and talk. This is one of the best examples of an objective group because, although I know this sounds odd, no one is judged in the bathroom.

Abby does not directly advocate that every girl has the power to transform the peer relationships that form their lives. Instead, she emphasizes how every person is always simultaneously in and out of overlapping worlds. But her focus on the power of objects, clothing, and locations like the bathroom to shape positive peer worlds reveals an understanding that certainly would support transforming actions in future social interactions.

The realization that one's words and actions with others can have an impact on the identities, relationships, and values of a world is a critical basis for transforming social worlds. Nilu also evidenced this consciousness in her essay about her inquiry into peer social worlds:

When I was little I had a best friend, Katie. We were always together, we would dance and sing and laugh and play, and she was the best. Our parents were best friends too, so that's how we met, lucky for us. Our parents would leave us on the floor together while they went to have their own, "grown up" discussions. They thought that we would just content ourselves with the silly little toys that they put around us, but nope, we had our own little discussions, about what kind of new tasty, and sometimes nasty, food that mommy or daddy had fed us that day, or the night before. It was quite fun. As we grew older, we grew closer, yet in some ways farther apart. As we hit the big Elementary school, we found out that we would be going to different schools, but that was ok, 'cause we saw each other every weekend. We both made new friends, but still had each other as best friends. The days past slowly, but then it was fifth grade, one more year and . . . *Middle School* . . . scary! In sixth grade, we were each on two separate teams, but still saw each other on the weekend, so that was ok, but something new was starting to happen. This word, this evil word, that attacks every kid on earth, at one point or another of his/her life hit me, it was *popularity*. In seventh grade everything began to suddenly change, anything anybody cared about was looks, the opposite sex and popularity. Katie and I grew further and further apart. Our parents still got together, and brought us along, but we no longer did fun things with each other, and in school we never talked. Eighth grade passed and nothing changed, only the fact that now our parents hardly ever brought us along with them, so we didn't really talk at all. Now its High School, she's in one of my classes this year, but I don't think that I have ever said more than "Hi, how are you?" to her this year. The last time that she was over at my house was when our parents got together this past summer, some of the old fun that we used to have came back in flashes, as it always does, but didn't stay, just came and went. And that's how friends are, they come into your life, flying in fast as a bird, and then leave just as quickly, sometimes without one word.

Throughout her explanation, Nilu explains how shared objects, space, time, discourse practices, and texts are essential to construct relationships in peer social worlds. She is also quite aware of how discourse practices involving popularity create contesting social worlds that divide peers. While at the end she embraces a value for old friends, she clearly knows how, if she so desired, to transform her social worlds to rebuild a social world with old friends.

In a very different social worlds project, Asqa represents similar ideas in a short story she wrote about two best friends divided by the desire of one of them for popularity. The story included pictures cut from magazines that illustrated story characters and events. The long fictional narrative constructed a conflict between peer social worlds that eventually helped the friend realize that her desire for popularity was a mistaken value, bringing the friends back together at the end of the story.

The social world of friends has many different conflicts involved. Such as friends who compete for grades but still remain friends, or friends who argue about what bands are "in" and what are "out." Or even friends who fight constantly, over little things, but still remain best friends. In the story, there was a conflict between two best friends, because one decided that the other one wasn't cool enough anymore. . . . It is not surprising to meet someone who acts one way in front of you, but differently in front of another. That's one thing people tend to do. Just to make friends, they act completely different than their normal selves, because they think this is the best way to be accepted into a clique. Some people, who are new in school, feel troubled by the way kids stare at them, so they make up stories, just so that people will like them, and accept them, and so they'll finally feel belonged. Many things go around in the social world of friends, such as conflicts, agreements, relationships, etc. That basically shows, in my opinion, that the world of friends is one of the most complicated social worlds to understand.

Kate explored the complicated emotions that friends feel when they are separated. For her inquiry project she created a book that included poems, responses to e-mail, photos, and refections on friendship: "The end of a friendship is not once the friend leaves, it could even start the beginning of a better relationship. Memories are something you will never forget, and as long as you have those memories the friend can never be forgotten." Kate realizes that social worlds are continually constructed, even when the participants are not physically together.

Nilu's, Asqa's, and Kate's analyses especially highlight their understanding of how peer social worlds are continually being constructed as overlapping, conflicting worlds. This consciousness will support their own agency in constructing the worlds that hold desired identities, relationships, and values.

8

School and Sports Worlds

OF THE DIFFERENT worlds students could study, the school or sports world is perhaps the most immediately accessible. (We have combined the school and sports worlds in one chapter because these two worlds often overlap.) That same accessibility, however, poses a challenge for students as it may be difficult for them to step back and achieve some distance from their own familiar school or sports cultures. They therefore may want to study a school setting or aspect of their school to which they have less attachment.

Students also may be reluctant to critique or consider transforming their school if they assume that their critiques or recommendations for change will be perceived negatively by teachers or school administrators. However, if they knew that their critiques or recommendations for change would be taken seriously by teachers or administrators, they might be more willing to conduct studies of school or sports worlds. Such is the case at Sharnbrook Upper School and Community College, which is located in Bedfordshire, England. "Students as Researchers" is a research and development project that has been in operation since 1996. Students are selected from all age groups (ages 13–18) to undertake research about areas on which the whole student body votes. They are trained in methods of research and evaluation in partnership with staff at the University of Cambridge and by participating staff at school. Students are broken into small groups of approximately eight or nine students to work with the staff on individual research tasks. Topics covered to date include: the student voice, school meals provision, the tutorial system, the use of trainee teachers in the classroom, careers education and guidance, what helps and hinders student learning, the use of ICT in the curriculum, extracurricular activities, industry links with school, and profiling and assessment.

In relation to *all* of these projects, reports are written and students make presentations to important stakeholders. This may include presenting to senior team, pastoral heads, whole-staff meetings, parents' forums, and even governing body meetings. The outcomes of each of the research projects have been taken extremely seriously and, indeed, feed school improvement at Sharnbrook. What is particularly unique about this project is that students, by definition, can feel that they can make a contribution to how the school is developed and improved. Students learn on many different levels from being involved in this kind of work. The way in which they work is non-hierarchical and relies on each person sharing and developing their skills with one another. The way that students work with staff is a completely new partnership, and external evaluation of this project carried out in 1998 by the University of Cambridge was extremely rewarding and promising.

IMMERSING IN A SCHOOL WORLD

In immersing themselves in a school or sports world, students observe and interview their peers or teachers. With teachers' permission, students can observe classrooms. Students in Barbara Lambert's journalism class at North High School, North St. Paul, Minnesota, each visited a local school and wrote a report of their visit for the high school newspaper, *Polar Prints*. Jenny Anderson (1999), a senior, shadowed a ninth-grade student, Ashley Chester, for a day, asking about her experiences as they moved from class to class. Ashley noted that "it's not that bad being a freshmen, but it's just the stereo-type we get that bugs me, but I can live with it." In sitting together in classes, they shared their perceptions about the fact that "the boys are pretty loud and try to act older than they are."

Nikki Peters shadowed her sister, Natalie, for a day at Natalie's college, St. Cloud State University. She was most struck by her sister's autonomy: "In college you have projects and tests, and it's up to you to be in class every day and to get it all done. To do well in your college classes, you have to be self-motivated, organized, and you need to have good time management." Ryan Foley shadowed his physical education teacher, Mr. Wallert, for a day, observing his work with students and perceptions about his job. Wallert explained to Ryan that he enjoyed his work because "I like to watch the kids improve day to day on just the basic skills of whatever unit we're on. It helps me as a person to know that I'm good at teaching somebody how to do something." Based on his observations, Ryan recognized that "it really isn't that easy of a job. They have to motivate some students who are virtu-ally unmotivated and highly immature. They deserve a lot more credit than they receive."

In observing their schools, students noted instances of how certain prac-tices foster learning in a school. For example, Diane Amsden and Katie Surrett observed four different aspects of a daycare center: environment, "being an insider," routine, and language. From these observations, they noted how the center revolved around accommodating the interests of children. They re-corded the different types of toys available on the playground:

Swing-sets, jungle gyms, slides, tricycles, sandboxes, and any other outside toy you could imagine. The classroom is divided into sections, all geared towards different activities that children would enjoy, like a dress-up area with a big mirror and lots of different shoes, little tables with crayons and coloring books, cabinets filled with craft supplies, and an individual reading area with tiny beanbags [and] . . . a million books, from Dr. Seuss to Mickey Mouse.

The students described how the daycare center also accommodates the size of the children: "Coat hooks were no more than two feet off the ground," as well as their own difficulty in sitting in kid-sized chairs: "We sat in these chairs during our observing and felt very cramped. Our knees were bent up close to our bodies." Similarly, based on her observation of a first-grade teacher interacting with children for a day, Becky Wilson noted:

You must have a lot of patience with all the kids. You also have to have a calm voice when getting frustrated. Although the kids ask simple questions, you must give them an answer politely. If one child doesn't understand something you must take the time to explain it to him/her. Usually the rest of the class is interested too.

Students also may immerse themselves in their school world by drawing maps of the different classrooms and other parts of their school—lunchroom, dean's office, auditorium, fields, and so on. They could then describe their perceptions of these different components in terms of positive versus negative feelings. Students also could keep a log or chart of their school day and, at certain times during the day, record their positive versus negative feelings and reasons for those feelings (Csikszentmihalyi & Larson, 1986).

In a similar process, Kyle, a State College Area High School freshman, explored his own experiences in various "extreme" sports. As a rock climber and dirt bike rider, he immersed himself into the many magazines and videos he had and could find about the sports. He also generated a reflective journal about his own experiences; one typical entry read:

When I go out to climb I try to think about my problems as little as I can, the only thing I worry about is whether I set up the anchor properly. . . . I enjoy riding my dirt bike through the fields and mountains around my house. It's a good way to relieve aggression and just to have fun and get away from my parents.

As students inquire into school or sports worlds, they need to gather their own reflections and observations, as well as others' thoughts through interviews or printed texts. These activities help students become immersed in the culture they wish to explore.

To help students understand the concept of "culture," 60 students in a reading/writing block taught by Jon Paulson and Kristen Konok at the Cross-winds Middle School (referred to in Chapter 6) participated in a "Digs 2" project. After discussing the concept of culture as a particular way of acting or thinking as evident in a group's clothing, food, recreation, religion, roles, values, and so on, students broke into groups and created their own fictional culture, requiring them to create artifacts and documents that portrayed the values of their imaginary culture. This immersing activity helped students become familiar with the idea of culture.

Then, to examine the concept of "diversity," students identified and mapped the different *actual* cultures to which they belonged. The teachers provided the initial question: "What is the typical Crosswinds student?" Students discussed the concepts of "typical," "normal," and "average." While this was a teacher-assigned topic, within it students had considerable leeway in selecting their own project for investigation.

To initiate their inquiries, students recorded their observations of peers' social practices in their homeroom period and at lunch in an observation journal, dividing the page in half and listing their observations of peers' behaviors, talk, dress, and gestures on one side, and their interpretations of these practices on the other side. Students also interviewed peers about their interests, leisure-time activities, hobbies, perceptions of self and others, and attitudes. For example, one group of students asked their peers the question, "Are you interested in dating?" As mentioned in Chapter 6, students also collected data by circulating surveys to classmates.

Students then shared with peers those cultures that were most important to them. They depicted those cultures as "cultural sandwiches" consisting of drawings or magazine cutouts pasted onto different pieces of colored paper and placed between two pieces of "bread." They then hung these sandwiches on classroom walls to display the range of diverse cultures represented in the Crosswinds student body.

IDENTIFYING CONCERNS, ISSUES, OR DILEMMAS ASSOCIATED WITH SCHOOL OR SPORTS WORLDS

Students are confronted daily with a range of concerns, issues, and dilemmas in their school or sports worlds that could serve as the basis of inquiry projects.

Students experience difficulties or frustrations with the issue of learning in a classroom, or participating in a sport, for a wide variety of reasons. They may not understand the subject matter, the purpose for classroom activities, the expectations for assignments, or the strategy of the coach and game, or they may not like the teacher or subject. They may organize an inquiry around questions such as: Will I have difficulty in a new course? What does my teacher think about me? Will I be hassled in the hallway? What do others think about my appearance? What do I have to do to be a starter on the team? What am I supposed to do in order to learn or succeed in this classroom or sport? What am I learning or not learning and why?

Level 8 students at the St. Ivo School in Cambridge, England, were concerned with their lack of learning associated with their peers' and teachers' difficulties in listening to each other (Report to 8KP, 1999). They and their teachers therefore conducted a study of instances of listening difficulties in the school. They recorded and analyzed classroom discussions and a listening lesson with a tutor from the University of Cambridge, and surveyed students and teachers with a questionnaire. They also met with teachers and discussed ideas for improving listening. The students noted that while there was a relationship between effective listening and the level of learning in a classroom, it was still difficult to listen in the classroom. They were frustrated with teachers who did not listen to their opinions and perspectives, implying a lack of respect for the students. They were also frustrated with peers who did not listen to teachers or with a few individual students who distracted them, resulting in unfair teacher reprimands of the entire class.

Students often express concerns about their discomfort in school. As one high school student noted: "People aren't comfortable in school . . . they then never learn the joy of putting everything they've got into learning" (Hersch, 1998, p. 222).

As part of their study of their own school, students in Kimberly Kosach's high school English class identified a number of concerns related to their safety and comfort in the school. They cited problems with uncollected trash; broken, older desks; lack of air-conditioning; missing lockers; graffiti; shortage of textbooks; the lack of a football field; a deteriorating soccer field; inadequate bathrooms; and broken roofs, windows, and walls. In writing about these problems, the students attributed some of them to lack of funding and proper maintenance, as well as their own behavior. As Donna Duenas noted:

> The reason why [the school] is missing a lot of lockers is because students mistreat the school lockers. They kick and write on them, so when they're broken, students can get new lockers. Students have to share lockers with their friends because there's not enough lockers for everyone. We should prevent students from destroying and damaging school property.

Students also may experience highly positive feelings of engagement in sports, music, art, or classes in which they assume responsibilities and display competence as active participants (Csikszentmihalyi & Larson, 1986). "At-risk" students participating in a high school "literacy lab" in a West Lafayette, Indiana, high school, who were bored with traditional academic schoolwork, were highly engaged in writing related to visual media, for example, writing a computer report of a movie or a video clip (O'Brien et al., 1998).

Students, particularly at the middle school level, express a concern with bullying by peers. About 10-20% of students in middle school self-report being bullies, and about 10-15% self-report being victimized (Smith & Sharp, 1994). To establish their superiority or dominance in a group, bullies will publicly display aggressive behavior, often by targeting peers who are physically weaker and perceived as victims by their teachers (Pellegrini, 1995; Pellegrini & Smith, 1998).

In teaching the novel *The 18th Emergency* (Byars, 1996) to his class at Harrold Priory Middle School, Bedfordshire, England, Rob Robson discovered that all the students in his class indicated that they had experienced some form of bullying. Robson found that the novel's portrayal of bullying served to foster discussion about students' experiences of bullying. In the novel, the main character, Mouse (a nickname for Benjie), constantly writes little signs throughout the school. He writes the name of the school bully, Marv Hammerman, on a poster at the school, with a little arrow pointing to a picture of a Neanderthal Man. Unknown to Mouse, Hammerman is standing behind him and threatens to beat him up. After many attempts to elude Hammerman, Mouse goes to find Hammerman, who does beat him up. Mouse is changed by this and people start to call him Benjie instead of Mouse.

In responding to the novel, students drew on their experiences and attitudes about bullying and stereotyping. As Robson notes:

> At first the class had a lot of sympathy for Mouse and his problem. In their first word drawings of Hammerman, he came out as the stereotypical bully figure, large, muscular, and stupid. Mouse came out as the "normal" pupil. As the book progressed, the class became rather frustrated with Mouse constantly avoiding the issue and running away. Their descriptive portraits of Mouse now saw him as a thin, weedy, and unappealing figure. Hammerman remained muscular but lost his stupidness. By the end of the book, Benjie was restored to class hero and became a "normal" pupil again. Interestingly, despite the fact that Hammerman had beaten up Mouse (described in graphic detail in the book), Hammerman did not become stupid again and indeed I felt amongst the class a sneaking admiration for a character who was, in their eyes, trying to defend his honor.

Robson's students increased their understanding about the concern of bully-ing through the process of connecting lived and represented social worlds.

Sports often play positive roles in students' lives, helping students over-come concerns, issues, or dilemmas. Students develop confidence in their abilities, make friends, and maintain physical fitness through sports. For ex-ample, the four members of a high school swim team portrayed in Chris Crutcher's *Stotan!* (1986) help each other cope with challenges in their per-sonal life. Teamwork is perhaps the biggest issue attributed to participation in a sport's social world. In separate inquiries into the world of high school, college, and NFL football, State College Area High School freshmen Michele, Jon S., and Nick concluded that learning to work together on a team was the most important consequence of the social world of sports:

> Everyone always has their own personal dreams and desires. Certain team records or league records. Now as a team you have records you want to accomplish as a team. You all work for the same goal. (Nick)

While participation in sports may lead to an increased commitment to or involvement in school, some argue that there is little evidence of increased academic performance or positive student self-concept (Griffin, 1998). More-over, some coaches and even parents promote a "win-at-all-costs" competi-tive orientation, placing students in moral dilemmas over whether to partici-pate in such a system. In *Running Loose* (Crutcher, 1983), the main character, Louie, faces a moral dilemma when his football coach orders players to in-jure star opponents.

CONTEXTUALIZING SCHOOL OR SPORTS WORLDS

Once students have identified their concerns, issues, or dilemmas, they then set up inquiry projects in which they study the components of school or sports worlds relevant to their questions.

Purpose

Many of the concerns, issues, or dilemmas associated with school/sports worlds revolve around questions of purpose for various practices—what are teachers, students, or administrators trying to accomplish? Students may ask teachers or administrators to describe the purpose of their school. In dis-cussing the purpose of a daycare center with its teachers, North High School students Diane and Katie noted that the school culture revolved around the purpose of socializing young children into the world of school and learning to interact with each other. They noted that "these children were very polite, and when they were mean to another one, the teacher would tell them to say sorry to their friends." If a child hurt another, or said "something bad," the teacher "would often correct them and put them in time out," strategies they perceived as designed to teach the children "politeness and kindness."

Roles

Students may examine the various roles operating in the school/sports world: student, teacher, dean, principal, coach, nurse, counselor, superintendent, athletic director, and so on. Within these roles, persons adopt certain identities. Within the student role, they may adopt the identities of "jock," "nerd," "burnout," "redneck," "druggie," "Motorhead," "Skater," "Micro-geek," and so forth. Given these categories, students often espouse stereotypical perceptions of peers.

In a study of the Knowledge Bowl Team of North High School, a team that competes in a televised competition involving knowledge of factual information, Dan Campbell and Rita Waheb observed and participated in team meetings, talked to team members and the coach, and attended a Knowledge Bowl Meet. In observing the students, they noted that they didn't "see many name brands like Abercrombie and Fitch, Tommy Hilfiger, Nautica, Fubu, The Gap, and Polo," brand names "worn by about 70% of the people at North High School," suggesting that these students "are concerned with more important things." They assumed that members of this team would conform to their stereotype of "someone wearing thick black glasses, carrying lots of books, reading them all the time so they can get straight As." As they began to interact with the students, Dan and Rita discovered a number of the students' discourse practices that contradicted their perception of team members as "nerdy." Team members talked about "Friday night and gossip," and described two couples on the bus, "one holding hands sweetly." This led Dan and Rita to infer that "they are not all nerdy brainiacs who stay home every afternoon and night, reading books and playing Final Fantasy." As they witnessed their team win the competition, they concluded that the team members' self-confident display of knowledge leads them to resist "mindless shallowness and commitment to fad."

In his inquiry project on football, State College Area High School freshman Austin reflected on the characteristics of the role players need to assume in football:

> Some may say it is just a game though most people who say that have probably never had a *role* as a football player. There are important

qualities that a player must have. You have to put in a considerable amount of time just to understand the parameters of the sport. . . . Even though some of the other players may be unruly but try to ignore it that shows good attitude and behaviors. Try not to let your accomplishments go to your head or your failures for that matter. The only way you'll learn is from your mistakes.

Students may perceive athletes as "dumb jocks" or female athletes as "manly." In conducting inquiry projects about sports, students may reflect on how these stereotypical assumptions shape their perceptions of participants. Before observing the North High Girls swimming and diving team, Karen James held "a few athletic stereotypes." She assumed that athletes "worked hard but that was about it." She observed their practices, noting in detail the layering of swimsuits, extensive warm-up stretching activities, use of equipment designed to improve their strength, and long hours of swimming laps. After observing these practices, she recognized that there is "more to [the swimmers] than I ever would have guessed." She also noted their hard work, driven by their sense of team spirit, in which "the success of their fellow colleagues was very important to them."

Rules

Students may study the rules operating in a classroom or school as well as the attitude of teachers and administrators toward enforcing these rules, an attitude that may reflect a prevailing ethos about the school. In writing about her visit to Southwest High School in Minneapolis, Ellen Brinkman of North High School noted:

> I couldn't believe how laid back of a school it was. All of the classes seemed very casual. The teachers didn't seem to mind the constant chatter. Teachers had a tardy policy, but they didn't enforce it. The students were free to leave class without a pass, but did not abuse this privilege. Southwest was very relaxed and it seemed that most of the students obeyed the general rules.

Beliefs

In studying how beliefs and attitudes shape social practices in a school, students may interview participants engaged in those practices. For example, to examine the belief that "sports build character," students may talk to players and coaches about what they think is the value of sports. They also may read excerpts from *Friday Night Lights* by H. G. Bissinger (1990), a Pulitzer Prize-winning journalist, who portrays one season of the Permian High School football team of Odessa, Texas. The book demonstrates the single-minded pressure exerted by the town on the team to win at all costs. Alumni assume the role of avid boosters who vicariously relive their former high school years through supporting the team. Team members take on the role of local heroes, while their girlfriends are forced to appear as less intelligent than the boys in order to maintain the boys' image as idols. Reading such books serves to model ways of achieving a critical distance from the often insular sports worlds and their obsession with winning.

History

Students may observe school events or rituals and how these events or rituals conform to or deviate from historical traditions. Or, they may attend high school reunions and interview returning alumni about their recollections of past traditions. Students then can determine how these traditions shape possible identities and relationships in their current school world.

In his social worlds unit project at State College Area High School, Paul examined hundreds of comic strips about life in school. His analysis focused on the common rituals related to romance, grades, and friends. The comics provided important clues about the traditional contexts of school because the humor in each one played off some common school discourse practice. The comics also provided a unique representational form for the presentation of findings.

REPRESENTING SCHOOL OR SPORTS WORLDS

In conducting inquiry projects, students may employ a range of different tools to represent their findings. For their final project, the Crosswinds Middle School students created a "Crosswinds Culture Magazine" that contained articles, advertisements, comic strips, surveys, horoscopes, charts/graphs, puzzles, photo journals, and editorials based on the results of their individual studies. Drawing on their instruction in math class, the students represented their quantitative analysis of interview responses using graphs and charts. The multigenre nature of this magazine encouraged students to present their results using a range of different tools.

Film offers a form of representation that has immense popularity and power with students. Ninth-grade students from State College Area High School often made connections between the social worlds represented in short stories and films. Many students used the computer to edit quicktime movies about school life and sports experiences.

An abundant number of films exist for students to use in studying representations of the world of sports. In examining films such as *Hoosiers, Rocky/Rocky II, The Karate Kid, Cutting Edge, The Mighty Ducks, Hoop Dreams,* or *Vision Quest,* students can analyze the values, identities, and relationships underlying the story development. These films often dramatize the unusual rise of an underdog team or individual who, with the help of a mentor employing unorthodox training methods, helps lead the team or individual to victory over far superior opponents. They may focus specifically on the role of the coach, who is portrayed both positively as someone who helps his players and negatively as someone who adopts a hard-line, authoritarian approach to disciplining players (Crowe, 1994).

Students also may study the representations of teachers in literature and the media. Shannon and Crawford (1998) identify a number of different representations of teachers as "caretakers," "jailers," "saviors," "drillmasters," "keepers of wisdom," "facilitators/guides-on-the-side," "technicians," "agents of social change," or "underpaid unionists," arguing that each of these representations portrays only a limited, partial perspective on the complex nature of teaching. For example, in the films *The Prime of Miss Jean Brodie* (1969), *To Sir, With Love* (1967), *Up the Down Staircase* (1967), *Dead Poet's Society* (1989), *Dangerous Minds* (1995), and *Good Will Hunting* (1997), teachers are portrayed as totally dedicated, loner saviors of students, who fight against the often repressive school to help their students. One limitation of this representation is that it "ultimately robs teachers of a life outside and inside their work and separates them from the rest of us who are charged with educating and socializing children" (Shannon & Crawford, 1998, p. 256).

Drama and role-play are also excellent and engaging tools for students to use in representing their experiences in school and sports social worlds. In acting out situations that concerned bullying, Rob Robson's students used specific real-life incidents from the playground. Robson noted that the students drew on their experiences with the *The 18th Emergency* to represent their perceptions of bullying:

> When the sketches were presented, the book's influence came out strongly again. The sketches showed pupils solving their own problems. At first I was worried by this because I felt that there was a message of "do it yourself" being accepted but I noticed a subtle twist as more work went on. The bullies sometimes won when the pupil victim stood up to them. It was obvious that the pupils did not see standing up to a bully as the only solution. More drama and discussion work made me realize that I had previously underestimated the skills that many pupils have in knowing when to seek outside help. I was fascinated to see a direct correlation between the seriousness of the incident portrayed and

the amount of help that was needed. For example, in the pupils' work a name calling situation would warrant an assertive and/or aggressive verbal response. Group teasing would need the extra help of peer-group friends whilst a sketch with punching or kicking nearly always portrayed the intervention of a teacher or older pupil.

Based on his experience with these sixth graders' perceptions of the need for teacher assistance in coping with bullying, he and another English teacher set up a program for eighth graders related to assertiveness as a means for coping with bullying. As with the sixth graders, the eighth graders acted out specific experiences based on actual incidents. Based on discussions about these role-play sessions, the students quickly moved from representing a social world into critiquing and transforming, when they believed that they actually could help other students cope with bullying.

The eighth-grade students also developed visual representations of their perceptions of a bully, using a computer cartoon library of drawings. Based on the sixth graders' stereotypical descriptions of bullies, the students generated nine character types: three thugs who look like violent people and who appear to fit the stereotype of bullies, two "normal" pupils, one "passive" person (a possible victim), two "look victims" (people who might be bullied because of the way that they looked), and a teacher. They then used these representations to critique stereotyping of bullies.

CRITIQUING AND TRANSFORMING SCHOOL OR SPORTS WORLDS

In critiquing school or sports worlds, students critically examine the forces shaping practices in these worlds. State College Area High School students Katie and Kelsey filmed a video about the life of a teen at basketball practice. The events of the practice created a critique of the pressure teens experience to perform at high levels of success in school sports. As Katie notes:

The expectations of an athlete can be high or low but in our play, just to show the extra pressure, we set them rather high. Since the teen in our skit was a good player who was only having an off day, she felt A TON of pressure from her coach and the other players. Players often are scolded at home, too, by their parents if they are not playing the best that they can. As you can see, there is plenty of stress due to pressure in a teen athlete's life. . . . I think that the one who plays on a team needs to discover their own identity. They should not let a coach or another member of the team tell them how far to push themselves, this is what happened in the play that we did. There was too much pressure on the teen to do well and because of this she could not play her best. Sometimes, it is easier to do your best when there is no one else around to see you or push you harder.

The girls' video critiques the values, identities, and relationships often constructed in the social world of team sports. They argue for individuals' agency to define their own identity through personally valued actions instead of always trying to act in ways others desire.

Based on their discussion of bullying, Rob Robson's eighth-grade students were critical of the level of bullying occurring in their school and believed that they could address this issue through taking action. They decided to develop a questionnaire to determine the amount of bullying in the school. In designing the questionnaire, they first generated the following definitions of bullying:

- A bully is somebody who deliberately prevents another person from having rights in order to get what he wants.
- Bullying has to have a bully and someone who is bullied, [they later accepted that the word *victim* might be useful to replace someone who is bullied]. It can be physically or mentally hurtful and can take many forms.

To these definitions, they added the statement: "The bully and the victim both need help."

Robson was pleased with these students' perceptions of bullying, noting that they reflected research that shows that "children do not feel bullying is an inevitable part of growing up. They want it to be stopped." As the students were discussing these perceptions, one student

raised a question which I hadn't foreseen. To paraphrase, it went something like this: "How can we ask other kids about bullying when it took us this long to decide what it is ourselves and we still don't all agree?" It was eventually decided by a huge majority (I was the only objector!) to drop the definitions and make up a questionnaire which did not mention bullying at all but rather questioned pupils about types of behaviour identified as bullying by 15 work groups (spread over four classes) and then edited into one worksheet by a team, one from each group and me.

In contemplating the results of his students' analysis of bullying, Robson hopes that, in the future, students will not only learn more about bullying, but also acquire strategies for coping with bullying, including the use of a "court" in which trained students provide feedback and counseling for bullies. In reflecting on the students' bullying project, Robson judges its success in terms of whether it serves to transform students' lives:

> A successful project whereby other pupils are helped and our Eighth Year grow in maturity and responsibility will give good grounds for expanding the work. A project that is judged to get in the way of the curriculum and/or is seen as a "trendy" waste of time could very well sound the death knell for future work. I cannot say that HPS has a serious bullying problem; I have not done enough long-term work to find out but I do know that personally I enjoy watching pupils help other pupils and in my opinion there is no better kind of help. If we can educate people to help and understand others rather than sitting in judgment on them, we will create society that actually does care instead of paying lip-service to it. We will be retaking the moral high-ground.

In addition to simply brainstorming alternatives, students could engage in activities in which they participate in making changes. For example, given their concern with public perceptions of schools as "failing," students could attempt to transform public perceptions by displaying their work to the public. The Museum of Art in Portland, Maine, mounts serious exhibits of students' artwork, poetry, and drama (Shannon & Crawford, 1998). Students could participate in school-wide forums designed to publicly address their concerns, issues, and dilemmas. Students in South High School in Minneapolis organized a series of forums for discussing ways of combating incidents involving written racial slurs in lavatories (Beach, 1997). Students could participate in service-learning or tutoring projects designed to assist others. By tutoring younger children in reading or writing, students begin to think about their own ways of reading or writing in having to teach these practices to others.

Students could engage in various writing and publishing projects to portray practices within school social worlds. They could create web pages to publish their work for access by parents and local citizens. State College Area High School ninth grader Briton authored an illustrated children's story titled "We Are All Different." In this story the young Black child doesn't realize he is different until he goes to school and begins to experience the exclusion of racism. The other children push him into the mud at recess. A teacher comes over to help him and he is excited to see that she is just like him. Now, even though the others still laugh at him for being different, he doesn't care. Briton cleverly uses the popular alien symbol at the very end of the story to represent the faces of all the other laughing children in school, making an ironic turn on who is really different.

And, beyond written tools for transforming social worlds, students could transform their worlds through their own individual actions and words—supporting efforts to open up participation in all sports regardless of gender, class, race, or disabilities, and discouraging coaches and players who condone a "winning-is-everything" belief.

Enacting new, and often contrary, discourse practices always requires the construction of a social world with others who share similar desired values, identities, and relationships. One cannot do it alone. However, in this book we have shared many instances of how students, when given responsibility for examining the ways in which their school is or is not serving their needs, develop a strong sense of agency and community as valued constituents who are contributing to the improvement of their social worlds through transforming actions and words.

9

Family and Romance Worlds

OF THE VARIOUS worlds described in this book, the family world perhaps plays the most important role in shaping adolescents' lives. The nature of social interaction with parents and siblings greatly influences their own sense of identity, the kind of human relationships they seek, and the values that guide their future. Given a recent shift toward both parents working, parents often have more difficulty devoting time and energy to everyday interactions with their children. Often the more important interactions involving play, working on school assignments, family outings, casual conversations about experiences, assisting adolescents in coping with problems or conflicts, participating in neighborhood events, and so on, are replaced by logistical interactions such as serving meals, monitoring children's whereabouts, transporting children, or organizing child care and nonfamily activities. Without parental support and attention, adolescents are left to their own limited resources to navigate life without the benefit of having more experienced parents participate in the construction of their social worlds (Finnegan, 1998; Hersch, 1998).

In his inquiry project on the conflicts between the family and work worlds, State College Area High School student Jeff noted how lack of parental support has detrimental effects on adolescents:

> Today many parents do not spend enough time with their kids.
> Parents are too exhausted from their jobs so they allow kids to
> watch TV or play video games. Also, parents are so busy busing their
> kid from one activity to another that they don't talk and share their
> lives. Quite often, a parent will work night shift. The children will
> rarely get to see and communicate with that adult. One result is
> some kids may have lower grades or get in trouble because the
> father or mother does not have time with the kid because they are at
> work or too tired to care.

In conducting inquiry about family worlds, students may explore a range of concerns, issues, or dilemmas associated with their interactions with families, both in their lived worlds and the represented worlds in literature and the media.

Interactions in the social world of romance revolve around the practices of being attracted to others, establishing initial relationships, organizing a date, issuing invitations, expressing one's feelings, complimenting/flattering the other, and so on. While these practices are designed to develop positive relationships, as with the family, they are linked to other worlds, leading to complications in relationships.

IMMERSING IN FAMILY OR ROMANCE WORLDS

To identify concerns, issues, or dilemmas related to the family/romance, students may observe various practices in their own or others' families or in their peers' romantic relationships. They may note the length of the interactions, the purpose or topic of the interactions, and the types of language employed. They also may interview both parents and children about their perceptions of their romantic or family interactions. From these findings, they then analyze the values for particular identities and relationships in family and romance social worlds.

For example, Cathy Witwicke of North High School, North St. Paul, Minnesota, conducted a study of her mother's first cousin's family of five who live on a farm. Knowing little about farming, she decided to spend some time studying the family and how farming served to define their lives. During her stay on the farm, she observed the daily routines of family members completing farm chores, interviewed family members about their perceptions of farming, and participated herself in doing the chores. Participating as if she were a member of the family provided her with a sense of how the family operated.

In conducting these studies, it is very important that, given potential invasion of privacy, students obtain family members' or couples' permission before engaging in a project. Ideally, they should involve other family members or couples as co-inquirers in reflecting on how they create their own social worlds. Through participating in these studies, family members or couples may share some perceptions of their lives that they otherwise might not, and these reflections may yield some insights into the challenges associated with family or romance worlds.

Given the difficulty of directly studying one's own family or love relationships, students may respond to literary portrayals of family or romantic relationships, using these responses to construct representations about their own lived world.

IDENTIFYING CONCERNS, ISSUES, AND DILEMMAS

Students face a range of concerns, issues, and dilemmas in their families or in their romantic relationships. Contrary to the popular conception of adolescence as a period of continual tension with parent(s), adolescents and parents actually experience relatively low levels of conflict (Steinberg, 1990). The majority of adolescents in the Sloan Institute survey perceived their parent(s) as supportive, loving, and accepting (Schneider & Stevenson, 1999). However, many in the survey were concerned about the lack of attention they received from parents: "Only a third said that they receive special attention and help when they have a problem. For most adolescents, problem situations are seen as times when parents are least likely to intervene or offer assistance" (Schneider & Stevenson, 1999, p. 143). Adolescents also are concerned about the quality of their communication with parents. One study found that 20% of adolescents had not had a substantive conversation of more than 10 minutes with parents within the past month (Beacon, 1993).

In communicating with parents, teens often are caught between wanting to maintain their respect and love for their parents, while at the same time needing to develop autonomy and independence from their parents. This creates a conflict between being accountable to parents versus the need to establish one's autonomy and a sense of self-worth. Analysis of adolescents' activities indicate that "about 80 percent of the time they feel they are doing the activity out of obligation (i.e., because they 'had to') rather than choice (i.e., because they wanted to)" (Csikszentmihalyi & Schmidt, 1998, p. 63). This gives them little time to "enjoy and seek out situations that make them feel competent and fully functioning. When such opportunities are lacking, they are driven to invent them" (Csikszentmihalyi & Schmidt, 1998, p. 63). Therefore adolescents often must choose between asserting their own independence against parental attempts to control them versus complying and being rewarded for their compliance.

Beyond family relationships, teens are especially concerned about establishing trusting and committed romantic relationships. Falling in love is perhaps one of the most important events of the adolescent years. As they enter into romantic relationships, students are concerned with establishing some level of trust or commitment necessary for sustaining a relationship (for narrative accounts of these difficulties, see Bode & Mack, 1994). Because many are experiencing romance for the first time, they may experience "peer shock" (Elkind, 1998) over perceived breakdowns in trust or commitment. They also discover that maintaining a commitment to a relationship requires an effort by both parties in the relationship.

Osseo High School student Mandy Statz conducted a study of her peers' relationships:

Now that I'm in a serious relationship, I want to know more about teenage relationships. I find them fascinating in many ways because there are so many things you have to do to make it work. A lot of teenagers get into relationships just to say they're in one because they think it makes them more popular, but this isn't always true. This can lead to good relationships, but it could also lead to bad relationships. You could meet the man of your dreams or you could meet an abusive boyfriend who ruins the most important years of your life.

To explore her concern, Mandy read material on some web sites devoted to discussions of relationships and interviewed another couple. She also created a survey consisting of eight questions:

Are you currently in a relationship? Do you wish you were in a relationship? Have you been in a relationship? Do you believe you have higher self-esteem when you're in a relationship? Do you know anyone who is in an abusive relationship? Do you like doing things with your friends when they're with their significant others? Do you think you should spend more time with your friends or significant others? How long do teenage relationships usually last?

Of the eighteen 16–18-year-old males and females she surveyed, only four noted they were currently in a relationship, while 10 indicated that they wished they were in a relationship. Six of the 18 indicated that they knew of someone in an abusive relationship. And, respondents noted that most relationships last for less than 6 months. Mandy was surprised by some of her results, which suggested the fragility of teen relationships.

In attempting to determine the long-term viability of their relationships, students may experience confusion about what constitutes "true love," conceptions derived from witnessing adults' relationships or media portrayals of relationships. Media representations mix sexual activity with issues of love and require extensive critique within student inquiries. Adolescents often are given the message in the media that it is legitimate to have sex without love. Adolescents therefore may engage in sex as a casual relationship with little concern for the emotional aspect of the relationship or for other motives.

A group of eighth graders at a Bronx middle school decided to study the topic of teenage sex/pregnancy (Schaafsma, Tendero, & Tendero, 1999). They read fiction and essays related to the topic, interviewed teenage mothers, and wrote essays and poems. Despite the difficulty of many of the texts, they "struggled through these texts because they cared passionately about the topic" (p. 30). They were also enthusiastic about the writing because they were producing a collection to be published for their peers and community adults: "Our So-Called Teen Years: Stories About Teenage Pregnancy from the Bronx." Their inquiry helped them to move from simply "writing about their lives—as they had been doing in writing workshop—to writing for their lives" (p. 29).

Given his concern with the issue of teen pregnancy, Mike Olsonoski, an Osseo High student, noted:

> People get together only for a couple of months until they have sex with each other. They then leave and never come back to see what ever happened to one another. They make each other feel loved, but then later they find out that they were only used as a play-toy. Teens don't care about the others' feeling just as long as they receive sex. The biggest question is, why don't they use a protective barrier, that way, they wouldn't have to worry about getting pregnant.

He then interviewed some of his peers about these relationships and concluded that teens hope to avoid the emotional and economic consequences of having sex.

CONTEXTUALIZING FAMILY OR ROMANCE WORLDS

In contextualizing family or romance worlds, students examine how the discourse practices of family life or romance construct the valued activities, the objects of desire, and the identities and relationships sought in social interaction.

Purpose

The basic purposes for families, courting, and marriages have changed over the centuries. William Doherty (1997) argues that the "institutional family" of the mid-nineteenth century was primarily concerned with maintaining parental authority, solidarity, religion, kinship ties, and economic survival. Thus, in a largely rural economy, families had many children in order to maintain the farm. In contrast, the purpose for the "psychological" family of the mid-twentieth century was to foster individual members' happiness, happiness that depends on providing and sharing love. This represents a major shift in parents' relationships with children, particularly for fathers, who, rather than serving as distant, patriarchal authoritarians, assumed a more involved relationship with their children.

However, Doherty notes that there are a number of challenges to fulfilling this purpose (Cummins, 1999). In contrast to the nineteenth-century family, the contemporary family often does not have the support of grandparents, many of whom live elsewhere, leaving child rearing solely to the "nuclear" family parents. The decline of the neighborhood community support system of familiar, respected people also leaves parents more on their own to raise children. For Doherty, the biggest challenge derives from a consumer culture in which parents are continually concerned about providing services for their children—camps, preschools, soccer lessons, computers, entertainment, and so on. Moreover, parents "have been told that children are fragile, that you can't be mad at them, that we have to protect their 'self-esteem' at all costs, that their being independent and 'authentically themselves' is most important" (Cummins, 1999, p. A13). Parents are therefore less willing to assert authority and more willing to accede to children's demands.

As students explore family and romance social worlds, they may find a host of purposes being negotiated within and across the diverse cultural groups that make up their community. Connecting these different purposes to different forms of social interaction will be their primary inquiry goal.

Roles

Students and parents adopt a range of roles and identities as family members or as lovers in a relationship. These roles and identities have shifted over the years given shifts in the prototypes for what it means to be an ideal mother, father, daughter, son, or lover, prototypes highly influenced by gender or class beliefs/attitudes (Solsken, 1993).

Some novels offer particularly good opportunities for students to examine the representation of family roles. As students read about mothers in novels such as *The Bean Trees* (Kingsolver, 1991), *I Know Why the Caged Bird Sings* (Angelou, 1969), or *A Yellow Raft in Blue Water* (Dorris, 1988); about fathers in *To Kill a Mockingbird* (Lee, 1960/1995) or *Death of a Salesman* (Miller, 1949/1999); or about lovers in *Pride and Prejudice* (Austen, 1813/1980), *Summer of My German Soldier* (Greene, 1973), or *Their Eyes Were Watching God* (Hurston, 1990), they can seek answers to the question: What does it mean to be a mother, father, daughter, son, or lover within a particular social world? These answers will help students contextualize the many roles they may find in inquiries into lived social worlds, and to critique both in terms of how prototypes are challenged.

In her study of the dairy-farm family, Cathy Witwicke found that much of the family's life revolved around adopting different roles related to maintaining the farm. While each member completed specific chores required in running the farm, however, some members of the family were more committed to farming than others.

Rules

Parents attempt to establish certain rules related to homework, curfews, operating automobiles, language use, space within a home, appropriate topics of discussion, and so on. Given their need to assert independence, students often resist these rules, particularly if the rules are perceived to be unfair or arbitrary.

At the same time, State College Area High student Nilu concluded that expectations should support friendly family relationships:

> There can be a family who has everything; money, food, a good house, and a good name, everything, except for a friendly relationship between family members. What is the use of having a mother that is not a friend? Having someone like a mother or a father to be able to talk to about adult subjects is great.

To study family rules, students could list the various expectations operating in their own families or relationships and then draw conclusions about how they support the values of the social world. Students also could role-play specific incidents in which parents or members of a relationship attempt to enforce certain rules. For example, students could role-play a situation in which a son or daughter arrives home after a designated curfew time and is confronted by a parent.

Beliefs

Students' beliefs about family or relationships often reflect differences in socioeconomic class. Michael Apted's BBC documentary series (see Singer, 1998), which began with *7-Up* and is currently at the point of *42-Up*, tracked various participants from different class backgrounds every 7 years. Participants from upper-middle-class backgrounds typically espoused the importance of careers and schooling in their family lives, while participants from working-class backgrounds focused more on the importance of family relationships.

As they interview family members or peers about reasons for specific discourse practices, students may infer certain underlying beliefs constructed in these discourse practices. A group of ninth-grade State College Area High School girls—Alyssa, Audra, Amanda, and Kim—pooled their own experiences with good and bad romantic relationships and created a video drama that illustrated the contrasting beliefs of romantic couples. Between scenes, they had sessions of real talk about what makes a relationship a good one or a bad one. In her essay about the video, Alyssa explained:

The relationships each portray their own set beliefs and morals. . . .
The difference is that the good couple communicated with each
other. They also had organized places they could go where they could
be together outside of school. The bad couple never communicated
and they didn't go out with each other that much.

History

Students also could examine families as affected by certain historical forces
or traditions. Until the eighteenth century, marriages were largely arranged
by parents, a practice that began to slowly change so that by the late nineteenth century, couples managed their own courting (Graff, 1999). However,
in many cultures, marriages are still arranged by parents. For example, the
novel *Shabanu* (Staples, 1989) portrays the resistance of an adolescent female to a forced marriage by her fundamentalist Muslim parents in Pakistan.
She is repulsed by the man she must marry, preferring punishment to forced
marriage.

Furthermore, the world of romance has changed from one of formal
courting practices supervised by parents, as portrayed in nineteenth-century
novels, to more casual dating practices of "going steady," and from resistance
to male sexual conquest in the 1940s and 1950s, as portrayed in Hollywood
movies, to the informal, group social interactions of the 1990s that allow for
a less artificial development of relationships.

REPRESENTING FAMILY OR ROMANCE WORLDS

In their inquiry projects, students represent their perceptions of family or
romance using a range of different tools that portray their concerns, issues,
or dilemmas. As in other social worlds projects, students often used posters
and collages to focus the results of their inquiry projects. In response to a
story about a deaf character who had difficulty communicating his love, ninth-
grade State College Area High School student Lina created a poster with the
following poem, in which the gaps of silence assumed their own meaning:

DEAF DONALD

Deaf Donald met talkie Sue, but . . . [silence]
was all he could do.
And Sue said, "Donald, I sure do like you."
But . . . [silence] was all he could do.
And Sue asked Donald

"Do you like me too? But . . . [silence]
Was all he could do
"Goodbye then Donald, I'm leaving you
but . . . [silence] was all he could do.
And she left forever so she never
Knew that . . . [silence] means I LOVE YOU.

Students could study the representation of romance in the "love-talk" lyrics of popular music. Most of the song lyrics in the 1950s, such as "Baby I Need Your Lovin," focused on emotional aspects of love. Then, starting in the 1960s, lyrics focused on other topics, and by the early 1980s only about 50% of songs dealt with love (Christenson & Roberts, 1998). In the late 1980s, there was an increase in focus on love, but with more attention to the physical than emotional aspects of love. Students also could examine the gender perspectives adopted in these songs, and the fact that, in one study, two-thirds of popular songs were performed by solo males or all-male groups (Roberts, Kinsey, & Gosh, 1993).

Mike explored how love is represented in music and he created a CD, complete with a cover and booklet of lyrics and illustrations, to represent the many different types of love that exist:

The social world of love ties together many different emotions including joy, sadness, excitement, despair, and anger. The songs I chose illustrate this very point well.

Students could represent their own experiences with romance through writing narratives or autobiographical incidents about past relationships. A student may recall a year-long relationship that culminated in a disagreement over the individuals' lack of commitment to each other. Or, students may create fictional romance stories based on their own experiences. Contrary to the assumption that this writing mimics formulaic story lines, students do explore the complexities involved in relationships, particularly in terms of dramatizing alternative perspectives on relationships (Moss, 1989). In one story, a female writes about a character attending a party and seeing her boyfriend with another girl (Moss, 1989). She portrays the character's conflicted feelings about this experience—the fact that she is angry, but also curious about her boyfriend's motives.

Students have used alternative media forms to represent the results of their inquiries into social worlds. During the social worlds unit at State College Area High, Debbie sewed a patchwork quilt with panels that signified 16 difficulties in love relationships. Each square used pink and blue hearts in a different arrangement for the particular difficulty. For example, two squares have two pink and two blue hearts to portray the problems of a girl liking a girl, or a boy liking a boy. A series of panels have three hearts to explore all the possible triangles of love. When students are permitted to use all of their talents to represent their ideas about social worlds, their participation in all phases of classroom activity increases dramatically.

Students also may employ a range of tools as they conduct their inquiry projects. To involve their families in their inquiry projects, students in a Bronx middle school wrote letters home describing their project and reasons for their interest in the project (Torres, 1998). For example, one student was studying the topic of AIDS. She wrote a letter to her father, an X-ray technician, in which she noted, "'This topic is important to me because I do not want to die of something I was not born with, meaning that I want to die normally'" (Torres, 1998, p. 61). Her father was so pleased with his daughter's interest in the topic, that he became involved with the project.

Students may write about autobiographical incidents as certain snapshot moments from their family histories to portray their relationships with their families, along with old photos, home movies/videos, letters, recipes, heirlooms, artwork, or artifacts that have particular meaning within their family world (Stillman, 1998).

Nicole studied the traditions and activities of her own family to describe that social world. To represent her conclusions, she selected particular pictures and hung them from a family tree. In her essay she described how she decided to represent family traditions:

> Most of the pictures I put on my tree represent bonding. . . . On my tree I placed the larger, more established traditions like Christmas at my grandma's or birthday parties closer to the trunk showing strong family traditions. . . . I placed younger traditions like going to the beach with my uncle further away from the trunk, on the weaker limbs.

Erin was another State College Area High freshman who used photographs to research her own family social world. As she developed several categories to express the significant roles, rituals, histories, and purposes of her family, she created different sections of a family photo album with subtitled explanations for each picture.

When students choose to study their families, it is important to create alternatives for the many students in a class who have no biological parents, who are adopted, or who have gay or divorced parents. For these students, the typical family history assignment that presupposes the traditional two-parent, heterosexual family is often a traumatic experience. One alternative to the family tree genealogy assignment as espoused by Maguire Pavao, head of the Center for Family Connections, is the idea of studying "'an orchard or a wheel that shows that everyone children are connected to is good'" (in Holloway, 1999, p. E2).

To contextualize the social world of families, students also could study the portrayal of families from different time periods and cultures, contextualizing the differences represented in family social worlds. In *One Bird* (Mori, 1995), a Japanese girl's parents' divorce, which, in 1975, was quite unusual. When her mother departs, the girl is left with a grandmother and a distant father, who has difficulty assuming the role of parent. In *Pride and Prejudice*, Elizabeth is under constant pressure to find a husband. Because she perceives her sisters entering marriages with men she does not respect, she refuses to accept just any suitor, and is even suspicious of the wealthy D'Arcy. In *My Brother, My Sister and I* (Watkins, 1994), a 13-year-old Japanese girl tells the true story of her and her siblings' difficult life as refugees in post-World War II Japan.

Students also could analyze how television dramas represent the family in terms of the current cultural beliefs contextualized in a historical time period. For example, programs in the 1990s such as *The Simpsons*, *Home Improvement*, *Brother's Keeper*, and *King of the Hill* portrayed fathers as bungling and ineffectual (National Fatherhood Initiative, 1999) and mothers as marginalized (Hewlett & West, 1998). Family shows from earlier decades portray quite different parent roles.

Many of these examinations of media and literary representations of family and romance social worlds help students contextualize the words and actions that construct these worlds' underlying values, identities, and relationships. As students examine these representations, they almost always engage simultaneously in a critique of the social worlds, or their (mis)representation.

CRITIQUING FAMILY OR ROMANCE WORLDS

Two State College Area High School students, Elise and Rachel G., inquired into teen romantic relationships by doing videotape interviews with several of their peers. They used the computer to edit this footage and created a quicktime movie in which many of the teens explained that relationships put too much pressure on teens. As Rachel noted:

> Relationships cause much stress, because they cause worrying about being dumped. When teens are involved in relationships, they are typically cautious of their attire. They don't want to let their significant other down.

Elise extended this critique of teen romance to describe the various actions and words of teens in romantic relationships that construct problematic identities and values:

> Many teens change their personalities when they enter into romantic relationships. They feel like they have to act the way their girl/boyfriend wants them to and because of that they act differently then they normally would. It is very common for teens to act like they don't have an opinion about various subjects when they are in a relationship. Usually this is caused by the teen not wanting to cause an argument with their girl/boyfriend. . . . Teenagers seem to believe that if they act a certain way, and say certain things, they will be able to keep up their relationship. Few teens realize that they are sacrificing their individuality when they do this. . . . As a result of all the compromises they make with their friendships, family, opinions and time, they begin to lose a part of themselves. Sometimes when they are alone, especially after a breakup, they feel like half of a person. This causes them to not even know themselves any more or know how to be the person they were before they entered the relationship.

While Rachel and Elise critiqued the loss of the individual in romantic worlds by interviewing their own peers, students could critique similar assumptions portrayed in television programs of the late 1990s such as *Dawson's Creek* or *Party of 5*, or novels such as *Ordinary People* (Guest, 1980), in which people have difficulty communicating because they hide behind a false outer mask and don't express their "inner feelings." The assumption is that if only people would be honest about expressing these inner feelings, then they would know each other better and problems would be solved. In some cases, expressing inner feelings proves successful, as in *Ordinary People*; when the mother is able to admit her feelings about the death of her son, she can begin to rebuild her relationships with her husband and other son.

However, in *A Yellow Raft in Blue Water* (Dorris, 1988), when Christine and her mother, Ida, openly express their dislike of each other, their relationship deteriorates. It is important to recognize that students may critique a discourse practice, or valued purpose or identity of a social world, yet not be aware of their own underlying beliefs and assumptions that contextualize their interpretations. Seeking other multiple interpretations, for example, about the value of expressing one's true individual character, is important.

Students also could critique the ways in which conflicts in family or couples' relationships are resolved. In situation comedies about the family or romance, problems often are resolved with a happy ending in a period of 30 minutes. Students could critique the nature or type of problem portrayed in a program, who has the power to solve the problem (which family member/ gender), what methods or tools they use to solve the problem (talk, physical action, money, etc.), and what value assumptions are inherent in the resolution ("father knows best," "parents are often blind to children's needs," etc.). One value assumption underlying these happy resolutions in situation comedies is the belief that achieving a consensus is preferable to perpetuating conflicts between individuals or deviant perspectives (Jones, 1992).

Students could critique the impact of various economic forces as well as various local, state, and national government policies related to the family— health insurance, business/corporate policies, welfare-to-work, employment opportunities, housing, transportation, taxes, and so on. In her study of the family farm, North High School student Cathy Witwicke found that the Lutz family was coping with the increasing shift to large, corporate farming and suburban sprawl that placed increased pressures on small family farms. As John Lutz noted:

> "A lot of houses are being built and old farms sold . . . your land becomes worth more so your taxes are raised. Sometimes they get too high that a farmer can't pay to keep his farm, so they have to sell it . . . now there are only four dairy farms left in Hugo. If one of them go then the others of us probably won't make it . . . we farmers help one another out. Instead of going out and buying big expensive equipment, like a $12,000 tractor, we share. I will go and bail a neighbor's field and he will come cut and grind my corn when I need him. That's how we go through things and we are always willing to help one another."

This led Cathy Witwicke to critique the influence of suburban sprawl on the family farm as threatened by increasing land values and taxes.

TRANSFORMING FAMILY OR ROMANCE WORLDS

Based on their critiques and representations, students can entertain alternative practices for participating in the family or romance worlds. Given their concern about communication in the family and relationships, students could role-play conflict situations—a parent who refuses to listen to a daughter or son; a daughter or son who consistently defies a parent; a partner in a relationship who is suspicious of the other partner's actions. Students could then reflect on alternative strategies for resolving these conflicts. In some cases, students may focus on the use of language, particularly judgmental "you-statements" used to label others. Students could entertain alternative uses of

"I-statements" in which one person describes his or her perceptions of the other person's practices, allowing that other person to make his or her own self-judgments (Gordon, 1973). For example, rather than state, "You're always late; you can't do anything right," a person may state, "When you're late, I get up upset because I don't know where you are." Students could script these alternative "I-statements" and then discuss their reactions to these statements.

Students also could discuss strategies for holding family meetings or forums or for couples to seek help from others to discuss difficulties or conflicts in relationships (Covey & Covey, 1998). Students could brainstorm procedures and guidelines for these meetings. For example, in a family, individual members could call a family meeting to discuss their concerns, issues, or dilemmas, followed by other members sharing their perceptions, which leads to consideration of strategies for dealing with the concerns, issues, or dilemmas.

To improve communication between family and school, students also could entertain ways to involve their parents more in their schoolwork and to make teachers more aware of students' family life (Schockley, Michalove, & Allen, 1995). Students could share their work or portfolio materials, as well as reflections on that work, with both parents and teachers so that both groups have some mutual understanding of their progress. As previously noted, teachers could invite parents to participate with students as co-inquirers in their inquiry projects. Parents could systematically meet with students to have them share their perceptions of their schoolwork.

Students also could discuss the topic of marriage in order to formulate beliefs about marriage. Students could discuss literary portrayals of marriage (see the textbook *The Art of Loving Well* by the Loving Well Project, 1995), as well as curriculum materials for what is known as the "partners course," developed by the American Bar Association, which focuses on the contractual elements of marriage (Morse, 1999). Based on these materials, Janet Mann of Natomas High School, Sacramento, California, has students role-play being bride and groom, writing wedding vows, planning a honeymoon, developing financial plans, and coping with marital conflicts (Morse, 1999). Students also could imagine themselves as future parents and generate some rules for how they would operate as a family.

Given their analysis of various families and their critique of government policies shaping the family, students could formulate government policies designed to provide support for families. Students could examine Hewlett and West's (1998) "Parents' Bill of Rights" for ideas in formulating their own recommendations. This "Parents' Bill of Rights" recommends that parents have "time for their children" through "paid parenting leave, family-friendly workplaces," and "a safety net"; "economic security" based on "a living wage, job opportunities, tax relief," and "help with housing"; "a pro-family electoral system" established through "incentives to vote" and "votes for children"; a "pro-family legal structure" that provides for "stronger marriage, support for fathers," and "adoption services"; "a supportive external environment" provided by "violence-free neighborhoods, quality schooling, extended school day and year, child care, family health coverage, drug-free communities, responsible media," and "an organizational voice"; and "honor and dignity" celebrated through "an index of parent well-being," "National Parents' Day," and "parent privileges" (pp. 231–232).

Students could determine the level at which each recommendation applied—their own family or neighborhood, local municipality, state, or national level. They could then invite speakers to address policies at each level, and write letters to officials or newspapers proposing consideration of their proposals.

Underlying all of these efforts is the ability to communicate one's own perspective and sense of self when faced with pressures from family members or partners in relationships. Conflicts between self and others in romantic and family worlds were conceptualized by one student as the influence of overlapping social worlds, with self as the primary and most important social world. To represent this social world of self (Figure 9.1), the artist painted a

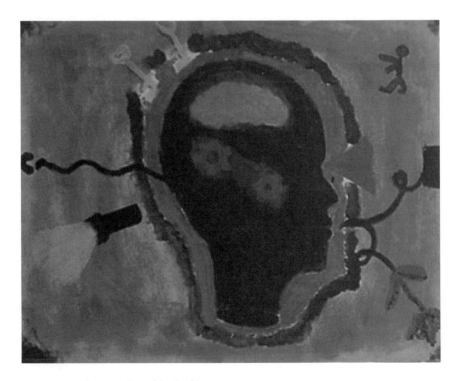

Figure 9.1. The social world of self.

person and provided the following description of the meanings of symbols within the painting:

> On my painting I showed a person with outstretched arms trying to communicate with the person inside. I showed keys by the brain inside the person to show how people are always trying to get inside someone's head and find out what he or she is thinking. I showed a mouth on the other side of the head to show communication through speech and how it reaches the inside of a person. The self is also showing speech which takes two different paths. One of the paths leads to a small box where his or her words are kept secret. This path would be when one tells a secret or no one is listening to what he or she is saying and words are lost. The other path leads to a flower where the words bloom. This path is where people listen to one's words and spread them to other people. Communication is the most prominent part of the self, since everything inside and out relies on communication.

We highlight this student's inquiry and representation because we believe it illustrates that the ability to transform one's social worlds requires the development of an inner dialectical consciousness in which a person considers the potential meanings of any act, word, or object within the context of multiple overlapping social worlds. The inner communication signified by the artist represents such consciousness and agency.

10

Community and Workplace Worlds

STUDENTS PARTICIPATE in a wide variety of community organizations such as the Boy/Girl Scouts, YMCA/YWCA, church groups, political organizations, service clubs, or volunteer groups. And a considerable number of students work in after-school jobs for a range of different reasons. Through their participation in these organizations and workplaces, students learn to develop relationships with adults, who provide them with support, role models, and perspectives on the future (Muller & Frisco, 1998, p. 154). They also learn to assume and fulfill responsibilities for various tasks, through which they gain a sense of competence and self-worth (Heath & McLaughlin, 1993). And they learn to define their identities as community and workplace members by displaying their competence in practices valued by a community (Wenger, 1998).

In conducting inquiries about their own or others' participation in these community organizations and workplaces, from our experience, students are particularly interested in the social practices of *becoming* new members of these worlds, as well as *belonging* to these worlds. In *becoming* new community or workplace members, they acquire a set of practices valued in a community or workplace, often with the help of a mentor, guide, or cultural broker. In *belonging* to a community or workplace, students display their competence in order to be recognized and included as legitimate, permanent members (Wenger, 1998). In studying a community or workplace, students may examine the extent to which the community or workplace helps them learn to become full members of the community or workplace (Wenger, 1998). For example, some workplaces provide extensive training for new employees, while others provide no training, adopting a sink-or-swim approach.

IMMERSING IN COMMUNITY AND WORKPLACE WORLDS

Students immerse themselves in community or workplace worlds by observing and interviewing participants engaged in activities associated with these worlds. In immersing themselves in the small-town, segregated world of

Lorain, Ohio, in the 1940s, portrayed in *The Bluest Eye* (Morrison, 1970), Kim Van Voorhees's students were engaged in a world quite different from their own. To understand the plight of the main character, 11-year-old, African-American Pecola Breedlove, they had to perceive her as the victim of various forces operating in her community. One of these forces is the privileged world of the White middle class in the town, a world that Pecola desires but never acquires. The students discussed Morrison's opening use of the "Dick and Jane" primer story populated by White middle-class characters that has little to do with the town's poor, African-American world. This led to a discussion of the topic of "White privilege," which Kim described as being "largely invisible for most White middle-class people who simply assume they are privileged without being aware of the fact that they are." Students noted the advantages derived from being privileged and considered whether Whites are aware of the fact that they hold certain privileges. They then studied the other images from White society contained in the book—Shirley Temple, Mary Jane, movie actresses, blue eyes, and their effects on Pecola's self-worth, noting that all of these images are from a world she did not experience or could not relate to.

To immerse themselves in adults' workplace worlds, students in Barbara Lambert's North High School English class interviewed people about their work experience. Valerie Reichel interviewed Angi Taylor, one of four morning talk-show hosts on station KDWB in Minneapolis. She found that because Angi, age 26, was younger than the other hosts, "it was hard at first because they were so different, but I think being younger than the rest of them really made our differences click and the show became very successful . . . the friction between us and our ages is what makes us so entertaining."

Sean interviewed his dad about his work as a firefighter. Sean discovered that "his station averages about 10–13 runs a day, each run lasting about one hour if not longer . . . on a slow night they might get 4 hours of sleep." When asked what is the worst thing about your job, Sean's dad described "all the pain and suffering that you see people go through with the loss of life and property . . . but the more rewarding things would have to be delivering babies because you are bringing a new life into the world."

Nicole Schmidt studied the work of Joel Kohout, a female criminal profiler, whose job is to "let the law enforcement agency know what type of person they are most likely looking for." Nicole discovered that the glamorous aspects of the job, as portrayed on television crime shows, do not match the reality of the work, the necessary years of training, and the lack of a personal life: "It's kind of hard to have any kind of a life . . . you might end up working day and night every weekend and be on the road for 3 months."

IDENTIFYING CONCERNS, ISSUES, OR DILEMMAS
IN COMMUNITY OR WORKPLACE WORLDS

Members of every community or workplace face a range of concerns, issues, or dilemmas in attempting to organize and mobilize participants to address problems of schooling, transportation, unemployment, poverty, health care, ecology, crime, and so on. Students may express concerns about the viability of their own local communities or workplaces in those communities. Many small rural communities are losing population to the point that they can no longer provide employment or support schools. Inner-ring suburbs and urban neighborhoods often lack a strong tax base and are struggling with high mobility and crime. Outer-ring suburbs are experiencing difficulties with sprawl and lack of mass transit. Reductions in support of local youth organizations or after-school programs means that students no longer have a place to go after school. For his inquiry project, Dan, a State College Area High School freshman, created a quicktime movie that presented the many places teens "hang out" downtown. His research dealt with local issues involving loitering versus the right of teens to have a place to spend time together. His project required him to take many pictures of the downtown locations as he analyzed the patterns of teen activity.

Unfortunately, teens' concerns about community space and activity often are identified in terms of simplistic, either/or, "we"/"them" categories, when, in fact, they involve a lot more complex sets of competing interests and agendas. This we/them dichotomy reflects a tension between individualism derived from a sense of personal freedom versus a communal commitment to the larger social good. Extreme individualism resists the idea of communities as built on shared trust. As David Kirp (2000) notes, "Individualism has acquired a harsh edge as people grow overly self-centered, uncivil, and civilly disengaged" (p. 15). This individualism conflicts with the fact that "no one is unencumbered by ties and obligations, whether to family, workplace, neighborhood, affinity group, or church . . . we live in a thick network of associations, a world where character counts" (p. 332).

This tension is compounded by the fact that people often identify the "them" or the "other" in terms of gender, race, or class. Attitudes toward public, taxpayer support for schools, housing, transportation, medical care, or job training for less privileged or poor people are shaped by ideological stances toward people perceived to be "different," that is, poor people of color.

In conducting their inquiries, ideally students learn to move beyond these simplistic categories as they engage issues of individualism, class, race, and gender in their community social worlds. High school and college students involved at the Community Literacy Center housed at Carnegie Mellon University engaged in inquiry about community issues such as housing disputes, gangs, or drug use (Flower, Long, & Higgins, 2000). They moved beyond simplistic perceptions and categories to entertain rival hypotheses about specific local issues. In doing so, the students made a "self-conscious attempt to treat one's presumptions, intuitions, and claims as a hypothesis among rivals" (p. 40). This required that the inquirers be open to a range of competing perspectives based on their experiences, rather than what John Dewey described as a "quest for certainty." For example, in a landlord and tenant project, students held a meeting with a tenant, landlord, community organizer, and mediator about a housing dispute. Students identified the different perspectives each of these people brought to the dispute, and how these perspectives reflected different interests and agendas.

Rather than simply bemoaning the "youth problem" of urban gang members, participants studying gangs addressed questions such as, "Where are the safe places in an inner city? Where are the social spaces that offer a basis for respect and identity for ordinary and even low-achieving students?" (p. 74). How does the material world support the construction of such identities and values?

The movement of many adolescents into the workplace to keep up with the demands of consumer values and family pressures makes inquiries into the social world of work valuable for students. During the 1990s, there was a large increase in the percentage of students working; some 80% of adolescents report working at least 15–20 hours a week (Schneider & Stevenson, 1999). In 1998, adolescents had a combined income of $121 billion from work, gifts, and parents, a 9% increase over 1997. They spent $141 billion, with the average male spending $84 a week and the average female spending $83 a week (Teenage Research Unlimited, 1999).

Most students hold minimum-wage service jobs in fast-food restaurants, department stores, shops, and so on, with minimum training, no benefits, few role models, low expectations about competency, and routine operations involving limited cognitive demands. While for the most part students do not perceive this work as related to their future careers, many enjoy working because they are given some degree of autonomy (Schneider & Stevenson, 1999).

Students may conduct inquiry projects about their own or their peers' perceptions of the benefits and liabilities of work. They may examine how work affects their ability to complete homework or participate in social activities. In her study of working secondary students who did not plan to go on to college, Susan Willis (1998) found that many of these students did not take their jobs very seriously, perceiving that "a job's a job." They did not necessarily enjoy their work, noting that they "had to work" to acquire spending money. Moving from job to job, they had little loyalty to their jobs and did not expect job security. They preferred jobs that involved little cognitive effort. As one student who worked in a photo printer shop noted, "'I want a job I don't have to think about. You know—like sleepwalking'" (p. 352).

CONTEXTUALIZING COMMUNITY AND WORKPLACE WORLDS

Students are members of communities in the form of neighborhoods, towns, suburbs, cities, states, regions, and countries, each with their own unique characteristics that students use to mark their own and others' identities as a southerner, New Englander, Texan, Canadian, midwesterner, New Yorker, and so on. Students could study how writers construct these unique qualities of a particular place and time. In "A Walk to the Jetty" from *Annie John*, by Jamaica Kincaid (1985), Annie describes a walk through her Antigua neighborhood on the way to board a boat to England. As she passes each neighbor's house, she recalls how they helped her in her life. In *House on Mango Street* by Sandra Cisneros (1986), Esperanza Cordero uses short vignettes and poems to describe the different neighbors and life in the Latino section of Chicago. Each of these vignettes and poems highlights an unusual aspect of a particular neighbor, aspects that reflected Esperanza's own concern about the neighborhood and her determination to eventually leave that neighborhood. Each text contextualizes people in terms of community purposes, roles, and histories.

In conducting inquiries about workplace worlds, students may examine the practices required to be successful in a particular job, the ways in which new employees acquire these practices, the workers' roles and relationships to each other, and the value or benefits of work for the person or for society.

Purpose

Individual community or workplace members construct a sense of community in terms of specific activities with their own sense of purpose. Students may study how these activities contribute to building a sense of shared purpose in a community or workplace. For example, the annual summer festivals in rural towns serve to define their shared sense of community. Through participation in these festivals, "regular citizens draw attention to themselves, celebrate themselves: 'look at us. This is our parade, our queen pageant, our way of having fun, our town, our people.' Indeed, the festival creates a space—an architecture—in a town that is all its own" (Lavenda, 1997, p. 43).

State College Area High School student Chris studied the world of his own workplace and arrived at several conclusions about how co-workers engage in particular activities in order to construct a similar sense of community belonging:

Friends give you something to keep you on task and help you to do
what you need to do. Even if you are doing something that you dislike,
friends make it seem fun. This is good, because not only does it make
a social world of friends at work, it also gives you something to look
forward to when you go to work.

Roles

Chris also noted some interesting findings about the different roles co-workers
assume at work versus roles other friends might assume elsewhere:

The friends in this social world act different than my other friends in
my home social world. . . . My friends at work are a joking kind. They
like to joke around, make jokes about each other, and fight. Practical
jokes are a big part of this social world. None of my other friends are
big jokers. This is another thing that makes this social world unique.

People assume a range of different roles associated with their participation in a neighborhood or community as leaders, organizers, facilitators, managers, council/board members, or volunteers. In his analysis of African-American neighborhoods in Philadelphia, Elijah Anderson (1990) identified two
different types of groups—the "decent" and the "street" people. The "decent"
people attempt to maintain positive practices in a neighborhood, in opposition to the "street" people, who are engaged in drugs, crime, or prostitution.
Anderson found that block clubs helped organize disparate members of a
neighborhood around a shared mission.

In responding to *The Bluest Eye*, Kim Van Voorhees's students discussed
the ways in which the community's social hierarchy shaped the characters'
perspectives. In discussing Pecola's mother, Mrs. Breedlove, who frequently
belittles Pecola, the students noted that in her service as a maid in a wealthy
White home and as a caretaker for the children in the home, Mrs. Breedlove
acquired a sense of importance she did not have in her own home in her relationship with her husband.

Rules

Communities often establish certain rules designed to regulate or control community practices. Students may examine the rules operating in a community or
workplace, noting who sets these rules and the level of adherence. In observing the legal procedures operating in a Ramsey County, Minnesota, traffic court,
Kirsten Egerstrom (1999) found that adolescents often have misconceptions
about the operation of the court. As one hearing officer, Robert Kraft, noted:

Teens often feel as though they are being persecuted because of their age. But they need to realize that police officers watch driving habits and equipment violations closely, and when teenagers play loud music and screech their tires, it causes attention. The police respond to this. Cops aren't trying to get kids. Kids put themselves in harm's way and don't realize the responsibility of driving a car.

Kirsten also observed a consequence of ignoring rules and exhibiting inappropriate practices in the court itself:

I witnessed a 17-year-old girl try to lecture the judge about police being rude to her when she was arrested for drunken driving. After interrupting the judge and yelling, the girl was given maximum fines and ordered to do community service work.

Students also may examine tensions between community rules and moral principles that transcend and challenge those rules (Kohlberg, 1984). For example, segregation laws in the South violated the principles of equality and human dignity. Students could study the tensions between community rules and larger moral principles as portrayed in Martin Luther King's *Letter from a Birmingham Jail* (1968), which contrasts just and unjust laws, and makes a moral argument for breaking unjust laws. Students also could discuss *The Giver* (Lowry, 1993), in which a 12-year-old boy, Jonas, lives in a completely controlled community, where all decisions are made for its members. Jonas is assigned to replace The Giver, who holds all memory of pain and the past. Through his training with The Giver, Jonas realizes that controlling society is a morally bankrupt practice that needs to be changed.

Beliefs

Communities may be organized around adherence to a single set of beliefs, with little tolerance for alternatives. Shirley Jackson's story, "The Lottery" (1948/1988), portrays a small town's blind conviction that one of its citizens needs to be sacrificed annually, a belief no one challenges.

In contrast to a unified belief system, members of a community may have totally different perceptions of the same community. Interviews with White and African-American working-class citizens of Buffalo and Jersey City found that "within the presumably 'same' community, African Americans will refer to local police with stories of harassment and fear while whites are far more likely to complain about a rise in crime and brag about a brother-in-law who's a cop" (Fine & Weiss, 1998, p. 266).

Many teens also believe that the real world exists only outside of school in the community and workplace. Cait and Kayelyn explored their many interactions, hobbies, and babysitting work and concluded that "after school real life begins." As students document the many activities beyond and within school, they must continually strive to uncover the underlying social values that support each activity.

History

Examining a community's history may help explain its current challenges. For example, in studying the community of south Chicago, St. Louis, Kansas City, Washington, Baltimore, Philadelphia, or Harlem, students may read about the migration of millions of African-Americans from the rural South into these urban centers (Cooper, 1995; Lemann, 1992). As they settled into urban areas, African-Americans had to transform their cultural practices imported from the South, such as dependency on their landowners.

A community's uniqueness derives from its history. In a series of essays about living in Harlem, *Still Life in Harlem*, Eddy Harris (1996) captures his sense of the historical traditions that shape his perceptions of Harlem and his identity:

> I felt that I was walking among the ghosts of Harlem's past, that I was coming here as they had come here, as Langston Hughes had come and Duke Ellington had come, as they all had come: the washerwoman and the seamstress; the heiress and the showgirl; the hard-laboring man and the vagrant; the high and mighty, the lowly and disregarded; the leaders and the followers; artists and intellectuals—coming home, coming to find peace, coming to gain in Harlem a sense of self and a new way of defining oneself, blackness, black culture, black awareness, that was independent of the white world's limiting influence and strictures and prying eyes. Here they and we and I could live completely within ourselves, in a world all black, all our own and of our own making. (pp. 50–51)

Students may access their own community's history by studying key events or notable people in their community. To study the traditions of his small, rural town of Boalsburg, Pennsylvania, State College Area High School student Taylor video interviewed several neighbors about community traditions and their hopes for the small town:

> Many people have dreams and hopes for Boalsburg as a neighborhood and town. Everybody interviewed wanted Boalsburg to remain small and a quaint village. They hoped Boalsburg expands to a degree for the better like adding parks and other things, but doesn't expand to the point that it becomes urban. They wanted to keep Boalsburg's

traditions and old artifacts of the town. They all hope the neighborhood stays safe and keeps looking like an old town. Many people said
that we should maintain Boalsburg's history. Many people said to
restore old homes rather than building new ones. In addition, people
said they wanted to keep Boalsburg clean and well-known for that.
Most people want Boalsburg to stay a small town village.

And, in studying the workplace, students could examine some of the
historical traditions shaping current workplace practices, as depicted in
interviews of workers from the 1950s and 1960s (Terkel, 1974) or women
workers (Hesse-Biber & Carter, 1999). They also could contrast work in
assembly-line factory jobs, as described in *Rivethead: Tales from the Assembly
Line* (Hamper, 1991), with more contemporary high technology workplaces.

REPRESENTING COMMUNITIES AND WORKPLACES

Students may study the ways in which writers represent communities to reflect their particular ideological biases and perspectives. For example, rural/
small-town communities may be represented idealistically, as in Garrison
Keillor's book, *Lake Wobegon Days* (1985), in which everyone knows everyone else and few of the economic or political problems facing rural America
are portrayed. In more realistic portrayals of small towns—*In the Lake of the
Woods* (O'Brien, 1994), *Hometown* (Kidder, 1999), *Main Street* (Lewis, 1937/
1992), *Our Town* (Wilder, 1938/1974), and *Winesburg, Ohio* (Anderson,
1969), as well as *The Last Picture Show*, *Whatever Happened to Gilbert
Grape*, *Unforgiven*, *Brother's Keeper*, and *Harlan County, U.S.A.*, the tensions between being isolated, remote, provincial, impoverished, or subject
to discrimination are balanced against the value of supportive, familiar, inti-
mate relationships between small-town people. The media may represent
suburban communities as either shallow, homogeneous, redundant worlds
or as pastoral, bucolic escapes from urban communities' blight and decay, as
represented on television crime shows or television news that highlights sen-
sationalist aspects of urban crime, with little or no contextual analysis of the
causes of crime (Suarez, 1999). Students could compare these television portrayals with more complex representations in the following books:

> *The Air Down Here: True Tales from a South Bronx Boyhood* (Alicea,
> 1995), which recounts a boy's life in a south Bronx neighborhood
> and his close relationship with his father after his mother's death
> *Basic Needs: A Year with Street Kids in a City School* (Landsman, 1993),
> which depicts the lives of homeless students

Boyz N the Hood, which is the story of two parents trying to keep their child from joining a gang in south central Los Angeles

Voices from the Streets: Young Former Gang Members Tell Their Stories (Atkin, 1996), which is a collection of interviews with young former gang members who left their gangs

To represent their perceptions of Pecola Breedlove's world in *The Bluest Eye*, Kim Van Voorhees's students created a "Dick and Jane" book (with a story and images) that Pecola could relate to. The students therefore had to envision themselves as early-elementary-age students who had been denied social practices and privileges. At the same time, they needed to, as is the case with this genre, author some sense of a positive outcome. In one story created by the students, the characters decide to use money they were going to spend on themselves to buy another friend a dress. This story was designed to provide Pecola with the idea that friends go beyond their own needs to assist others.

Rob Robson's students in Harrold Priory Middle School, described in Chapter 8, used role-play to examine issues of homelessness in the community. In the role-play, students were divided into two groups—a small number of homeless teenagers who bonded with one another, and a group of counselors who specialized in helping homeless adolescents. Before the drama scenario (of six runaway children brought to social services by the police) started, pupils could volunteer to have a "trial run" in which a teacher played the role of the person being counseled, and the pupil played the role of counselor. This was watched by others and positively criticized afterward. Mistakes were discussed and corrected in this fashion. Robson reflected on the students' interactions:

> The skills that the pupil counselors developed were extraordinary. A team leader ensured that none of the ground rules was being broken but after a few problems at the beginning, both the team leaders in the classes that I was working with became virtually redundant. The difficult art of gently coaxing information from people seemed to come naturally to the counselors and they made good use of agencies that could help the "victims" they were counseling. The counselors quickly established boundaries and would not promise things they could not provide. I was delighted with the maturity that this age group showed in the exercise (my colleague reported similar success). I want them to use these skills that they have developed so well in real situations to help other pupils.

Such role-playing activities provide students an opportunity to reflect on how their representations in social interaction construct positive relationships and identities.

In studying representations of the workplace, particularly on prime-time television drama programs, students may note how various professions are portrayed. These programs often depict characters working collaboratively as "workplace families" whose work often provides more satisfaction than their homelife and can conflict with their family or personal lives (Pungente & O'Malley, 1999).

Over and over again we have recommended that students deconstruct media representations to examine how social worlds are constructed and to engage in critiques of the representations. Because teens spend an enormous amount of time consuming video representations, it is essential that they begin to use the technology tools to produce their own video representations. While these technologies will be discussed more in Chapter 11, it is interesting to note how State College Area High School student Chris combined images and audio to convey ideas about his workplace social world. Chris was very deliberate in the construction of a quicktime video about his workplace. For the soundtrack he chose a song by Smashing Pumpkins titled "Today Is the Greatest Day I've Ever Known," because every day that he goes to work is really great. To this soundtrack he synchronized many images from the work environment. Chris spends his working time in a chemical lab with hundreds of small test tubes. The final scene of his movie is a tray of test tubes, and fitting the humorous atmosphere of work that he documented, a smile face is created by using two different-colored liquids in the tubes.

CRITIQUING COMMUNITY AND WORKPLACE WORLDS

As students critique the discourse practices and representations of community and workplace worlds, they should strive to explicate the values, identities, and relationships that are constructed through words, symbols, objects, and activities. For example, in studying community issues such as smoking, alcohol, or pollution, they may examine the public relations campaigns launched by tobacco and alcohol companies, as well as corporations involved in pollution, in an attempt to offset negative images. As reported in *Marketing Madness* (Jacobson & Mazur, 1995), "the Miller Brewing Company reportedly spent twice as much publicizing its support of the Thurgood Marshall Scholarship Fund as it spent on the original donation" (p. 92).

Students conducting a project on the issue of sprawl and the expansion of suburban developments in their community may critique current zoning laws regarding lot size and housing design, as well as attempts by real estate developers to promote new development. They could study the influence of sprawl on air pollution by comparing ozone levels across different communities with varying levels of sprawl, information that is available from the Environmental Protection Agency.

Students also may examine the organizations or interest groups behind these various representations. For example, when President Clinton proposed a national health insurance plan, the private insurance industry launched a massive advertising campaign designed to mobilize public opposition to the plan, which, for various reasons, was defeated in Congress. Or, when Congress was debating the 1996 Communications Act, which gave the major television network broadcasters free access to several billion dollars worth of public air waves, the broadcasters provided little coverage of the topic on their new broadcasts so that the public had little knowledge of what was being passed.

Students also could critically examine utopian and distopian versions of communities as portrayed in literature or film (*1984*, *Fahrenheit 451*, *Brave New World*, *The Truman Show*), as well as attempts to construct ideal communities, for example, the utopian town of Celebration, Florida, designed by the Disney Corporation to integrate housing, school, work, and recreation.

Based on their observation and analysis of a workplace, students could critique some of its limitations. Students may discover that workers are reluctant to voice their own criticisms for fear of repercussions. Willis's (1998) study of adolescent workers found that, despite the lack of benefits and advancement/career opportunities, or poor working conditions, the workers had little sense of the value of or need for any organized, collective action that would address these problems. She contrasts this lack of collectivity on the job with their collectivity in peer-group or virtual worlds:

> Teens cope by inventing individual solutions to their job situations and collective solutions to their culture. They float from job to job, binge on work and leisure, hedge their bets with certification scams, all the while channeling their desire for community into music and fashion styles associated with subcultural affiliation. The dramatic separation between the individual practices that teens develop to cope with employment and the collective practices that they invent in their off-the-job cultural lives underscores the desire expressed by many of my informants to preserve themselves and their leisure as somehow "free." (Willis, 1998, p. 356)

Students may note problems in communication between workers and their managers; workers may not clearly understand what they are supposed to do. Or, they may find that workers are expected to engage in practices for which they have had no training. For example, workers may be expected to work in teams, but have had no collaboration training.

As described earlier, Chris studied his workplace and developed a critique of workers' relationships. He decided that "there is a unique bond between us (workers). It is kind of a strange friendship, because we don't seem to be friends outside of work, but we seem to be friends inside of work. Once we leave it is like the friendship was broken. This is strange how we are only friends in work, which also makes this unique." Chris might be encouraged to explore even further why this friendship seems to be contained only within the space and time of work.

Students also may critique some of the idealized representations of the workplace in the media. For example, in situation comedy portrayals of "workplace families," conflicts between workers often are solved in a 20-minute period. Or, characters' social lives assume greater significance than their work.

In these critiques, students analyze deficiencies of communities or workplaces in providing people with the necessary supporting activity. Noting these deficiencies lays the groundwork for students to entertain ways of improving conditions operating in these communities or workplaces.

TRANSFORMING COMMUNITY WORLDS

Based on their critiques of community worlds, students also could construct their own ideal community, including a map that represents various design principles, a charter defining a mission and purpose, and a constitution defining roles, rules, and beliefs. (See Chapter 11 for examples of how students can employ the computer program *Sim City* to explore different aspects of creating an alternative community.) In constructing an ideal community, students may consider the extent to which their proposed policies or practices will effectively address their concerns, issues, or dilemmas. For example, given the issue of joblessness in inner-city urban areas, would a proposed program of housing and school construction in the inner city actually create more jobs for inner-city residents?

As part of their inquiry projects, students also may engage in community service or service-learning projects. A group of students in Mark Woolley's social studies class at Scio Middle School in Scio, Oregon, participated in a project to help preserve covered bridges in their town (Woolley, 1995). They sent letters and drawings to local county commissioners who were deciding on whether to designate the bridges as protected by the National Register of Historic Places. Over a 2-year period, the students organized a series of petition-drive campaigns to help save several bridges from demolition.

Students in the Detroit summer program worked each summer beginning in 1992 on reconstructing parks, designing murals, painting and rebuilding homes, building community gardens, and receiving training in small-business development (Breitbart, 1998). Members of the Dudley Street Neighborhood Initiative in Boston were involved in designing a greenway between two community centers and in redesigning an avenue (Breitbart, 1998).

Central to transforming community worlds is the process of organizing and lobbying for change. To understand lobbying, students may role-play their town's or city's review board to which they make proposals for policy changes. In proposing these changes, students need to consider their justification for funding relative to funds available and potential cuts in other areas. Students also need to consider the clarity and succinctness of their proposals in making their case for needed changes.

Students also may organize a fund-raising project designed to assist people in need (Zimbalist & Driggs, 1999). They could read about the "Souper Bowl" project designed to help feed the hungry, a fund raiser held in conjunction with the Super Bowl (Smith, 1999). Students could discuss and write about the purpose for raising funds, who would benefit and in what ways, the tools they could employ, how they would represent and advertise their fund raiser, and how their project connects to other similar projects.

Based on their study of a workplace, students could propose some alternative operating practices. If they found that the work was routine or monotonous, they could entertain ways of making it more engaging. If they found that workers needed more training, they could propose new training programs.

In all of these activities, students challenge stereotypes about themselves and their worlds in ways that can transform them through their work. As one member of the Detroit summer project noted: "We have not yet made this city what it could be or should be just by painting some houses and planting some gardens for free . . . more importantly, we have created hope that before didn't exist" (Breitbart, 1998, p. 325).

11

Virtual Worlds

Wɪᴛʜ ᴛʜᴇ ɪɴᴄʀᴇᴀsᴇᴅ use of technology in recent years, a new set of social worlds has emerged that offers numerous possibilities for inquiry projects. We define these worlds as virtual worlds, a concept derived from the idea of "virtual reality." For the purpose of this book, we define "virtual worlds" to mean those worlds in which students are engaged in some interactive manner with electronic text or mediated communication such as radio and television talk shows, video and audio editing, Web Zines, Internet chat groups, computer games, and hypertext/hypermedia computer productions. Virtual worlds also could include actual sites such as "entertainment-retail" stores, amusement or "fantasy theme" parks, or music clubs/rock concerts in which students assume active roles as participants and consumers. The key term is "interactive"—students go beyond simply responding to electronically produced texts to actively participating in the creation of the texts and artifacts that construct a sense of reality in the virtual worlds.

Adolescents are devoting increasing time to participating in virtual worlds. A survey by the Annenberg Public Policy Center (1999) found that, on a daily basis, children ages 10–17 spend 2-½ hours watching television, and another 2 hours with video games, computers, music, or VCR. Many adolescents participate in "instant messaging" AOL chat rooms with people from all over the country, people whom they do not know and never will know. Consequently, they are not necessarily accountable for what they say to the degree they would be in "lived" conversations. They often create new identities to explore various relationships and values in these virtual communities.

Adolescents' participation in these virtual worlds has become increasingly suspect, particularly in terms of the vicarious experience of violence in playing computer games, which occurs without the consequences associated with violence in lived worlds. These concerns have led to considerable debate over how to conceive of the relationship between the "virtual" and the "real" or lived-world experience. One conception of the virtual is that it is a photocopy or "never anything more than a pale imitation of the real: a mere simulation" (Doel & Clarke, 1999). From this perspective, the virtual may never measure up to the complex reality it attempts to imitate. Adopting this perspective, critics note that chat-room participants are engaged in inauthentic forms of conversation that can never match the authenticity of lived-world conversation. This conception of the virtual as false imitation or approximation of reality presupposes a correspondence theory of representation—that artistic or technological forms need to bear some direct iconic relationship to reality. We believe that this is a questionable assumption.

Another conception of the virtual is that it is not a copy of reality, but is a more attractive alternative to the everyday, humdrum lived world (Doel & Clarke, 1999). From this perspective, the virtual is celebrated as an improvement over or even a solution to reality. As Doel and Clarke note, "The virtual is to the real as the perfect is to the imperfect. Here, it is the real that is figured as partial, flawed, and lacking, while the virtual promises a rectification and final resolution to come . . . sadly, reality rarely suffices" (p. 268). For example, computer games based on *PlayStation2* are advertised as being more engaging than the reality they are based on. This somewhat utopian conception of the virtual is still based on the need to compare the virtual with the real.

A third conception posits the idea that the virtual is its own "hyper-reality" (Baudrilland, 1994) divorced from any need to correspond or connect to a lived-world reality—the idea that the virtual creates its own form of reality (Doel & Clarke, 1999). One problem with this conception is that, in attempting to define a possible world of its own, it cannot ultimately divorce itself from juxtaposition with and influence from lived worlds.

These different conceptions of virtual worlds suggest that while the virtual is more than simply an artificial, fake version of lived-world reality, it still bears some relationship to that reality. Participating in virtual worlds also differs from simply responding to "represented worlds," such as literature or video, in that in hypertext or interactive versions of literature or video, readers or viewers often assume an active role in constructing the material presence or sequence of the texts. For example, in responding to a hypertext novel or computer game, students make decisions about the direction of the plot or character development. As Molly Travis (1998) notes, "The more interactive that hypertextual literature becomes and the closer it moves to virtual reality, the more the reader becomes a role-player in 'real-time' dramatic performance with other readers" (p. 12).

Through participation in on-line chat rooms or collaborative computer games, students experience a sense of virtual community. Many adolescents are turning away from the represented worlds of broadcast media, which "created a world awash in events but largely devoid of shared experiences" (Travis, 1998, p. 114), to participate in the shared communal experiences of interactive media, especially as these activities bring participants together over the Internet. In these virtual worlds, they also can experiment with different roles and stances by using alternative forms of language without concern for the constraints of physical gender, class, race, age, or disability markers that inhibit their participation in lived-world, face-to-face interaction.

IMMERSING IN VIRTUAL WORLDS

In participating in and observing their own and others' engagement in the virtual worlds described in this chapter, students reflect on the practices involved in constructing these worlds—the ways in which people interact in these worlds; the language, signs, and images they employ; the roles they adopt; the links they make to lived and represented worlds; as well as why these practices are appealing to avid participants. (In this chapter, unless noted, all of the student projects described were conducted by State College Area High School students.)

Students participate in a range of different types of computer/video games. In "shooter games" such as *Quake, Doome*, and others, players use various weapons to destroy their opponents. Some critics argue that these games serve as a form of training or "killology" similar to that in the military in which soldiers are conditioned to use guns to kill (Grossman & DeGaetano, 1999). Others argue that these are simply games and not lived-world military training. In their inquiry into video game playing, Brett and Justin videotaped themselves playing games, then analyzed their own activity. Their conclusions corresponded to those of some experts about the violent aspect of games:

> Behaviors are also largely affected by video games, and this can be a bad aspect of video games. Think, for example, that "Geoff" goes home after a very bad day at school. He lies down on the couch and turns on "killing and mutilation 2," while feeling sorry for himself. He might see images of death and people shooting and stabbing each other, because these types of video games are available. He might (not very likely) go to school the next day and shoot a group of people that he dislikes. This is similar to the Columbine incident, in which the killers went home every day after school, reportedly and played the video game "Doome" on their computer. This video game no doubt influenced them in some way, shape or form. As you can see, some video games do have a negative effect on people, however I would not use that reason to deter anyone from playing a video game.

In other games, such as *Sim City 3000, Populous*, and *Alpha Centauri*, students are involved in constructing different aspects of community—housing, transportation, shopping, business, schooling, waste disposal, day care, and so on. For example, in *Sim City 3000*, if players do not zone for incinerators or landfills, the city piles up with trash (Taylor, 1999). Using *Sim City 3000*, students participate in future-city contests that are judged by design engineers (Taylor, 1999).

Computer games operated with Sony's *PlayStation2* add highly realistic graphics and allow players to become active participants in games in which characters respond to the players' own emotions:

> The graphics allow characters in the games to respond to the ways in which the use controls them. Over time, they learn about the player: if he or she is going badly, the character may become agitated or annoyed. The best Tomb Raider [a computer game] may be "rewarded" with flirtatious behavior from Croft [a main character]. . . . The programmers are able to mimic every nuance of a player's body language so that using the machine becomes more like watching, or even taking a part in, a film. (Islam, 1999, p. 11)

In web-based computer games, players participate with other players with varied abilities and expertise, a characteristic that mirrors the reality of lived worlds. Within this social hierarchy, players advance as they learn new practices and strategies. For example, Buskin (1999) describes one high school freshman, Terry Timmons, who spends about 2 hours a day playing computer games and prefers a game in which one team attempts to steal the other team's flag to return it to their home base:

> The game generates any number of characters, including snipers, scouts, engineers, demolition men, spies, heavy-weapons men and soldiers, and players can assume the roles of any one. . . . Terry performed impressively enough as a soldier to be invited a couple of years ago to join a clan, a circle of players who organize matchers and practice and play together as a team. . . . After experiencing life in several different clans, Terry refined his game enough to go into a more elite group called a guild. Guilds also arrange matches and practices and play as a team, but all members of the guilds play as a single type of character. (p. 4)

In studying these games, students may examine participants' perceptions of differences and similarities between playing the game as a virtual reality and experiences in similar lived-world realities.

Students also participate in on-line chat rooms within AOL or other sites, as well as MOOs (multi-user dimension object oriented), a subgroup of MUDs (multi-user, interactive fantasy games). In these chat rooms, students carry on conversations with others. For example, within AOL, they may employ the instant messaging (IM) option for short, casual, real-time communication with other on-line participants listed on the screen. They also may employ shorthand acronyms or lingo in order to keep pace with the fast-moving conversation, for example, AYT (Are you there?), YIAH (Yes, I am here.), Pmfji (Pardon me for jumping in.), BRB (Be right back.), PG11 (Parent nearby.), GTG (Got to go.), CYA (See ya.), POOF (Gone, left the chat room.) (Ruane, 2000).

Many call-in, morning radio programs geared for adolescents consist of "shock/jock" talk radio in which hosts engage listeners in "hot-button," provocative topics only to subject them to ridicule or challenge as a form of entertainment. Sports talk shows often consist of callers sharing technical expertise about players, rules, and stats. These radio talk shows serve as a virtual world of conversation in that students potentially could call in and participate in a conversation; however, unlike in lived-world conversations, students have little or no control over the direction of the conversation. Hosts may marginalize, trivialize, or dismiss guests' comments or create an adversarial stance that reflects what Deborah Tannen (1998) has described as a "culture of argument." Many male hosts of these programs also demean women in an attempt to maintain a male audience.

Students may contrast the topics, conversational modes, and roles on these shows, again, as with chat-room talk, comparing it to lived-world talk.

Students also participate in various teen e-zines or web pages geared for adolescents; for example, *Teenink* (*www.teenpaper.org*) and *Grip Magazine* (*www.gripvision.com*) contain material written entirely by adolescents. *Teen Voices* (*www.teenvoices.com*) and *New Moon* (*www.newmoon.org*), written primarily for females, represent alternatives to traditional female teen magazines. *Teenreads: The Book Bag* (*www.teenreads.com*) contains information about young adult novels, authors, and entertainers. *Writes of Passage* (*www.writes.org*) and *Yo! Youth Outlook* (*www.pacificnews.org/yo*) address current issues of concern to adolescents. *Wave* (*www.wavemag.com*) contains short stories and poems.

In studying these e-zines or web pages, students may examine how they appeal to adolescent audiences and reasons for their interest or engagement. One of Richard's students, Margaret Hamilton (1999), studied adult males' and females' perceptions and recollections of reading Nancy Drew novels. As part of the study, she had participants respond to a story on the Nancy Drew web page (*www.nancydrew.com*). As Nancy Drew solves a mystery during the course of the story, readers can choose one of three optional directions for the plot to take. Hamilton noted that the choices for readers were rigged so that if a reader "chooses one of the other two alternatives, the plot dead-ends and takes him or her back to the preferred plot choice. Thus, the interactive plot devices function as a means of conditioning the reader to act like Nancy Drew" (p. 8). She found that many of the adults did not identify with the more current version of Nancy Drew as portrayed in her language and appearance, reflecting their nostalgic recollection of older versions of the character.

Adolescents may engage in shared public response to music at music clubs or rock concerts. We categorize these as virtual worlds because, unlike traditional concerts, participants are actively engaged as a group through dance, singing along, or karaoke singing. In an analysis of adolescents' "clubbing" in rock clubs, Ben Malbon (1998) examines how participation in highly sensuous dancing in the club creates an alternative sense of space:

> Dancing can provide a release from many of the accepted social norms and customs of the "civilized" spaces of everyday life, such as social distance, conformity and reserve or disattention. Dancing might be seen as an embodied statement by the clubber that they will not be dragged down by the pressures of work, the speed and isolation of the city, the chilly interpersonal relations one finds in many of the city's social spaces. (p. 271)

Malbon noted that in congregating together in large numbers in the club, adolescents created a tribe-like sense of communal, ritual participation through their dance and dress. In the dark lighting, they perceived each other in a different manner. And, within the continuous, pervasive sound of the music, they experienced a mesmerizing sense of "'losing it' or 'losing yourself'" (p. 274).

Students may observe the ways in which participants in music concerts are transformed through various practices and their perceptions of being in an alternative sense of space. Taylor R. and Candice studied the social world of music at concerts and as members of a band. Through their own immersion in the concert experience, they were able to describe the important practices:

> At punk, ska, or any hardcore, fast and crazy concert, people traditionally start a mosh pit. During the moshing, people pick you up, and you can crowd surf. That is really fun because you are riding on top of lots of people carrying you until you fall. If you get lucky, the singer or one of the band members will pick you up onto the stage, and you can stage dive back onto the crowd, and surf the people again. (Candice)

Students spend a lot of time hanging out in shopping malls, largely because there are few alternative public spaces available in which adolescents can congregate. The largest of these malls have become more virtual communities, containing everything from banks, health clubs, schools, libraries, churches, entertainment parks, movie theaters, conference centers, hotels, restaurants, bars, and so on. They differ from lived-world communities in that, although they may be supported by tax dollars, they are privately owned and operated and even enforce their own rules of conduct. They also differ from cities in that they are controlled, heavily monitored worlds and are therefore perceived to be safer.

Within these malls, "entertainment-retail" stores entice consumers to make purchases by having them sample products in the store (Nelson, 1998). For example, at the Mall of America in Bloomington, Minnesota, the Oshman's Super Sports U.S.A. store contains a batting cage, boxing ring, racquetball court, video golf course, and small basketball court. In the same mall, a Lego store, containing a 70-foot-high virtual town built out of Legoblocks, invites children to build their own Lego models. Behind this simulation is the reality of merchandising and the creation of consumer needs. Furthermore, most of these stores, unlike local neighborhood businesses, are part of global, corporate chains. Stores in one mall may look the same as stores in malls throughout the world, thereby divorcing these virtual worlds from any connection to a local, particular culture.

Students could study the ways in which these malls and entertainment-retail stores create consumer demands by promoting themselves as appealing alternatives to other forms of shopping.

Theme or amusement parks such as Disney World, Disneyland, or the 6 Flags chain attempt to simulate realities, but often in highly controlled, artificial ways. As visitors to Disney World, a group of academics (Project on Disney, 1995) noted that while they were being told that they were entering into a "magic" set of virtual worlds, their experiences were continually positioned or mediated by a highly controlled environment. As one of them noted:

> The erasure of spontaneity is so great that the spontaneity itself has been programmed. On the "Jungle Cruise," khaki-clad tour guides teasingly engage the visitors with their banter, whose apparent spontaneity has been carefully scripted and painstakingly rehearsed. Nothing is left to the imagination or the unforeseen. (p. 184)

As visitors in these parks, students could observe various attempts to simulate lived-world realities and their own reactions to any disparities between the simulation and these realities.

IDENTIFYING CONCERNS, ISSUES, OR DILEMMAS IN VIRTUAL WORLDS

In studying virtual worlds, students may be intrigued with the question, "What is reality?" When they are playing a computer game or going on an African safari boat ride in Disney World, are they engaged with "reality" or simply a simulation of "reality"? How can they determine the difference? What features distinguish the two—authenticity, genuineness, level of engagement, concern with consequences? Why is some alternative reality preferable to the "real world"? What aspects of virtual worlds provide pleasure? To explore these questions, students may study their or others' experience in a virtual world and then reflect on questions about the authenticity or genuineness of engagement with that experience.

Participants in virtual worlds may or may not be accountable for any real-world consequences of their actions in virtual worlds. They may adopt different identities because they perceive no need, in a virtual world, to consider the consequences of their actions. As Bill Teel, who runs a chat monitoring service, noted, "In teen chat rooms, all the girls are cheerleaders and all the boys have muscles . . . for the majority of kids, this kind of fibbing is healthy, allowing kids to pretend to be whatever they think is cool" (Santo, 2000, p. 9). Based on her extensive study of MUD participants, Sherry Turkle (1996) found that "you are who you pretend to be" by experimenting with different identities/roles. She quotes one participant:

> "You can completely redefine yourself if you want. You can be the opposite sex. You can be more talkative. You can be less talkative. Whatever. You can just be who you want really, whoever you have the capacity to be. You don't have to worry about the slots other people put you in as much. It's easier to change the way people perceive you, because all they've got is what you show them. They don't look at your body and make assumptions. They don't hear your accent and make assumptions. All they see is your words." (p. 158)

At the same time, adopting alternative identities as romantic lovers or provocateurs without concern for actual social consequences can be dangerous. Kimberly Young, director of the Center for On-Line Addiction (*http://www.netaddiction.com*), cites the example of a 15-year-old female who posed as a 30-year-old man for 6 months in chat rooms. She "dated" a number of women, one of whom wanted to divorce her husband to marry this "man" (Santo, 2000). Or, pedophiles may pose as adolescents to gain access to unknowing adolescent participants. These examples reflect the larger issue of how, in a virtual world, certain rules or ethical codes of conduct can operate when there are no actual consequences for one's actions.

This potential to construct multiple identities, however, does not mean that others do not judge people on the Internet and take action to silence those who abuse others. Nick noted the practice of judging others in his study of an Internet community:

> The Internet has a certain value system that differs from the real world. On-line, we choose not to judge people by what age, race, or gender. We choose to judge one another by the way we "act" on-line, the way we respond and talk to others. In this sense we are all equals, and we show that by giving others a chance to make a good name for

themselves. Although there are those who could care less about how others feel and they make the Internet a potentially dangerous place.

Nick's assertion also evidences a high level of critique of others' language, and an awareness of how words can transform relationships and construct values in a social world.

Many of the virtual worlds noted in this chapter are driven by commercial agendas reflecting the commodification of culture. Simulations of different cultural contexts are designed for commercial purposes as opposed to providing the actual experience of cultural difference. Visitors in shops in Disney World representing different countries of the world, unlike visitors to real countries, have no interaction with the culture that produced the products sold in these shops (Project on Disney, 1995). As a result, they may perceive the real world as a "global marketplace . . . where goods flow freely and are free exchanged" (p. 42), a distorted version of reality in which people must produce products within the constraints of economic forces and barriers.

In participating in virtual worlds, students often are caught in the dilemma of not knowing whether they are simply escaping from lived-world realities into a fantasy version of reality or breaking out of their "reality-bound" lived world to entertain new, more effective ways of experiencing the world. For example, in experimenting with different voices or ideas in chat rooms, students may be using that experience to escape the realities of their lived experiences. At the same time, they may be taking risks necessary for exploring and developing new aspects of their identity. Justin and Brett noted this in their study of the human impact of video games:

> We found that people tend to "tune out" of life and their way of thinking when they are playing video games. People might use this as an escape from the pressures of everyday life. The games sometimes engulf the person to the point where they forget what they were doing before and concentrate only on the video game. This can be a fun part of video games if you had a bad day, or just want to "get out of it all."

They place some value on the stress-relieving experience of playing video games. At the same time, they also noted that players may substitute their long hours of playing games for coping with reality.

CONTEXTUALIZING VIRTUAL WORLDS

Given these concerns, issues, or dilemmas, students could examine the various components shaping these virtual worlds.

Purposes

Understanding the various purposes for participation in virtual worlds may explain the appeal of the worlds. One purpose may be to engage in a pleasurable, ritual-like experience that connects participants with larger, mythic, collective dramas (Real, 1996). For example, soccer fans viewing World Cup soccer television broadcasts as a social group engage in the following ritual-like social practices: a "fanship dimension and the desire to 'thrill in victory,'" a "learning dimension"—acquiring information about the teams and players, a "release dimension"—the "opportunity to 'let loose'" or "get psyched up," a "companionship dimension"—sharing time with friends and family, and a "filler dimension"—the use of sports viewing to "kill time" (Wenner & Gantz, 1998, p. 237). The appeal of virtual worlds therefore may lie in participants' need to transcend the everyday through collective rituals. Allen studied the social world of home entertainment, describing the need to participate with others as "hanging out": "I hang out on the computer and on the net a lot. The Internet is where I can talk and hang out with friends, far or close."

Nick interviewed members of an on-line community, and the following response highlights the ability to share thoughts, feelings, and experiences with the world of video games as a key purpose achieved by participating in this community:

> No one has mentioned why the DBB rulez so much tho. for one thing, or speling kan suk, nd no 1 wil care, cuz we still kno wut yur trying 2 say! Also, we have those nifty 'lil smiley guys to make our emotions a little clearer, where it is mostly impossible otherwise. Finally, eveyone is pretty much equal here. Unless you're admin. Then you are a demigod. NO, correction. The Moderators are demigods Admin is who all the other gods worship . . . no offense, Finally, everyone is frinedly, helpful, and fun to hang with! Ok, the finale of the finallys (sp?) WE can talk about useless chatter, and get away with it. And now for the encore finally, EVERYONE GO BUY D#!!! A great game, and it will likely only take 90% of your free time from you! . . . Welcome to the DUHQ pond . . . DBBDT Organizer WaHoo The official cheer of the DBBDT.

Another possible purpose for participating in virtual worlds is to experiment with alternative identities and relationships by trying out different forms of language expression. In their study of Sam, a 13-year-old female participant in AOL IM interactions, Lewis and Fabos (1999) found that she experimented with a range of voices in order to build social ties both with her friends and with strangers. In talking with her close friend, Sam adopted what she described as a "softer and sweeter" tone, while giving shorter, more pointed answers to peers with whom she did not want to talk; she also mimicked the language of another participant who accidentally got onto her buddy list to maintain the connection:

> SAM: This girl, she thinks I'm somebody else. She thinks I'm one of her friends, and she's like "Hey!" and I'm like "Hi!" and I start playing along with her. She thinks that I'm one of her school friends. She doesn't know it's me. She wrote to me twice now.
>
> BETTINA: So she's this person that you're lying to almost . . .
>
> SAM: Yeah, you just play along. It's fun sometimes. It's comical. Because she'll say something like "Oh [a boy] did this and we're going to the ski house," or whatever, and I'm like "Oh God!" and like and I'll just reply to her. I'll use the same exclamations where she uses them and I'll try to talk like they do. (Lewis & Fabos, 1999, p. 7)

Sam and her close friend, Karrie, both find that they are less socially awkward in IM chat than in face-to-face conversations, particularly with boys:

> SAM: You get more stuff out of them. Yeah. They'll tell you a lot more, cause they feel stupid in front of you. They won't just sit there and . . .
>
> BETTINA: So it's a different medium and they can test themselves a bit more and . . .
>
> SAM: So they know how we react and they don't feel stupid cause they don't have to think about the next thing to say. I can smile (using an emoticom [a visual icon representing an emotion]) or I can say something to them. (Lewis & Fabos, 1999, p. 8)

Students observe specific aspects of participants' conversations in these chat rooms. In his study, Nick emphasized the awareness of language gained by participants: "We judge each other by the way we 'act' and by the way we express ourselves. This is important because it is the basis for social interaction on-line." Through experimenting with language, Sam and Nick are developing confidence in employing different language styles, which may or may not transfer to the ability to express themselves, and to construct and transform roles that may transfer to other lived worlds.

Roles

In participating in virtual worlds, students construct identities through adopting practices associated with alternative roles in these worlds. *Star Trek* fan club members construct their own identities as "Trekkies" by using the *Star Trek* register, wearing costumes, or displaying their knowledge of programs or the actors' and actresses' personal lives (Jenkins, 1992). Soap opera fans display pictures of soap opera actors in their bedrooms, write letters to the actors, or attend social events to meet the actors (Harrington & Bielby, 1995).

Justin and Brett noted that many young players of video games construct future possible identities through play:

> Sometimes a young child will fantasize about being the basketball player or soccer star that they are controlling in the video game, and they will learn to love and idolize that player for the rest of their life. That is a way that video games shape a person's dreams or identities.

Another aspect of roles is belonging to a group. Of course, on-line communities construct roles for the various members, but they also have the same subgroups, or cliques, associated with lived social worlds. This was highlighted in Nick's study of DBB:

> This community even has groups within it, often referred to as Squads or Clans. And to a point: To prove that on-line communities are not just a fad, they are real, and make a difference: As of tommorow, the Squad I founded will be 4 YEARS old founded Nov. 18 of 1995, making us one of the oldest.

Rules

Virtual worlds operate according to their own rules or conventions. For example, learning to play a computer game or learning to navigate through a hypertext novel involves learning to attend to cues implying rules or conventions operating in that game or novel. Chat-room participants also adhere to rules of "netiquette," constituting appropriate topics, modes of decorum, and civility. Hamilton (1999) found that the Nancy Drew chat room formulated explicit rules discouraging users from providing full names or using "bad words."

Chat rooms also may follow certain implicit rules regarding appropriate topics. One of Richard's students, Judy Ward (1996), studied 35 computer newsgroup participants' responses to the television program *X-Files*. She found that there were certain unspoken rules regarding inappropriate posting, such as making irrelevant, off-topic statements, bashing or spreading false rumors about the two celebrity stars of the show, posting sexually explicit or violent messages, or misusing the newsgroup. When a participant began spreading false rumors about the female star of the show, she was immediately castigated and told, "'Either get with it and get some netiquette or please keep your computer turned off'" (p. 8).

Beliefs

Science fiction films or novels often portray futuristic versions of computer-driven virtual worlds, examining some of the beliefs shaping those worlds. For example, the film *The Matrix* portrays a "lived" world of the 1990s constructed entirely by a set of futuristic computer minds who use technology to simulate and maintain their own artificial intelligence by living off humans' desire for a consumer culture. The main characters live outside this computer reality and move in and out of it to challenge these villains and the tyranny associated with the controlled virtual society. In the young-adult science fiction novel, *Interstellar Pig* (Sleater, 1984), the main character copes with aliens who are engaged in a life-or-death game. In *This Perfect Day* by Ira Levin (1970), UniComp is a computer god who makes all the decisions for a society so that its citizens are not allowed to think for themselves. And, in *2001: A Space Odyssey*, the computer HAL is programmed to destroy the members of a spaceship crew. In these fictional versions of virtual worlds, students can deconstruct the representations to explicate how optimistic beliefs about advancing society through technology are frustrated by distopian versions, yet ultimately are reconstructed through the protagonists' heroic social interactions.

As part of the rebellion inquiry projects conducted in Leo Bickelhaupt's class in the St. Paul Open School, Elliot examined the themes in a science fiction novel that portrays a rebellion and war between two universes in the years 3025–3030. He described the rebellion led by the daughter of a former ruler of one of the "houses" of the universe against another "house." From studying this rebellion, he noted, "I learned that not [all] rebellions are because of oppression or tyranny . . . some are just a grab for power and for the benefit of civilians."

History

In commercialized virtual worlds, "reality" often is mediated by the producers' own ideological versions of history and community, often masking complex cultural or political issues. Members of the Project on Disney (1995) found that history in Epcot exhibits in Disney World was portrayed primarily as a continuous improvement of the world through technology and corporate agents (who are also sponsors of the exhibits). For example, in an exhibit on "The Land" sponsored by Kraft, "no relationship to the land other than commercial use by business is posited as possible or even desirable" (p. 59). In an exhibit on "Universe of Energy," sponsored by Exxon, there is no reference to energy shortages, oil spills, or solar power. Representations of American history emphasize "unity" and "equality" achieved through global capitalism, while masking over references to conflicts associated with gender, class, race, or cross-cultural differences between societies. The future is portrayed as a world populated by intact, heterosexual families—"in 'Tomorrowland Theater' the chorus tells us that 'Disney World is a wonderland for girls and boys and moms and dads'" (p. 69). The prevailing narrative in these historical representations is one of "capitalist expansion masquerading as science fiction in which the heroes of the next century are not people but machines, with faith placed not in courage but in technology" (p. 86).

REPRESENTING VIRTUAL WORLDS

Participants in virtual worlds learn to use a range of different tools to construct these worlds. As previously mentioned, rather than reading in a linear fashion, responding to computer hypertext novels or web documents allows students to actively construct their own version of the text by clicking on text, icons, or addresses to move between different texts (Bolter, 1991; Joyce, 1995). Or, in composing "multigenre" papers, they incorporate links to various images, texts, sounds, music, videoclips, documents, and so on, to construct a similar hypertext experience for their readers (Davis & Shadle, 2000; Moulton, 1999; Romano, 2000). In conducting studies of shopping malls, amusement/theme parks, or media events, students may employ photography or video as a tool for representing their own experiences in and perceptions of these virtual worlds. Their own images can be set in contrast to the often glamorized publicity images associated with these worlds.

In her analysis of Disney World, Karen Klugman, a professional photographer, observed that most visitors were carrying cameras and that they were constantly taking pictures (Project on Disney, 1995). She was intrigued by the fact that people were taking pictures of what was an artificial environment. She explained this as reflecting a need "to preserve the magic . . . the notion that what is represented in their pictures is reality itself and not some fiction framed by technology" (p. 24). Klugman's own photos in the book portray bored visitors tired of the artificiality of Disney World. Similarly, as part of her ethnographic study of Super Bowl XXVI held in Minneapolis in 1992, Dona Schwartz (1998) employed photos to portray a more realistic, behind-the-scenes analysis of the less glamorous, ironic side of this media event—photos of department store mannequins wearing football helmets or a group of Native Americans protesting the Washington Redskins' logo.

Students also may study how participants use various tools to construct virtual worlds. For example, in studying the *X-Files* listserve, Judy Ward (1996) found that participants learned to use language and narrative retelling in ways that established their reputations within the group of active participants.

Several participants, who were particularly adept at recounting previous episodes of the program in a colorful, entertaining style, assumed the status of celebrities within the group.

Students who have studied various worlds of music find that playing a fiddle or guitar, or singing, provides a new tool for constructing a shared virtual world through engaging audiences in alternative experiences. Candice noted this after her study of playing guitar in a band and participating in hard-rock concerts:

> Through music, you can express your feelings to others and yourself. This was an important idea in my journal because that is how music is made—by instruments. And people play the instruments. The kind of music that they play reflects on their moods, feelings, and personalities that create this social world with other beings.

CRITIQUING AND TRANSFORMING VIRTUAL WORLDS

Trisha provided one of the most important critiques of the technology tools that create virtual social worlds when she wrote that "technology is changing the way people think and act, and it's playing a big role in society." It is critically important that students study how new forms of technology construct the many virtual worlds available today or in the future. Mike studied the world of robotics and described what the future holds when NANO technology produces robots as small as blood cells:

> NANO technology will change the world and introduce the world to new possibilities. NANO technology can improve everything from surgery to cars that can fly. Most everything will be computerized and will respond via voice command. You will have a little card about the size of a credit card that will have all your personalized settings and the card setting can change where the chair reclines, what channel the HDTV turns on to, the light setting, and everything.

Another central focus of inquiry projects on virtual worlds is the extent to which virtual worlds provide a valid representation of lived-world experiences. While virtual worlds need not replicate lived worlds exactly, they also should not distort lived worlds in a deceptive, misleading manner. Moreover, rather than being ideal societies, the virtual worlds of chat rooms or computer-game networks can be closed, limiting spaces that simply mimic rather than transform the limitations of real-world communities (Nunes, 1997).

Students could critique instances of misleading or deceptive web sites, particularly those promoting a certain ideological orientation. They also may examine the commercialization of the web, exploring the underlying economic forces shaping advertising and marketing on the web. In studying computer games or web sites, students may critique stereotyped portrayals of gender, class, or racial roles in computer games, web sites, or chat rooms; for example, the gender or racial stereotyping in "shooter" games.

They also may critique their own or others' potential for on-line addiction, examining the extent to which such addiction is "harmful" or not. One potential harm has to do with whether, in adopting alternative roles in a chat room, participants simply are adopting identities that conform to the immediate virtual context without any reference to a consistent lived-world self.

Based on their critiques of computer games, or multimedia production, students could entertain or actually construct their own alternative versions that address some of the limitations found in their inquiry projects. For example, having critiqued the gender stereotypes in "shooter" computer games, they may create their own version of a computer game that subverts these gender stereotypes.

Throughout this book we often have highlighted quicktime movies, edited music, digital photographs, and web sites created by students to represent ideas they have identified in a social world. As they construct these representations, the students learn to use the virtual tools of new technologies to critique ideas about lived, represented, and virtual worlds through authoring the sequence and juxtaposition of images, text, and audio. What we haven't noted is that the actual work with the technology tools on the computer, and the experience of the final project "texts" produced, also creates a new social world. In this world, students experience high levels of excitement and motivation as they feel a sense of power to create multimedia texts just like the many texts they experience in everyday virtual and lived worlds. This new world of using virtual tools also supports their ability to critique existing multimedia texts because they have been "inside" as authors of multimedia. Several students who worked with cameras and multimedia computer representational tools highlight the thinking involved in multimedia authoring:

> NICK (quicktime video on Internet communities): This unit was an
> entirely new experience except for reading a class book. In
> previous years, we simply wrote on the book that we read.
> GARRETT (quicktime video connecting romance and sports): It required
> more deep thinking, reflections, and comparison to personal
> experiences.

In exploring and constructing virtual worlds, students are transforming their lived-world experiences into alternative versions of reality. In studying their own or others' activities, students reflect on how their participation in these activities involves changes in ways of knowing or perceiving. For example, in constructing web-based links revolving around the theme of different kinds of friendship, Jenny noted that the very activity of constructing links helped develop her very perceptions about friendship. Hopefully, all students will experience how the act of representing aspects of a social world generates a sense of constructive agency to transform social worlds.

12

Conclusion: Critical Consciousness Through
Inquiry into Social Worlds

WE CANNOT AVOID the construction of social worlds. The key question remains, What are the kinds of worlds in which we hope to live? Our words and actions with others will determine the answer to this question. The material world already present to us, its objects, symbols, and discourse practices will play a major role in what we believe we can possibly say or do at each moment. The pull of different groups, with their alternative values and identities, often will turn each interaction into the overlapping negotiation of contesting social worlds. We have no choice but to develop our abilities to represent and to critique our social worlds in order to gain fuller agency in our interactions as we continually construct, negotiate, and seek to transform with others our lived worlds.

WHAT'S THE VALUE OF PARTICIPATING
IN A SOCIAL WORLDS CURRICULUM?

As we worked with teachers and students engaged in various inquiry projects related to social worlds, we learned a number of things about the value of having students participate in a social worlds curriculum.

Immersing themselves in worlds different from their own helped students recognize alternative perspectives. Given increasing cultural diversity, students need to embrace difference rather than conformity as they examine social worlds and how they are constructed. By immersing themselves in different lived and represented worlds, students grapple with unfamiliar beliefs and discourse practices that challenge their own familiar perspectives. They may then be less likely to frame others' actions and words in terms of fixed world views, and be more willing to explore and participate with others in cultural practices that construct new worlds across the limiting boundaries of class, race, and gender. In their analyses of social worlds represented through literature, media, and personal experience, the State College Area High School students continually recognized the difficulty and injustice created by these boundaries.

Students were particularly engaged in inquiry projects when they framed those activities in terms of concerns, issues, or dilemmas. Framing inquiry projects around concerns, issues, or dilemmas implies that there are problematic, conflicting perspectives and agendas operating in a social world. Having to deal with a "real" problematic, conflicted situation, as opposed to an assigned topic or theme, motivated students to seek possible explanations of and resolutions to a situation, as was the case with Sarah's students' concern with the plight of women in the medieval period. Projects were highly purposeful and pragmatic in terms of the students' own everyday social interactions.

Contextualizing people's and characters' actions in terms of purposes, roles, rules, beliefs, and history helped students understand how language and action contribute to the larger discourse practices of a social world. Rather than focus simply on people's or characters' actions and words in terms of individualistic psychology and fixed identities, students learned to perceive words and actions as both contributing to and constituted by larger discourse practices made up of socially negotiated purposes, roles, rules, beliefs, and traditions. Throughout their analyses of the social worlds constructed in short stories, the State College Area High School students articulated how the characters' identities, relationships, and values both shaped and were shaped by their social interactions and discourse practices.

> I thought this was different from what I've done in other English classes in one key way. Thought. I think I did a lot more in-depth thought in this unit than in years past. You were really required to think and analyze different aspects of life. (Brett)

When Kim's students juxtaposed lived experiences with historical representations to analyze the myths of the American West, they appreciated how beliefs are continually negotiated through the process of sharing and critiquing alternative representations of social life.

Studying how tools are employed to represent worlds helped students recognize the power of tools to convey meaning. In studying the ways in which worlds are represented through tools, students began to understand how language, narratives, images, signs, and other tools are used to achieve specific purposes. When the meaning for a particular word, image, or interaction was multiple, they began to identify contesting purposes from overlapping social worlds. They came to recognize the important idea that the uses of tools are purpose-driven and functional and not just fixed forms to be reproduced in school assignments.

I liked how the social worlds unit made me look at the interactions of characters. I have never had a unit that looked at this aspect of writing before this. (Ian)

Through using a range of different multimedia tools to represent their own perceptions of worlds, as did the State College Area High School ninth graders, students learned how to combine signs, images, and sound with language and narrative to communicate meaning. This further supported their ability to deconstruct media messages and critique underlying ideologies.

The ability to change worlds depends on the quality of critiques of those worlds. Students recognized that to change worlds, they needed to build specific, substantive critiques to warrant the need to change. By defining particular problems in how worlds operate, or by identifying specific forms of interaction, language, and action, they could define particular changes for improving those worlds. Moreover, when students are given the authority to recommend changes, as was the case at Sharnbrook School, they are more likely to seriously engage in careful inquiry and critique.

Collaborating through co-inquiry, students and teachers learn how to mutually construct shared understandings of worlds. In some of the projects, students and teachers worked together as collaborative, co-inquiry teams. In doing so, they learned how to each contribute their own particular expertise and knowledge to the overall project. Such collaboration and sharing of ideas created a classroom community in which students felt like fully valued participants in determining the direction of thinking and activity. Learning how to work collaboratively with others may be just as valuable as the final products that result from that work.

Framing the English classroom as inquiry into social worlds actually improved the achievement of traditional literacy goals. When the students explored how identities and relationships were constructed and maintained in the social worlds represented in literature and media, they engaged in analysis of characterization. When students explored the activities of participants in a social world—how characters struggled to belong in various, sometimes conflicting social worlds, and how characters sought greater agency and consciousness within their worlds—the students examined plot. When students explored the values constructed in social worlds for objects, purposes for activities, and desired identities and relationships, they encompassed the idea of theme. When students explored the symbolic meanings and uses of language, object, action, and text, and how these meanings were layered through characters' ongoing interactions with others and self, they explored imagery, metaphor, and symbolism. When students examined how different linguistic patterns of speech constructed different identities, relationships, and values, how characters used words to achieve purposes and desires, and how authors represented this role of language in the construction of social worlds, they identified aspects of discourse style and point of view. When the students explored how language, symbols, objects, and actions created tension, ambiguities, or pleasure in characters' social interactions and readers' responses, they examined mood and tone.

What the social worlds curriculum did quite effectively is bridge the process of interpreting literature and media texts with the students' process of meaning making in their own lived worlds. Suddenly the ideas about social worlds were everywhere, in every text, at every moment, and the whole mix became a connected resource for negotiating the best understanding about any one instance of human word or action. As one student put it:

> It was much more creative and made me think more than I normally would in English. Instead of parts of speech we were actually doing something useful. I think we were supposed to realize how complex society is; like a web, and also to get us to think more about the environment(s) we are in. (Abby)

In addition, with all the emphasis on multimedia and alternative forms for representing meaning in this book, we do not devalue the act of writing, or the power of printed texts. We have, in fact, found that when students represent their worlds through multimedia, their written efforts improve and become more effective because they begin to analyze and frame their writing in terms of socially valued purposes beyond a school grade.

Public sharing and specifying criteria for completing projects fostered students' self-evaluation during work on a project. A practice-oriented curriculum is based in continual negotiation of participants' subjective understandings. The State College Area High School students appreciated the opportunity to share ideas and experience the many artifacts class members created to represent ideas about social worlds. In the words of one of these ninth graders:

> I liked the freedom to make an artifact and not being told exactly what to make and how to make it. I also liked the relaxed way in which we presented the artifacts to the class. (Rich)

Through this continual sharing, the students co-constructed a classroom discourse practice that moved the assessment of quality into a public forum rather than the traditional teacher–student matching of an authorized form that comes from some external realm of ideal answers.

Given the open-ended, constructive nature of these projects, students also benefited from specific, descriptive criteria for use in guiding their different inquiry projects. For example, students found helpful the different handouts used to structure their thinking as they identified specific words or actions in stories or life, contextualized the interactions in terms of the components and practices of a social world, and then critiqued the identities, relationships, and values constructed. The students also appreciated the criteria that encouraged them to represent their ideas using the complete range of different representational tools.

LEARNING THROUGH ACTIVE CLASSROOM PARTICIPATION

Students must be full participants in the negotiation of both discourse practices and meanings in the classroom social world. In their social worlds beyond the school classroom, adolescents most often feel like they are equal members, fully contributing to the meanings for valued activities. They know what it feels like to co-construct their social worlds. The traditional discourse practices of school tend to position adolescents with little, if any, power to determine meanings and activities with the prescribed academic content. By denying adolescents the opportunity to co-construct meaning within a classroom social world through curricular texts and inquiry activities, we prevent them from developing the discourse practices and critical consciousness needed for positive participation in all their social worlds. It is no wonder that a great many adolescents value nonacademic social worlds in which they may experience greater opportunities for agency and shared meaning making.

Consciousness is a consequence of representing the world. It is the great legacy of language. A curriculum focused on inquiry into how language, symbols, and action constructs our social worlds must be full of opportunities to produce and critique representations. Negotiating these representations with others moves us beyond our own subjectivities and constructs the intersubjectivity that is the core of our cultural existence. As we enter social worlds, we always encounter readymade representations embedded in established discourse practices through which we can realize our identities and relationships and values. Yet we must always choose to enact these discourse practices, and some should be closely critiqued for their human value before being adopted.

There is always room for agency. It is a dialectic—not a balance between the social and individual—because neither exists separately, but each creates the other, back and forth, negotiated in each and every social interaction and in each and every reflection we have about experience. As students develop this understanding through their inquiries into lived and represented social worlds, their participation in all social worlds can result in the construction of a greater sense of belonging and of a more just and equitable democracy.

References

Alicea, G. (1995). *The air down here: True tales from a south Bronx boyhood*. New York: Chronicle Books.

Anderson, E. (1990). *Streetwise: Race, class, and change in an urban community*. Chicago: University of Chicago Press.

Anderson, J. (1999, October 1). Life as a freshman. *Polar Prints*. North High School, North St. Paul, MN.

Anderson, S. (1969). *Winesburg, Ohio*. New York: Viking Press.

Anderson, S., & Cloud, C. (1999, December 16). A royal visit. *Polar Prints*. North High School, North St. Paul, MN.

Angelou, M. (1969). *I know why the caged bird sings*. New York: Random House.

Annenberg Public Policy Center. (1999). *Media in the home*. Philadelphia: University of Pennsylvania, Annenberg Public Policy Center.

Atkin, B. (1996). *Voices from the streets: Young former gang members tell their stories*. New York: Little, Brown.

Austen, J. (1980). *Pride and prejudice*. New York: Penguin. (Original work published 1813)

Austin, J., & Willard, M. N. (Eds.). (1998). *Generations of youth: Youth cultures and history in twentieth-century America*. New York: New York University Press.

Bakhtin, M. (1981). *The dialogic imagination: Four essays* (M. Holquist, Ed.). Austin: University of Texas Press.

Barthes, R. (1974). *S/Z* (R. Miller, Trans.). New York: Hill & Wang.

Bazerman, C. (1994). Systems of genres and the enactment of social intentions. In A. Freedman & P. Medway (Eds.), *Genre and the new rhetoric* (pp. 79-101). Philadelphia: Taylor & Francis.

Baudrilland, J. (1994). *Simulacra and simulation*. Ann Arbor: University of Michigan Press.

Beach, R. (1997). Students' resistance to engagement with multicultural literature. In T. Rogers & A. Soter (Eds.), *Reading across cultures: Teaching literature in a diverse society* (pp. 69-94). New York: Teachers College Press.

Beach, R., & Anson, C. (1988). The pragmatics of memo-writing: Developmental differences in a writing role-play. *Written Communication, 5*, 157-183.

Beach, R., & Freedman, K. (1992). Responding as a cultural act. In J. Many & C. Cox (Eds.), *Reader stance and literary understanding* (pp. 162-190). Norwood, NJ: Ablex.

Beach, R., & Marshall, J. (1991). *Teaching literature in the secondary school.* Belmont, CA: Wadsworth.

Beacon, P. (1993). *The troubled journey: A portrait of 6th-12th grade youth.* New York: Free Spirit Press.

Berkenkotter, C., & Huckin, T. (1995). *Genre knowledge in disciplinary communication: Cognition, culture, power.* Mahwah, NJ: Erlbaum.

Bissinger, H. G. (1990). *Friday night lights: A town, a team, and a dream.* Reading, MA: Addison Wesley.

Bode, J., & Mack, S. (1994). *Heartbreak and roses: Real-life stories of troubled love.* New York: Delacorte.

Boesky, A. (1994). A veil of water. In B. Emra (Ed.), *Coming of age: Short stories about youth and adolescence* (pp. 223–227). Chicago: National Textbook Company.

Bolter, J. (1991). *The writing space: The computer, hypertext, and the history of writing.* Hillsdale, NJ: Erlbaum.

Breitbart, M. M. (1998). "Dana's mystical tunnel": Young people's designs for survival and change in the city. In T. Skelton & G. Valentine (Eds.), *Cool places: Geographies of youth cultures* (pp. 305–328). New York: Routledge.

Brown, B., & Theobold, W. (1998). Learning contexts beyond the classroom: Extracurricular activities, community organizations, and peer groups. In K. Borman & B. Schneider (Eds.), *The adolescent years: Social influences and educational challenges. 97th Yearbook of the National Society for the Study of Education* (pp. 109–141). Chicago: University of Chicago Press.

Brown, J. (2000). Creating a censorship simulation. *ALAN Review, 27*(3), 27–30.

Buskin, J. (1999, March 29). The players. *The Asian Wall Street Journal, 56,* 4.

Byars, B. (1996). *The 18th emergency.* New York: Viking Press.

Christenson, P., & Roberts, D. (1998). *It's not only rock and roll: Popular music in the lives of adolescents.* Cresskill, NJ: Hampton Press.

Christian-Smith, L. K. (1990). *Becoming a woman through romance.* New York: Routledge.

Cisneros, S. (1986). *House on Mango Street.* New York: Vintage.

Cisneros, S. (1994). Eleven. In B. Emra (Ed.), *Coming of age: Short stories about youth and adolescence* (pp. 3–6). Chicago: National Textbook Company.

Cole, M. (1996). *Cultural psychology.* Cambridge, MA: Harvard University Press.

Collier, E. (1994). Marigolds. In B. Emra (Ed.), *Coming of age: Short stories about youth and adolescence* (pp. 137–146). Chicago: National Textbook Company.

Cooper, M. (1995). *Bound for the promised land: The great black migration.* New York: Dutton.

Cormier, R. (1986). *The chocolate war.* New York: Dell.

Coval, J. (1999). Snowboarding: A lay person's guide to infiltrating the core. Unpublished paper, University of Minnesota, Minneapolis.

Covey, S., & Covey, S. (1998). *The 7 habits of highly effective families.* New York: Golden Books.

Crowe, C. (1994). The coach in YA literature: Mentor or dementor. *ALAN Review, 22,* 47–50.

Crutcher, C. (1983). *Running loose.* New York: Greenwillow.

Crutcher, C. (1986). *Stotan!* New York: Bantam.

Csikszentmihalyi, M., & Larson, R. (1986). *Being adolescent: Conflict and growth in the teenage years.* New York: Basic Books.

Csikszentmihalyi, M., & Schmidt, J. (1998). Stress and resilience in adolescents: An evolutionary perspective. In K. Borman & B. Schneider (Eds.), *The adolescent years: Social influences and educational challenges. 97th Yearbook of the National Society for the Study of Education* (pp. 42–64). Chicago: University of Chicago Press.

Cummins, H. J. (1999, June 13). Oral history: Interview with William Doherty. *Minneapolis Star Tribune*, 28(70), A13.

Cushman, K. (1994). *Catherine called Birdy.* New York: HarperCollins.

Davis, R., & Shadle, M. (2000). "Building a mystery": Alternative research writing and the academic act of seeking. *College Composition and Communication, 51*(3), 417–446.

DeSantis, J. (1991). *For the color of his skin: The murder of Yusuf Hawkins and the trial of Bensonhurst.* New York: Pharos Books.

Dillon, D., & Moje, E. (1998). Listening to the talk of adolescent girls: Lessons about literacy, school, and life. In D. Alvermann, K. Hinchman, D. Moore, S. Phelps, & D. Waff (Eds.), *Reconceptualizing the literacies in adolescents' lives* (pp. 193–224). Mahwah, NJ: Erlbaum.

Doel, M., & Clarke, D. (1999). Virtual worlds: Simulation, suppletion, s(ed)uction and simulacra. In M. Crang, P. Crang, & J. May (Eds.), *Virtual geographies: Bodies, space, and relations* (pp. 261–283). New York: Routledge.

Doherty, W. (1997). *The intentional family: How to build family ties in our modern world.* Reading, MA: Addison Wesley.

Dorris, M. (1988). *A yellow raft in blue water.* New York: Warner.

Duncombe, S. (1998). Let's all be alienated together: Zines and the making of underground community. In J. Austin & M. N. Willard (Eds.), *Generations of youth: Youth cultures and history in twentieth-century America* (pp. 427–452). New York: New York University Press.

Edelsky, C. (1999). On critical whole language practice: Why, what, and a bit of how. In C. Edelsky (Ed.), *Making justice our project: Teachers working toward critical whole language practice* (pp. 7–36). Urbana, IL: National Council of Teachers of English.

Egerstrom, K. (1999, January 19). A day in court. *Polar Prints.* North High School, North St. Paul, MN.

Elkind, D. (1998). *All grown up and no place to go: Teenagers in crisis.* Reading, MA: Addison Wesley.

Emra, B. (Ed.). (1994). *Coming of age: Short stories about youth and adolescence.* Chicago: National Textbook Company.

Engestrom, Y. (1987). *Learning by expanding: An activity-theoretical approach to developmental research.* Helsinki: Orienta-Konsultit.

Engestrom, Y. (1999). Innovative learning in work teams: Analyzing cycles of knowledge creation in practice. In Y. Engestrom, R. Miettinen, & R. Punanaki (Eds.), *Perspectives on activity theory* (pp. 377–404). New York: Cambridge University Press.

Ensico, P. E. (1998). Good/bad girls read together: Pre-adolescent girls' co-authorship of feminine subject positions during a shared reading event. *English Education, 30,* 44-62.

Fairclough, N. (1989). *Language and power.* New York: Longman.

Fairclough, N. (1995). *Media discourse.* London: Edward Arnold.

Felsen, H. G. (1994). A private talk with Holly. In B. Emra (Ed.), *Coming of age: Short stories about youth and adolescence* (pp. 113-116). Chicago: National Textbook Company.

Finders, M. J. (1997). *Just girls: Hidden literacies and life in junior high.* New York: Teachers College Press.

Fine, M., & Weiss, L. (1998). *The unknown city: The lives of poor and working-class young adults.* Boston: Beacon Press.

Fine, M., Anand, B. T., Jordan, C. P., & Sherman, D. (1998). *Off track: Classroom privileges for all* [Video]. New York: Teachers College Press.

Finnegan, W. (1998). *Cold new world: Growing up in a harder country.* New York: Random House.

Fitzgerald, F. S. (1980). *The great Gatsby.* New York: Scribners. (Original work published 1925)

Fitzgerald, F. S. (1996). Bernice bobs her hair. In *Bernice bobs her hair and other stories* (pp. 11-32). New York: Signet. (Original work published 1951)

Flower, L., Long, E., & Higgins, L. (2000). *Learning to rival: A literate practice for intercultural inquiry.* Mahwah, NJ: Erlbaum.

Foucault, M. (1980). *Power/knowledge.* New York: Pantheon.

Freire, P. (1973). *Education for critical consciousness.* New York: Seabury Press.

Gaines, D. (1991). *Teenage wasteland: Suburbia's dead end kids.* New York: HarperPerennial.

Gee, J. P. (1996). *Social linguistics and literacies: Ideology in discourses.* London: Taylor & Francis.

Gee, J. P. (2000). New people in new worlds: Networks, the new capitalism and schools. In B. Cope & M. Kalantzis (Eds.), *Multiliteracies: Literacy learning and the design of social futures* (pp. 43-68). New York: Routledge.

Gelder, K., & Thornton, S. (Eds.). (1997). *The subcultures readers.* New York: Routledge.

Gordon, T. (1973). *Parent effectiveness training.* New York: P. H. Wyden.

Graff, E. (1999). What's love got to do with it. *Utne Reader, 93,* 65-67.

Greene, B. (1973). *Summer of my German soldier.* New York: Dell.

Griffin, R. (1998). *Sports in the lives of children and adolescents: Success on the field and in life.* Westport, CT: Praeger.

Grossman, D., & DeGaetano, G. (1999). *Stop teaching our kids to kill.* New York: Crown.

Guest, J. (1980). *Ordinary people.* New York: Ballantine.

Hamilton, M. (1999). Deciphering the rhetoric of Nancy Drew. Unpublished paper, University of Minnesota, Minneapolis.

Hamper, B. (1991). *Rivethead: Tales from the assembly line.* New York: Warner.

Harrington, C. L., & Bielby, D. (1995). *Soap fans: Pursuing pleasure and making meaning in everyday life.* Philadelphia: Temple University Press.

Harris, E. L. (1996). *Still life in Harlem*. New York: Henry Holt.

Heath, S. B., & McLaughlin, M. W. (Eds.). (1993). *Identity and inner-city youth*. New York: Teachers College Press.

Hersch, P. (1998). *A tribe apart: A journey into the heart of American adolescence*. New York: Fawcett Columbine.

Hesse-Biber, S., & Carter, G. (1999). *Working women in America*. New York: Oxford University Press.

Hewlett, S. A., & West, C. (1998). *The war against parents*. New York: Houghton Mifflin.

Hinton, S. E. (1980). *The outsiders*. New York: Dell.

Holloway, L. (1999, March 10). Family tree assignments become more flexible for the '90s. *Minneapolis Star Tribune, 28*(80), E2.

Howey, K., Sears, S., DeStefano, J., Berns, R., & Pritz, S. (1998). *Preparing teachers to use contextual teaching and learning strategies to enhance student success in and beyond school*. Columbus: College of Education, Ohio State University.

Hunt, R. A., & Vipond, D. (1991). First, catch the rabbit: Methodological imperative and the dramatization of dialogic reading. In R. Beach, J. Green, M. Kamil, & T. Shanahan (Eds.), *Multidisciplinary perspectives on literacy research* (pp. 69–90). Urbana, IL: National Conference on Research in English/National Council of Teachers of English.

Hurston, N. Z. (1990). *Their eyes were watching God*. New York: Perennial.

Ianni, F. (1989). *Search for structure: A report on American youth today*. New York: Free Press.

Islam, F. (1999, March 22). Sony banks on an interactive future. *The Japan Times, 89*, 11.

Jackson, S. (1988). The lottery. In J. Pickering (Ed.), *Fiction 100: An anthology of short stories* (pp. 702–708). New York: Macmillan. (Original work published 1948)

Jacobson, M., & Mazur, L. (1995). *Marketing madness: A survival guide for a consumer society*. Boulder, CO: Westview Press.

Jenkins, H. (1992). *Textual poachers: Television fans and participatory culture*. New York: Routledge.

Jones, G. (1992). *Honey, I'm home! Sitcoms*. New York: Grove Weidenfeld.

Joyce, M. (1995). *Of two minds: Hypertext pedagogy and poetics*. Ann Arbor: University of Michigan Press.

Keillor, G. (1985). *Lake Wobegon days*. New York: Viking Press.

Kincaid, J. (1985). A walk to the jetty. In J. Kincaid, *Annie John* (pp. 130–148). New York: Penguin Books.

Kidder, T. (1999). *Hometown*. New York: Random House.

King, M. L. (1968). *Letter from a Birmingham jail*. Stamford, CT: Overbrook Press.

Kingsolver, B. (1991). *The bean trees*. New York: HarperCollins.

Kirp, D. (2000). *Almost home: America's love-hate relationship with community*. Princeton, NJ: Princeton University Press.

Kohlberg, L. (1984). *The psychology of moral development: The nature and validity of moral stages*. San Francisco: Harper & Row.

Kretschmer, S. (1994). And summer is gone. In B. Emra (Ed.), *Coming of age: Short stories about youth and adolescence* (pp. 206–209). Chicago: National Textbook Company.

Labov, W. (1972). *The language of the inner city*. Philadelphia: University of Pennsylvania Press.

Landsman, J. (1993). *Basic needs: A year with street kids in a city school*. Minneapolis: Milkweed.

Langer, S. (1957). *Feeling and form: A theory of art*. New York: Scribners.

Lankshear, C. (1997). *Changing literacies*. Philadelphia: Open University Press.

Lave, J., & Wenger, E. (1991). *Situated learning: Legitimate peripheral participation*. New York: Cambridge University Press.

Lavenda, R. (1997). *Cornfests and water carnivals: Celebrating community in Minnesota*. Washington, DC: Smithsonian Institution Press.

Lee, H. (1995). *To kill a mockingbird*. New York: HarperCollins. (Original work published 1960)

Lemann, N. (1992). *The promised land: The great black immigration and how it changed America*. New York: Vintage.

Leonard, M. (1998). Paper planes: Travelling the New Grrrl geographies. In T. Skelton & G. Valentine (Eds.), *Cool places: Geographies of youth cultures* (pp. 101–118). New York: Routledge.

Levin, I. (1970). *This perfect day*. New York: Random House.

Lewis, C., & Fabos, B. (1999, December 3). *Chatting on-line: Uses of instant message communication among adolescent girls*. Paper presented at the National Reading Conference, Orlando.

Lewis, S. (1992). *Main Street*. New York: Library of America. (Original work published 1937)

Loving Well Project. (1995). *The art of loving well: A character education curriculum for today's teenagers*. Boston: Boston University, School of Education.

Lowry, L. (1993). *The giver*. New York: Bantam Doubleday Dell.

Lucas, T. (1998). Youth gangs and moral panics in Santa Cruz, California. In T. Skelton & G. Valentine (Eds.), *Cool places: Geographies of youth cultures* (pp. 145–160). New York: Routledge.

Maasik, S., & Solomon, J. (1994). *Signs of life in the U.S.A.: Readings on popular culture for writers*. Boston: St. Martin's Press.

Macrorie, K. (1988). *The I-search paper*. Portsmouth, NH: Boynton/Cook.

Malbon, B. (1998). The club: Clubbing, consumption, identity and the spatial practices of every-night life. In T. Skelton & G. Valentine (Eds.), *Cool places: Geographies of youth cultures* (pp. 266–286). New York: Routledge.

McCarthy, C., Hudak, G., Miklaucic, S., & Saukko, P. (1999). *Sound identities: Popular music and the politics of education*. New York: Peter Lang.

McCormick, K. (1999). *Reading our histories, understanding our cultures: A sequenced approach to thinking, reading, and writing*. Boston: Allyn & Bacon.

McCullers, C. (1994). Sucker. In B. Emra (Ed.), *Coming of age: Short stories about youth and adolescence* (pp. 102–112). Chicago: National Textbook Company.

McKillop, A. M., & Myers, J. (1999). The pedagogical and electronic contexts of composing in hypermedia. In S. DeWitt & K. Strasma (Eds.), *Contexts, intertexts, and hypertexts* (pp. 65-116). Cresskill, NJ: Hampton Press.

McKinley, E. G. (1997). *Beverly Hills, 90210: Television, gender, and identity*. Philadelphia: University of Pennsylvania Press.

McRobbie, A. (1991). *Feminism and youth culture: From "Jackie" to "Just Seventeen."* Boston: Unwin Hyman.

Miller, A. (1999). *Death of a salesman*. New York: Penguin. (Original work published 1949)

Moffatt, M. (1989). *Coming of age in New Jersey: College and American culture*. New Brunswick, NJ: Rutgers University Press.

Moore, J. (1998). Street signs: Semiotics, Romeo and Juliet, and young adult literature. *Theory into Practice, 37*, 211-219.

Mori, K. (1995). *One bird*. New York: Henry Holt.

Morrison, T. (1970). *The bluest eye*. New York: Plume.

Morse, J. (1999). Hitched in home room. *Time, 153*(24), 54-55.

Mosenthal, P. B. (1998). Reframing the problems of adolescence and adolescent literacy: A dilemma-management perspective. In D. E. Alvermann, et al. (Eds.), *Reconceptualizing the literacies in adolescents' lives* (pp. 325-352). Mahwah, NJ: Erlbaum.

Moss, G. (1989). *Un/popular fictions*. London: Virago.

Moulton, M. C. (1999). The multigenre paper: Increasing interest, motivation, and functionality in research. *Journal of Adolescent and Adult Literacy, 42*(7), 528-545.

Muller, C., & Frisco, M. (1998). Social institutions serving adolescents. In K. Borman & B. Schneider (Eds.), *The adolescent years: Social influences and educational challenges. 97th Yearbook of the National Society for the Study of Education* (pp. 142-159). Chicago: University of Chicago Press.

Myers, J. (1988). Self-discovery through literature: Fluency not Lit. Crit., Every student should be in the novel. *English Journal, 77*(2), 28-34.

National Fatherhood Initiative. (1999). What does prime-time network television say about fatherhood. Gaithersburg, MD: Author. http: //www.fatherhood.org

Nelson, E. (1998). *Mall of America: Reflections of a virtual community*. Lakeville, MN: Galde Press.

Norris, L. (1994). Shaving. In B. Emra (Ed.), *Coming of age: Short stories about youth and adolescence* (pp. 117-124). Chicago: National Textbook Company.

Nunes, M. (1997). What space is cyberspace? The Internet and virtuality. In D. Holmes (Ed.), *Virtual politics: Identity and community in cyberspace* (pp. 163-178). Thousand Oaks, CA: Sage.

O'Brien, D., et al. (1998, December 2). *Beyond literacy, illiteracy, and aliteracy: Celebrating the multiple literacies of "at risk" adolescents*. Paper presented at the meeting of the National Reading Conference, Austin, TX.

O'Brien, T. (1994). *In the lake of the woods*. New York: Houghton Mifflin.

O'Connor, S. (1996). *Will my name be shouted out? Reaching inner city students through the power of writing*. New York: Touchstone.

Ostermann, A. C., & Keller-Cohen, D. (1998). "Good girls to to heaven; bad girls . . ."
    learn to be good: Quizzes in American and Brazilian teenage girls' magazines.
    Discourse & Society, 9(4), 531–558.

Palladino, G. (1996). *Teenagers: An American history.* New York: Basic Books.

Peck, R. (1994). I go along. In B. Emra (Ed.), *Coming of age: Short stories about
    youth and adolescence* (pp. 190–196). Chicago: National Textbook Company.

Pellegrini, A. (1995). The rough play of adolescent boys of differing sociometric sta-
    tus. *International Journal of Behavioral Development, 17,* 525–540.

Pellegrini, A., & Smith, P. (1998). Physical activity play: The nature and function of a
    neglected aspect of play. *Child Development, 69,* 577–598.

Phelan, P., Davidson, A., & Yu, H. (1998). *Adolescents' worlds: Negotiating family,
    peers, and school.* New York: Teachers College Press.

Plath, S. (1994). Initiation. In B. Emra (Ed.), *Coming of age: Short stories about youth
    and adolescence* (pp. 239–249). Chicago: National Textbook Company.

Project on Disney. (1995). *Inside the mouse: Work and play at Disney World.*
    Durham, NC: Duke University Press.

Pungente, J., & O'Malley, M. (1999). *More than meets the eye: Watching television
    watching us.* Toronto: McClelland & Stewart.

Real, M. (1996). *Exploring media culture: A guide (communication and human
    values).* Thousand Oaks, CA: Sage.

Reinertsen, C. (1993). *Girls' night out: An ethnography of females' responses to
    Beverly Hills 90210 and Melrose Place.* Unpublished paper, University of Min-
    nesota, Minneapolis.

Report to 8KP. (1999). *Report to 8KP.* Cambridge: University of Cambridge, St. Ivo
    School and School of Education.

Roberts, D., Kinsey, D., & Gosh, S. (1993). *Themes in top 40 songs in the 1980's.*
    Unpublished raw data.

Rogoff, B. (1995). Observing sociocultural activity on three planes: Participatory
    appropriation, guided participation, and apprenticeship. In J. Wertsch, P. Del
    Rio, & A. Alvarez (Eds.), *Sociocultural studies of mind* (pp. 129–164). New York:
    Cambridge University Press.

Romano, T. (2000). *Blending genre, altering style: Writing multigenre papers.* Ports-
    mouth, NH: Boynton/Cook.

Ruane, M. (2000, January 10). Chatspeak. *St. Petersburg Times,* p. 12.

Rubinstein, B. (1995). *Dress codes: Meanings and messages in American culture.*
    Boulder, CO: Westview Press.

Salomon, G. (1993). No distribution without individuals' cognition: A dynamic inter-
    actionalist view. In G. Salomon (Ed.), *Distributed cognition: Psychological and
    educational considerations* (pp. 11–118). New York: Cambridge University
    Press.

Santo, C. (2000, February 13). Teen chatting: Trouble on the line? *ACCESS,* p. 9.

Schaafsma, D., Tendero, A., & Tendero, J. (1999). Making it real: Girls' stories, social
    change, and moral struggle. *English Journal, 88*(5), 28–36.

Schneider, B., & Stevenson, D. (1999). *The ambitious generation: America's teen-
    agers motivated but directionless.* New Haven: Yale University Press.

Schockley, B., Michalove, B., & Allen, J. (1995). *Engaging families: Connecting home and school literacy communities*. Portsmouth, NH: Heinemann.

Schwartz, D. (1998). *Contesting the super bowl*. New York: Routledge.

Seitz, J. (1999). *Motives for metaphors: Literacy, curriculum reform, and the teaching of English*. Pittsburgh: University of Pittsburgh Press.

Shakur, S., AKA Monster Kody. (1993). Can't stop, won't stop: The education of a Crip warlord. In S. Walker (Ed.), *Changing community* (pp. 239-260). St. Paul, MN: Graywolf.

Shannon, P., & Crawford, P. (1998). Summers off: Representations of teachers' work and other discontents. *Language Arts, 75*(4), 255-264.

Short, K., & Harste, J. (1996). *Creating classrooms for authors and inquirers* (2nd ed.). Portsmouth, NH: Heinemann.

Short, K., & Kauffman, G. (2000). Exploring sign systems within an inquiry curriculum. In M. Gallego & S. Hollings (Eds.), *What counts as literacy* (pp. 42-61). New York: Teachers College Press.

Singer, B. (Ed.). (1988). *42 up: "Give me the child until he is seven and I will show you the man": A book based on Michael Apted's award-winning documentary series*. New York: New Press.

Sleater, W. (1984). *Interstellar pig*. New York: E. P. Dutton.

Smagorinsky, P., & O'Donnell-Allen, C. (1998). Reading as mediated and mediating action: Composing meaning for literature through multimedia interpretive texts. *Reading Research Quarterly, 33*, 198-227.

Smith, B. (1999, January 31). Banking on super bowl to help feed the hungry. *New York Times Sunday Magazine*, pp. 14-17.

Smith, P., & Sharp, S. (1994). The problem of school bullying. In P. Smith & S. Sharp (Eds.), *School bullying* (pp. 1-19). New York: Routledge.

Solsken, J. (1993). *Literacy, gender, and work in families and in school*. Norwood, NJ: Ablex.

Staples, S. (1989). *Shabanu*. New York: Knopf.

Steinberg, L. (1990). Autonomy, conflict, and harmony in the family relationship. In S. Feldman & G. Elliott (Eds.), *At the threshold: The developing adolescent* (pp. 248-272). Cambridge, MA: Harvard University Press.

Steinberg, L., Brown, B., & Dornbusch, S. (1996). *Beyond the classroom: Why school reform has failed and what parents need to do*. New York: Simon & Schuster.

Stillman, P. (1998). *Families writing* (2nd ed.). Portland, ME: Calendar Islands.

Suarez, R. (1999). *The old neighborhood: What we lost in the great suburban migration: 1966-1999*. New York: Free Press.

Sumara, D. J. (1996). *Private readings in public: Schooling the literary imagination*. New York: Peter Lang.

Tannen, D. (1998). *The argument culture: Moving from debate to dialogue*. New York: Random House.

Taylor, C. (1999, March 1). Playing god. *Time, 153*(8), 52.

Taylor, M. (1976). *Roll of thunder, hear my cry*. New York: Dial.

Teenage Research Unlimited. (1999). *Report on adolescent youthwork*. Chicago: Yankelovich Partners.

Terkel, S. (1974). *Working: People talk about what they do all day and how they feel about what they do.* New York: Pantheon.

Torres, M. (1998). Celebrations and letters home: Research as an ongoing conversation among students, parents, and teacher. In A. Egan-Robertson & D. Bloome (Eds.), *Students as researchers of language and culture in their own communities* (pp. 59-68). Cresskill, NJ: Hampton Press.

Transworld. (1995). Snowboarding, p. 35.

Travis, M. (1998). *Reading cultures: The construction of readers in the twentieth century.* Cardondale: Southern Illinois University Press.

Turkle, S. (1996). Parallel lives: Working on identity in virtual space. In D. Grodin & T. Lindlof (Eds.), *Constructing the self in a mediated world* (pp. 156-175). Thousand Oaks, CA: Sage.

van Dijk, T., Ting-Toomey, S., Smitherman, G., & Troutman, D. (1997). Discourse, ethnicity, culture, and racism. In T. van Dijk (Ed.), *Discourse as social interaction* (pp. 144-180). Thousand Oaks, CA: Sage.

Van Oers, B. (1998). The fallacy of decontextualization. *Mind, Culture, and Activity, 5*(2), 135-142.

Vygotsky, L. (1978). *Mind in society: The development of high psychological processes.* Cambridge, MA: Harvard University Press.

Ward, J. (1996). *Don't watch it alone! An ethnography of the alt.tv.e-file newsgroup.* Unpublished paper, University of Minnesota, Minneapolis.

Watkins, Y. (1994). *My brother, my sister and I.* New York: Bradbury Press.

Watson, L. (1993). *Montana, 1948.* Minneapolis: Milkweed.

Wells, G. (1999). *Dialogic inquiry: Toward a sociocultural practice and theory of education.* New York: Cambridge University Press.

Wenger, E. (1998). *Communities of practice: Learning, meaning, and identity.* New York: Cambridge University Press.

Wenner, L., & Gantz, W. (1998). Watching sports on television: Audience experience, gender, fanship, and marriage. In L. Wenner (Ed.), *Mediasports* (pp. 233-251). New York: Routledge.

Wertsch, J. V. (1998). *Mind as action.* New York: Oxford University Press.

Wilder, T. (1974). *Our town: A play in three acts.* Avon, CT: Limited Editions Club. (Original work published 1938)

Wilhelm, J. D., & Edmiston, B. (1998). *Imagining to learn: Inquiry, ethics, and integration through drama.* Portsmouth, NH: Heinemann.

Willis, S. (1998). Teens at work: Negotiating the jobless future. In J. Austin & M. N. Willard (Eds.), *Generations of youth: Youth cultures and history in twentieth-century America* (pp. 347-357). New York: New York University Press.

Woolley, M. (1995). Community service learning: A bridge to meaning. In M. Burke-Hengen & T. Gillespie (Eds.), *Building community* (pp. 187-202). Portsmouth, NH: Heinemann.

Young, C. (1994). Adjo means good-bye. In B. Emra (Ed.), *Coming of age: Short stories about youth and adolescence* (pp. 71-75). Chicago: National Textbook Company.

Zimbalist, A., & Driggs, L. (1999, February 1). Tackling hunger on "souper bowl" Sunday: Helping out in your community through fundraising [Daily lesson plan]. *http://www.nytimes.com/learning/teachers/lessons/990201monday.html*

Index

About the Authors

Richard Beach is Wallace Professor of English Education at the University of Minnesota. He is author of *A Teacher's Introduction to Reader Response Theories* and co-author of *Teaching Literature in the Secondary School* and *Journals in the Classroom: Writing to Learn*. He conducts research on response to literature, composition, and inquiry instruction. He is a former president of the National Conference on Research in Language and Literacy and a member of the Board of Directors of the National Reading Conference.

Jamie Myers is an Associate Professor of Language and Literacy Education at Pennsylvania State University. His writing and teaching explore the social contexts of literacy and how curricular activities can best promote the collaborative generation and critique of representations of self, others, and the world, and the negotiation of these representations to construct knowledge valued within, between, and across multiple communities. Recent publications have focused on his collaborative work with student hypermedia authoring and the consequences of a professional development school model for English teacher education.

We hope that teachers will find the curriculum framework in this book to be helpful, and we encourage them to share the results of their own projects with Richard (rbeach@.umn.edu) or Jamie (jmm12@psu.edu). These results could then be posted to the web page that has many of the multimedia examples shared in this book (www.ed.psu.edu/k-12/socialworlds).

—R. B. and J. M.